triumphlearning™

Mathematics 5

Coach®

Table of Contents

Domain 1

Operations and Algebraic Thinking

Domain 1: Diagnostic Assessment for Lessons 1–5

Domain 1: Cumulative Assessment for Lessons 1–5

Domain 1: Diagnostic Assessment for Lessons 1–5

1. Evaluate: $5 - (2 + 1)$

   A. 4

   B. 3

   C. 2

   D. 1

2. Evaluate: $2 \times (7 + 2)$

   A. 16

   C. 20

   B. 18

   D. 22

3. What is the next term in the pattern below?

   7, 12, 17, 22, _?_

   A. 25

   C. 29

   B. 27

   D. 31

4. Which represents the expression below?

   $(10{,}652 + 410) - 515$

   A. 515 subtracted from the sum of 10,652 and 410

   B. 515 subtracted from the product of 10,652 and 410

   C. 515 subtracted from the difference of 10,652 and 410

   D. 515 subtracted from the quotient of 10,652 and 410

5. Evaluate: $[12 \times (4 + 1)] + 8$

   A. 44

   C. 50

   B. 56

   D. 68

6. Which represents the description below?

   4 more than 12 times 3

   A. $(12 \div 3) + 4$

   B. $(12 - 3) + 4$

   C. $(12 \times 3) + 4$

   D. $(12 \times 4) + 3$

7. Two patterns start at 0. The rule for the first pattern is to add 7. The rule for the second pattern is to add 14. Which ordered pairs show the corresponding terms from the patterns?

   A. (0, 0), (7, 14), (14, 14), (21, 28), (28, 42)

   B. (0, 0), (7, 14), (14, 28), (21, 42), (28, 56)

   C. (0, 0), (7, 14), (7, 28), (7, 42), (7, 56)

   D. (0, 0), (7, 28), (14, 42) (21, 56), (28, 0)

8. What is the rule for the pattern below?

32, 16, 8, 4, …

A. subtract 16

B. subtract 8

C. multiply by 2

D. divide by 2

9. Evaluate: $212 - [(9 \times 4) + 8]$

_____

10. Two patterns start at 0. The rule for the first pattern is add 1. The rule for the second pattern is add 3.

A. Write ordered pairs using the corresponding terms from each pattern. Then graph the ordered pairs.

_____

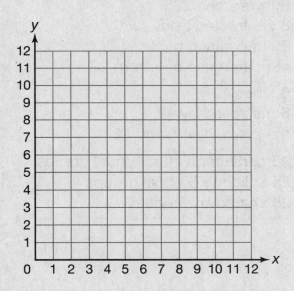

B. Explain how the corresponding terms in the patterns are related.

_____

_____

_____

Write and Interpret Expressions

Getting the Idea

An **expression** is a combination of numbers and operation signs such as +, −, ×
and ÷. To write a numerical expression from words look for the relationship between
the words and the numbers in the situation.

Operation	Problem	Numerical Expression
addition	3 more than 10 the sum of 10 and 3 3 increased by 10 the total of 10 and 3 3 combined with 10	3 + 10
subtraction	20 minus 8 8 fewer than 20 8 subtracted from 20 20 decreased by 8 the difference of 8 from 20	20 − 8
multiplication	5 times 12 5 multiplied by 12 the product of 5 and 12	5 × 12
division	25 partitioned into 5 equal groups 25 split into 5 equal groups 25 shared by 5 equally	25 ÷ 5

Example 1

Write a numerical expression to represent the problem below.

A box of 36 character cards is shared equally among 3 friends.

Strategy **Use a strip diagram to represent the problem.**

Step 1 Represent the problem using a strip diagram.

36		
?	?	?

Step 2 Write the expression.

$36 \div 3$

Solution **A numerical expression that represents the problem is 36 ÷ 3.**

Sometimes you may need to write a numerical expression using more than one operation. For example, "the sum of 45 and 35, multiplied by 3" can be written as $(45 + 35) \times 3$.

Example 2

Write a numerical expression to represent the problem below.

Subtract 3 from 12, then multiply by 4.

Strategy **Separate the problem into two parts. Write a numerical expression for each part.**

Step 1 The comma separates the problem into two parts.

Write a numerical expression for the first part "subtract 3 from 12."
$(12 - 3)$

Step 2 Write a numerical expression for the second part "then multiply by 4."
$\times 4$

Step 3 Combine the parts.
$(12 - 3) \times 4$

Solution **The expression is (12 − 3) × 4.**

Example 3

How does the expression $4 \times (27 - 12)$ compare to $27 - 12$?

Strategy   **Look how the expressions are the same and different.**

Step 1   Look to see how the expressions are the same.

   Both expressions have $27 - 12$.

Step 2   Look to see how the expressions are different.

   The expression $4 \times (27 - 12)$ shows the common part multiplied by 4.

   So, $4 \times (27 - 12)$ is 4 times as many as $27 - 12$.

Solution   **The expression $4 \times (27 - 12)$ is 4 times as many as $27 - 12$.**

Coached Example

Write a numerical expression to represent the problem below.

   Divide 30 by 5, then add 12.

Write a numerical expression for "divide 30 by 5."

   (_____ ____ _____)

Write a numerical expression for "then add 12."

   ____ _____

Combine the parts.

   (_____ ____ _____) ____ _____

The expression is (_____ ____ _____) ____ _____.

Lesson Practice • Part 1

Choose the correct answer.

1. Marty picked 3 times as many quarts of strawberries as Dora. Dora picked 2 quarts. Which expression could be used to find the number of quarts Marty picked?

   A. $3 + 2$

   B. $3 \div 2$

   C. $3 - 2$

   D. 3×2

2. Which expression means 6 fewer than 15?

   A. $15 - 6$

   B. $15 \div 6$

   C. 15×6

   D. $15 + 6$

3. Which represents the problem below?

   Mike has 4 brothers. Donna has 2 more brothers than Mike.

   A. $4 - 2$

   B. $4 \div 2$

   C. $4 + 2$

   D. 2×4

4. Which represents the expression below?

   $2 \times (465 + 371)$

   A. 2 more than 465 plus 371

   B. 2 times 465 plus 371

   C. 2 less than 465 plus 371

   D. 2 fewer than 465 plus 371

5. Which represents the problem below?

   Multiply 7 and 6, then subtract 5.

   A. $5 - (7 \times 6)$

   B. $(7 - 6) \times 5$

   C. $(7 + 6) - 5$

   D. $(7 \times 6) - 5$

6. A group of 4 friends was at a restaurant. They each ordered an $8 meal. Then the group ordered a $6 dessert to share. Which expression represents this situation?

   A. $(4 \times 6) + 1$

   B. $(4 \times 6) + 8$

   C. $(4 \times 8) + 6$

   D. $(4 \times 8) + 1$

7. Which represents the problem below?

3 more than 6, times 8

A. $(3 \times 6) + 8$

B. $(8 \times 3) + 6$

C. $(8 \times 6) + 3$

D. $(6 + 3) \times 8$

8. Which problem represents the expression below?

$(15 - 9) - 1$

A. Joe brought $15 to the supermarket and spent $9 on fruit. Then he donated $1.

B. Joe brought $15 to the supermarket and spent $1 on fruit. Then he donated $9.

C. Joe brought $15 to the supermarket. He gave the cashier $9. His change was $1.

D. Joe brought $15 to the supermarket. He gave the cashier $15. His change was $9.

9. Joanne picked 15 more than twice as many apples as her sister. Her sister picked 35 apples.

A. Write a numerical expression to represent the situation.

_____

B. Joanne ate 3 of her apples. Write a new numerical expression to represent the number of apples Joanne has now.

_____

Lesson Practice • Part 2

Choose the correct answer.

1. How does the value of $5 \times (7 + 6)$ compare to the value of $7 + 6$?

   A. The value of $5 \times (7 + 6)$ is 5 times as many as the value of $7 + 6$.

   B. The value of $5 \times (7 + 6)$ is 5 more than the value of $7 + 6$.

   C. The value of $5 \times (7 + 6)$ is $\frac{1}{5}$ the value of $7 + 6$.

   D. The value of $5 \times (7 + 6)$ is 5 less than the value of $7 + 6$.

2. Which expression can be expressed as "multiply 4 and 9, then subtract 8"?

   A. $4 \times 9 - 8$

   B. $4 \times (9 - 8)$

   C. $8 - 4 \times 9$

   D. $8 - (4 \times 9)$

3. Which expression can be expressed as "add 12 and 9, then multiply by 6"?

   A. $6 \times 12 + 9$

   B. $6 \times (12 + 9)$

   C. $6 \times 9 + 12$

   D. $6 + (12 \times 9)$

4. Which expression can be expressed as "subtract 6 from 18, then divide by 3"?

   A. $18 \div (6 - 3)$

   B. $18 - (6 \div 3)$

   C. $18 - 6 \div 3$

   D. $(18 - 6) \div 3$

5. Which can be represented as $(19 + 11) \div 5$?

   A. divide the sum of 19 and 11 by 5

   B. divide 11 by 5, then add 19

   C. divide 5 by 19, divide 5 by 11, and add the quotients

   D. divide 19 by 5 and then add 11

6. Rachel bought and downloaded 6 songs on Friday and 8 more songs on Saturday. Each song cost $2. Which expression represents the amount of money that Rachel paid?

   A. $6 \times 8 \times 2$

   B. $6 \times 8 + 2$

   C. $2 \times 6 + 8$

   D. $2 \times (6 + 8)$

7. How does the value of 8 + (12 × 5) compare to the value of 12 × 5?

   A. The value of 8 + (12 × 5) is 8 less than the value of 12 × 5.

   B. The value of 8 + (12 × 5) is 8 times as many as the value of 12 × 5.

   C. The value of 8 + (12 × 5) is 8 more than the value of 12 × 5.

   D. The value of 8 + (12 × 5) is $\frac{1}{8}$ the value of 12 × 5.

8. How does the value of (48 − 34) ÷ 2 compare to the value of 48 − 34?

   A. The value of (48 − 34) ÷ 2 is 2 times as many as the value of 48 − 34.

   B. The value of (48 − 34) ÷ 2 is 2 more than the value of 48 − 34.

   C. The value of (48 − 34) ÷ 2 is $\frac{1}{2}$ the value of 48 − 34.

   D. The value of (48 − 34) ÷ 2 is 2 less than the value of 48 − 34.

9. The prices at Enzo's Lunch Truck are shown.

   A. A group ordered 3 cheeseburgers, 2 chicken sandwiches, and 4 drinks. Write an expression to represent the total cost.

Enzo's Lunch Truck

Item	Cost
Cheeseburger	$3
Chicken Sandwich	$5
Salad	$4
Drink	$1

   B. Another group ordered 4 of everything. Write an expression to represent the total cost.

10. Circle the operation sign that makes the expression true.

    5 more than 13

    13 [× − +] 5

11. Decide which operation sign is needed to write each expression. Write the problem in the correct box.

5 less than 9	12 shared equally among 3 people	32 minus 25
18 divided by 6	15 divided by 5	22 decreased by 7

Use ÷	Use −

12. Use numbers from the box to complete the expression "8 fewer than 10, times 3."

(_____ − _____) × _____

3
8
10

13. Which problems represent the expression below? Circle all that apply.

   $(12 + 9) \div 3$

   A. Aretha painted 12 plates on Monday and 9 plates on Tuesday. Then she packed the same number of plates in each of 3 boxes.

   B. Hoyt sent 12 postcards to friends and 9 postcards to family each day for 3 days in a row.

   C. Twelve collie puppies and 9 poodle puppies were born at a shelter. The puppies were divided evenly among 3 families.

   D. Twelve red roses and 9 yellow roses were picked, but 3 roses died before the flowers were delivered.

   E. Twelve acorns fell from a tree. Birds ate 9 of them. The remaining acorns were shared equally among 3 squirrels.

14. Look at each expression. Does it represent "3 times the sum of 4 and 7"? Select Yes or No.

   A. $3 + (4 \times 7)$ ○ Yes ○ No

   B. $3 \times (4 + 7)$ ○ Yes ○ No

   C. $(4 + 7) \times 3$ ○ Yes ○ No

   D. $(4 \times 7) + 3$ ○ Yes ○ No

15. Decide whether the expressions are the same. Select True or False.

   A. 8 more than 4 $4 + 8$ ○ True ○ False

   B. 5 fewer than 12 $5 - 12$ ○ True ○ False

   C. the sum of 3 and 6 3×6 ○ True ○ False

   D. 24 divided by 6 $24 \div 6$ ○ True ○ False

Order of Operations

Getting the Idea

When evaluating an expression with more than one operation, use the **order of operations**. The order of operations is a set of rules used for evaluating an expression with more than one operation.

Order of Operations

1. Operate inside the grouping symbols.

2. Multiply and divide from left to right.

3. Add and subtract from left to right.

Example 1

Evaluate this expression: $14 - 6 \div 3$

Strategy   **Use the order of operations.**

> **Step 1**   There are no grouping symbols, so multiply and divide from left to right.
>
> $14 - 6 \div 3$
>
> $14 - 2$

> **Step 2**   Add and subtract from left to right.
>
> $14 - 2$
>
> 12

Solution $14 - 6 \div 3 = 12$

Example 2

Evaluate this expression: $2 + 3 \times 8 \div 2$

Strategy   **Use the order of operations.**

Step 1   There are no grouping symbols, so multiply and divide from left to right.

Multiply.

$2 + 3 \times 8 \div 2$

$2 + \quad 24 \quad \div 2$

Divide.

$2 + 24 \div 2$

$2 + \quad 12$

Step 2   Add and subtract from left to right.

Add.

$2 + 12$

14

Solution $2 + 3 \times 8 \div 2 = 14$

Example 3

Evaluate this expression: $64 \div 8 + 15 \times 3 - 16$

Strategy   **Use the order of operations.**

Step 1   There are no grouping symbols, so multiply and divide from left to right.

Divide.

$64 \div 8 + 15 \times 3 - 16$

$\quad 8 \quad + 15 \times 3 - 16$

Multiply.

$8 + 15 \times 3 - 16$

$8 + \quad 45 \quad - 16$

Step 2 Add and subtract from left to right.

Add.

8 + 45 − 16

53   − 16

Subtract.

53 − 16

37

Solution   64 ÷ 8 + 15 × 3 − 16 = 37

Coached Example

What is the value of the expression shown below?

100 − 60 ÷ 5 × 8 + 17

Use the order of operations.

Divide, then multiply.

100 − 60 ÷ 5 × 8 + 17

100 − _____ × 8 + 17

100 − _____ + 17

Subtract, then add.

_____ + 17

_____

100 − 60 ÷ 5 × 8 + 17 = _____

Lesson Practice • Part 1

Choose the correct answer.

1. Evaluate: $8 + 12 \div 4 - 3$

   A. 2   **C.** 14

   B. 8   **D.** 44

2. What is the value of the expression below?

   $20 - 5 \div 5 + 3$

   A. 2   **C.** 16

   B. 8   **D.** 22

3. Evaluate: $9 \times 5 - 16 \div 2$

   A. 7   **C.** 37

   B. 9   **D.** 39

4. Which expression has a value of 3?

   A. $18 - 4 \times 3 - 2$

   B. $1 + 1 \times 2$

   C. $6 - 2 \times 2$

   D. $7 + 4 \div 4$

5. Evaluate: $3 + 2 \times 4 + 36$

   A. 47   **C.** 60

   B. 56   **D.** 290

6. What is the value of the expression below?

   $15 - 3 \times 12 \div 4$

   A. 36   **C.** 7

   B. 12   **D.** 6

7. What is the value of the expression below?

   $5 \times 16 - 4 + 2 \div 2$

   A. 77   **C.** 40

   B. 61   **D.** 39

8. Evaluate: $4 \times 9 \div 3 + 8 - 6$

   A. 10   **C.** 26

   B. 14   **D.** 110

9. John's answer to the test question below was 10.

Evaluate: $11 + 7 - 2 \times 3 + 8 \div 2$

A. Evaluate the expression. Show your work.

B. Is John's answer correct? Explain.

_____

_____

_____

Lesson Practice • Part 2

Choose the correct answer.

Use this expression for questions 1 and 2.

$$7 - 3 + 4 \div 2 \times 6$$

1. What is the first step in evaluating the expression above?

   A. $7 - 3$ **C.** $4 \div 2$

   B. $3 + 4$ **D.** 2×6

2. What is the value of the expression above?

   A. 16   **C.** 36

   B. 24   **D.** 96

3. What is the value of the expression below?

   $$32 - 8 \div 4 \times 2$$

   A. 3

   B. 12

   C. 28

   D. 60

4. Evaluate: $10 \times 6 + 24 \div 4$

   A. 14

   B. 66

   C. 75

   D. 120

Use this expression for questions 5 and 6.

$$16 + 18 \times 9 \div 3 - 1$$

5. What is the second step in evaluating the expression above?

   A. $16 + 162$ **C.** $162 \div 3$

   B. 34×9 **D.** $3 - 1$

6. What is the value of the expression above?

   A. 101   **C.** 71

   B. 97   **D.** 69

7. Evaluate: $7 + 4 \times 9 - 6 \div 3$

   A. 17   **C.** 41

   B. 31   **D.** 97

8. What is the value of the expression below?

   $$24 - 8 \times 6 \div 2 + 4$$

   A. 4

   B. 16

   C. 52

   D. 112

9. Evaluate: $12 + 24 \div 6 - 3$

  A. 3

  B. 9

  C. 12

  D. 13

10. What is the value of the expression below?

$2 + 2 \times 2 - 2$

  A. 2

  B. 4

  C. 6

  D. 8

11. Will gave his classmates this expression to evaluate.

$48 + 4 \times 12 \div 3 - 15$

  A. Evaluate the expression. Show your work.

  B. Why is it necessary to follow the order of operations? Use the expression above as an example.

  _____

  _____

  _____

12. Select True or False for the value of each expression.

  A. The value of $4 + 3 \times 2$ is 14.   ○ True   ○ False

  B. The value of $2 + 6 \div 2 - 2$ is 3.   ○ True   ○ False

  C. The value of $5 \times 3 - 2 \times 4$ is 7.   ○ True   ○ False

  D. The value of $12 - 8 \div 2 - 2$ is 2.   ○ True   ○ False

13. Use numbers from the box to complete an expression that has a value of 5.

_____ + _____ ÷ _____

1
2
3
9

14. Draw a line from each expression to its value.

A. $3 + 4 \times 2 - 2$ •   • 12

B. $9 + 5 \times 4 - 9$ •   • 9

C. $18 - 24 \div 4$ •   • 15

D. $12 - 2 + 15 \div 3$ •   • 20

15. Evaluate each expression. Write the expression in the correct box.

$8 + 2 \times 5$	$2 + 5 \times 4 - 6$	$3 + 24 \div 3 + 7$

$4 \times 5 - 6 \div 3$	$11 \times 2 - 12 \div 2$	$19 - 9 \div 3$

The value of the expression is 16.	The value of the expression is 18.

16. Which expressions have a value of 7? Circle all that apply.

    A. $6 + 4 \div 2 - 1$

    B. $3 \times 2 + 6 - 5$

    C. $4 \times 5 - 3 \times 4$

    D. $3 \times 9 - 4 \times 5$

17. Circle the operation sign that makes the expression have a value of 21.

$$12 + 6 \boxed{\begin{array}{c} \times \\ - \\ + \end{array}} 2 - 3$$

18. Use numbers from the box to complete an expression that has a value of 34.

$$3 + \underline{\hspace{2cm}} \times \underline{\hspace{2cm}} + \underline{\hspace{2cm}}$$

2

4

6

7

Evaluate Expressions with Grouping Symbols

Getting the Idea

You can use the order of operations to evaluate an expression with grouping symbols. First operate in parentheses ( ), then brackets [ ], then braces { }.

For example:

$8 \times \{3 + [5 - (3 - 2)]\}$

$8 \times \{3 + [5 - 1]\}$

$8 \times \{3 + 4\}$

$8 \times 7 = 56$

Example 1

Evaluate this expression: $[(2 + 3) \times 8] \div 2$

Strategy **Use the order of operations. Work inside the grouping symbols first.**

Step 1 Operate within the parentheses.

$[(2 + 3) \times 8] \div 2$

$[\ \ \ 5 \ \ \ \times 8] \div 2$

Step 2 Operate within the brackets.

$[5 \times 8] \div 2$

$40 \ \ \ \div 2$

Step 3 Multiply and divide from left to right.

$40 \div 2$

20

Solution **$[(2 + 3) \times 8] \div 2 = 20$**

Example 2

Evaluate this expression: $87 \div 3 - [15 - (4 \times 3)] + 2$

Strategy	**Use the order of operations. Work inside the grouping symbols first.**
Step 1	Operate inside the parentheses. $87 \div 3 - [15 - (4 \times 3)] + 2$ $87 \div 3 - [15 - \quad 12 \quad] + 2$
Step 2	Operate inside the brackets. $87 \div 3 - [15 - 12] + 2$ $87 \div 3 - \quad 3 \quad + 2$
Step 3	Multiply and divide from left to right. $87 \div 3 - 3 + 2 = 29 - 3 + 2$
Step 4	Add and subtract from left to right. $29 - 3 + 2 = 26 + 2 = 28$

Solution $87 \div 3 - [15 - (4 \times 3)] + 2 = 28$

Example 3 below shows the evaluation of the expression from Example 2 without grouping symbols. Notice that the answer is not the same as in Example 2.

Example 3

Evaluate this expression: $87 \div 3 - 15 - 4 \times 3 + 2$

Strategy	**Use the order of operations.**
Step 1	Multiply and divide from left to right. $87 \div 3 - 15 - 4 \times 3 + 2$ $29 \quad - 15 - 4 \times 3 + 2 = 29 - 15 - 12 + 2$
Step 2	Add and subtract from left to right. $29 - 15 - 12 + 2$ $14 \quad - 12 + 2 = 2 + 2 = 4$

Solution $87 \div 3 - 15 - 4 \times 3 + 2 = 4$

Example 4

Evaluate this expression: $9 \times [(4 + 2) \div 3]$

Strategy   **Use the order of operations.**

Step 1   Operate inside the parentheses.

$$9 \times [(4 + 2) \div 3]$$
$$9 \times [\quad 6 \quad \div 3]$$

Step 2   Operate inside the brackets.

$$9 \times [6 \div 3] = 9 \times 2$$

Step 3   Multiply.

$$9 \times 2 = 18$$

Solution $9 \times [(4 + 2) \div 3] = 18$

Coached Example

Evaluate this expression: $[(4 + 3) \times 2 - 8] \div 3$

Use the order of operations.

Operate inside grouping symbols.

$$[(4 + 3) \times 2 - 8] \div 3$$

$$[\underline{\hspace{1.5cm}} \times 2 - 8] \div 3$$

$$[\underline{\hspace{1.5cm}} - 8] \div 3$$

$$\underline{\hspace{1.5cm}} \div 3$$

Divide.

$$\underline{\hspace{1.5cm}} \div 3$$

$$\underline{\hspace{1.5cm}}$$

$[(4 + 3) \times 2 - 8] \div 3 = \underline{\hspace{1.5cm}}$

Lesson Practice • Part 1

Choose the correct answer.

1. Evaluate: $(8 + 12) \div 4 - 3$

   A. 2

   B. 8

   C. 14

   D. 44

2. Which expression has a value of 4?

   A. $(8 - 4) \times (3 - 2)$

   B. $1 + (1 \times 2)$

   C. $(6 - 2) \times 2$

   D. $(7 + 1) \div 4$

3. Evaluate: $5 \times [16 - (4 + 2)] \div 2$

   A. 20

   B. 25

   C. 35

   D. 40

4. Evaluate: $2 \times [6 \div (9 - 8)] - 6$

   A. 12

   B. 9

   C. 6

   D. 3

5. Evaluate: $(21 - 5) \div (5 + 3)$

   A. 1

   B. 2

   C. 18

   D. 23

6. Evaluate: $9 \times (5 - 1) \div 2$

   A. 18

   B. 21

   C. 27

   D. 72

7. Evaluate: $3 + 2 \times (4 + 36)$

   A. 83

   B. 60

   C. 47

   D. 40

8. Evaluate: $[(15 - 3) \times 12] \div 4$

   A. 42

   B. 36

   C. 27

   D. 6

9. Sean's answer to the test question below was 10.

   Evaluate: $\{[11 + 7 - (2 \times 3)] + 8\} \div 2$

A. Evaluate the expression. Show your work.

B. Is Sean's answer correct? Explain.

   _____

   _____

   _____

Lesson Practice • Part 2

Choose the correct answer.

Use this expression for questions 1 and 2.

$16 + 12 \div (4 - 2) + 3$

1. What is the first step in evaluating the expression above?

   A. $16 + 12$

   B. $12 \div 4$

   C. $4 - 2$

   D. $2 + 3$

2. What is the value of the expression above?

   A. 8   C. 20

   B. 17   D. 25

3. Evaluate: $6 \times [36 \div (9 - 3)] + 8$

   A. 84

   B. 44

   C. 29

   D. 14

4. Evaluate: $8 + [24 \div (3 \times 2)] - 12$

   A. 0   C. 20

   B. 12   D. 32

Use this expression for questions 5 and 6.

$\{[12 + 20 - (2 \times 4)] + 32\} \div 2$

5. What is the first step in evaluating the expression above?

   A. 2×4

   B. $4 + 32$

   C. $20 - 2$

   D. $32 \div 2$

6. What is the value of the expression above?

   A. 4   C. 34

   B. 28   D. 40

7. Evaluate: $6 \times (4 - 2) \div 2 + 1$

   A. 24   C. 8

   B. 12   D. 7

8. Which expression has the greatest value?

   A. $64 - 4 \times 6 \div 2 + 8$

   B. $64 - 4 \times (6 \div 2) + 8$

   C. $(64 - 4) \times 6 \div 2 + 8$

   D. $64 - [4 \times (6 \div 2)] + 8$

9. Evaluate: $5 + [9 \times (6 + 8)] \div 2$

   A. 36

   B. 46

   C. 68

   D. 98

10. Which expression has the greatest value?

    A. $6 \times 40 + 16 \div (4 - 2)$

    B. $6 \times [(40 + 16) \div 4] - 2$

    C. $6 \times (40 + 16) \div 4 - 2$

    D. $6 \times 40 + (16 \div 4) - 2$

11. Ashley gave her classmates this expression to evaluate.

    $$\{[64 + (8 - 4)] \times 12 - 6\} \div 2$$

    A. Evaluate the expression. Show your work.

    B. Evaluate the expression with all of the grouping symbols removed. Show your work.

12. Evaluate each expression. Write the expression in the correct box.

$32 - 3 \times (3 + 4)$	$2 + 3 \times (12 - 6)$	$(32 + 4) \div 3 - 1$
$8 + (15 - 6) \div 3$	$6 \times 5 - (4 + 6)$	$16 + (9 - 1) \div 2$

The value of the expression is 11.	The value of the expression is 20.

13. Draw a line from each expression to its value.

    A. $12 + 4 \times (8 - 2)$ •   • 30

    B. $[2 + (9 \div 3)] \times 4$ •   • 15

    C. $15 \times [26 - (12 \times 2)]$ •   • 36

    D. $(12 - 2) + 15 \div 3$ •   • 20

14. Use numbers from the box to complete an expression that has a value of 6.

_____ ÷ (_____ − _____)

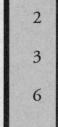

2

3

6

18

15. Which expressions have a value of 16? Circle all that apply.

    A. $10 + 12 \div (4 - 2)$

    B. $3 \times (2 + 6) - 5$

    C. $4 \times 5 - (3 + 4)$

    D. $36 - [(10 - 5) \times 4]$

16. Circle the operation sign that makes the expression have a value of 35.

$$27 + [20 \begin{array}{|c|} \hline \times \\ - \\ + \\ \hline \end{array} (2 \times 6)]$$

17. Use numbers from the box to complete an expression that has a value of 19.

    _____ $+ (4 +$ _____ $) \div$ _____

$$\begin{array}{|c|} \hline 2 \\ 6 \\ 10 \\ 12 \\ \hline \end{array}$$

18. Select True or False for the value of each expression.

    A. The value of $(14 + 12) \div 2$ is 13.   ○ True   ○ False

    B. The value of $3 \times (14 - 3) + 6$ is 45.   ○ True   ○ False

    C. The value of $2 \times (22 - 6) - 4$ is 28.   ○ True   ○ False

    D. The value of $12 - [8 \div (15 - 11)]$ is 1.   ○ True   ○ False

Patterns

Getting the Idea

A **pattern** is a series of numbers or figures that follows a **rule**. The rule of the pattern tells you how to get from each number in the pattern to the next number. The rule can also help you find a missing number in a pattern.

The pattern below is an increasing pattern. The rule is add 3.

5, 8, 11, 14, 17, …

The pattern below is a decreasing pattern. The rule is subtract 5.

100, 95, 90, 85, …

You can create a new pattern using a rule and a starting number. Each number in a pattern is called a **term**.

Example 1

Write a new pattern that starts with 3, has 6 terms, and uses the rule add 4.

Strategy   **Use the rule to write a new pattern.**

Step 1   Start with the first term.

The first term is 3.

Step 2   Use the rule to extend the pattern.

Add 4 to the first term to find the second term.

$3 + 4 = 7$

The second term is 7.

Step 3   Continue to extend the pattern until there are 6 terms.

Add 4 to each sum.

$7 + 4 = 11$

$11 + 4 = 15$

$15 + 4 = 19$

$19 + 4 = 23$

Step 4   Write the terms in the pattern.

3   7   11   15   19   23

Solution   **The new pattern is 3, 7, 11, 15, 19, 23.**

Example 2

Write a new pattern starting with 3 that has 6 terms and uses the rule multiply by 4.

Strategy   **Use the rule to write a new pattern.**

Step 1   Start with the first term.

The first term is 3.

Step 2   Use the rule to extend the pattern.

Multiply the first term by 4 to find the second term.

$3 \times 4 = 12$

The second term is 12.

Step 3   Continue to extend the pattern until there are 6 terms.

Multiply each product by 4.

$12 \times 4 = 48$

$48 \times 4 = 192$

$192 \times 4 = 768$

$768 \times 4 = 3,072$

Step 4   Write the terms in the pattern.

3   12   48   192   768   3,072

Solution   **The new pattern is 3; 12; 48; 192; 768; 3,072.**

Look back at Examples 1 and 2. Even though they start with the same term, the multiplication pattern increases much faster than the addition pattern.

You can create two patterns to form a relationship between the corresponding terms.

Example 3

Create two patterns with 5 terms that both start with 0. Pattern A uses the rule add 2. Pattern B uses the rule add 8. Make a table to show the corresponding terms. How are the terms in the two patterns related?

Strategy   **Use the rules to write two new patterns.**

Step 1   Write the terms for Pattern A.

Use the rule add 2. Start with 0.

0, 2, 4, 6, 8

Step 2   Write the terms for Pattern B.

Use the rule add 8. Start with 0.

0, 8, 16, 24, 32

Step 3   Make a table to show the corresponding terms.

Pattern A	0	2	4	6	8
Pattern B	0	8	16	24	32

Step 4   Compare the terms.

$8 \div 2 = 4$

$16 \div 4 = 4$

$24 \div 6 = 4$

$32 \div 8 = 4$

Each term in Pattern B is 4 times the value of the corresponding terms in Pattern A.

Solution   **The terms in Pattern B are always 4 times the value of the corresponding terms in Pattern A.**

Coached Example

Create two patterns each with 5 terms that both start with 0. Pattern A uses the rule add 4 and Pattern B uses the rule add 12. What is the relationship between the patterns?

Create the pattern with the rule add 4.

0, 0 + 4 = _____, _____, _____, _____.

The first 5 terms of Pattern A are 0, _____, _____, _____, _____.

Create the pattern with the rule add 12.

0, 0 + 12 = _____, _____, _____, _____.

The first 5 terms of Pattern B are 0, _____, _____, _____, _____.

Complete the table.

Pattern A	0				
Pattern B	0				

Find the relationship between the patterns.

Divide each term in Pattern B by the corresponding term in Pattern A.

_____ ÷ _____ = _____

_____ ÷ _____ = _____

_____ ÷ _____ = _____

_____ ÷ _____ = _____

The relationship is that each term in Pattern B is _____ the value as each corresponding term in Pattern A.

Lesson Practice • Part 1

Choose the correct answer.

1. What is the next term in the pattern below?

   45, 36, 27, 18, _?_

   A. 10
   B. 9
   C. 8
   D. 7

2. What is the rule for the pattern below?

   32, 36, 40, 44, …

   A. add 8
   B. subtract 4
   C. add 4
   D. subtract 8

3. What is the missing term in the pattern below?

   2, _?_, 18, 54, 162

   A. 3
   B. 6
   C. 8
   D. 9

4. The pattern below uses the rule subtract 7.

   77, 70, 63, _?_, 49

   What is the missing term?

   A. 58
   B. 57
   C. 56
   D. 55

5. What is the rule for the pattern below?

   2, 4, 8, 16, 32, …

   A. add 2
   B. multiply by 4
   C. add 4
   D. multiply by 2

6. What is the next term in the pattern below?

   1, 2, 3, 4, 5, 6, _?_

   A. 7
   B. 8
   C. 9
   D. 10

7. What is the missing term in the pattern below?

     24, 26, <u>?</u>, 30, 32

A. 27

B. 28

C. 29

D. 31

8. What is the rule for the pattern below?

     5, 10, 15, 20, 25

A. multiply by 2

B. add 10

C. multiply by 3

D. add 5

9. Create two patterns starting with the term 45 and ending with the term 5.

A. Use the rule subtract 5.

_____

_____

_____

_____

_____

B. Use the rule divide by 3.

_____

_____

_____

Lesson Practice • Part 2

Choose the correct answer.

1. Lilly wrote two rules that both have 0 for the first number. The first rule was add 3 and the second rule was add 15. Which sentence is true about the numbers in Lilly's patterns?

   A. The second rule has a number that is always 5 more than the corresponding number of the first term.

   B. The second rule has a number that is always 5 times as many than the corresponding number of the first term.

   C. The second rule has a number that is always 12 more than the corresponding number of the first term.

   D. The second rule has a number that is always 12 times as many than the corresponding number of the first term.

2. Two patterns start at 0. The rule for Pattern A is add 2. The rule for Pattern B is add 3. What is the value of Pattern B when Pattern A has a value of 12?

   A. 13   C. 18

   B. 15   D. 21

3. Aaron wrote two rules. The first rule is add 3 and starts at 0. The second rule is multiply by 3 and starts at 3. Which sentence is true about the numbers in Aaron's patterns?

   A. The number from the second rule is always 3 times as many as the corresponding number from the first rule.

   B. The difference between the second number and the first number remains the same as the pattern continues.

   C. The number from the second rule is always 3 more than the corresponding number from the first rule.

   D. The difference between the second number and the first number increases as the pattern continues.

4. Two patterns start at 0. The rule for Pattern C is add 6. The rule for Pattern D is add 4. Which number is a term in both patterns?

   A. 12   C. 18

   B. 16   D. 20

5. Pattern E starts at 2 and uses the rule add 4. Pattern F starts at 6 and uses the rule add 3. Which is the first term in which the number in Pattern E is greater than the corresponding term in Pattern F?

   A. fourth term

   B. fifth term

   C. sixth term

   D. seventh term

6. Pattern G starts at 12 and uses the rule multiply by 4. Pattern H starts at 6 and uses the rule multiply by 6. Which is the first term in which the number in Pattern H is greater than the corresponding term in Pattern G?

   A. fifth term

   B. fourth term

   C. third term

   D. second term

7. Two patterns start at 0. Pattern J uses the rule add 12. Pattern K uses the rule add 6.

   A. Write the first 6 terms of Pattern J.

   _____

   _____

   B. Write the first 6 terms of Pattern K.

   _____

   _____

   C. What is the relationship between Patterns J and K? Explain your reasoning.

   _____

   _____

8. Which patterns use the rule add 4? Circle all that apply.

    A. 4, 8, 16, 32, …

    B. 3, 7, 11, 15, …

    C. 4, 8, 12, 16, …

    D. 5, 20, 80, 320, …

    E. 11, 15, 19, 23, …

9. Draw a line from each pattern to the next term in the pattern.

    A. 4, 7, 10, 13, ?   ●   ● 162

    B. 64, 32, 16, 8, ?   ●   ● 46

    C. 2, 6, 18, 54, ?   ●   ● 4

    D. 70, 64, 58, 52, ? ●   ● 16

10. Determine the rule for each pattern. Write the pattern in the correct box.

2, 9, 16, 23, …	6, 24, 96, 384, …	2, 8, 32, 128, …
3, 12, 48, 192, …	6, 13, 20, 27, …	4, 11, 18, 25, …

Rule: Add 7	**Rule: Multiply by 4**

11. Look at each pattern. Is the next term 36? Select Yes or No.

    A. 2, 4, 8, 16, <u>?</u>   ○ Yes   ○ No

    B. 68, 60, 52, 44, <u>?</u>   ○ Yes   ○ No

    C. 7, 14, 21, 28, <u>?</u>   ○ Yes   ○ No

    D. 20, 24, 28, 32, <u>?</u>   ○ Yes   ○ No

12. The pattern below uses the rule divide by 3. Use numbers from the box to complete the pattern.

324, _____, 36, _____, _____

4
12
16
108

13. Decide whether the underlined number is the correct term in the pattern. Select True or False.

    A. 128, <u>64</u>, 32, 16, 4   ○ True   ○ False

    B. 13, 17, <u>22</u>, 25, 29   ○ True   ○ False

    C. 3, 15, 75, <u>425</u>, 1,875   ○ True   ○ False

    D. 70, 61, <u>52</u>, 43, 34   ○ True   ○ False

Graph Patterns

Getting the Idea

You can show the relationship between two values in a graph. You can graph the values as **ordered pairs** on a **coordinate plane**.

(**Note:** Look ahead to Lessons 30 and 31 for more information on coordinate planes.)

An ordered pair (*x, y*) is a pair of numbers used to locate a point on a coordinate plane.

The first number in an ordered pair is called the **x-coordinate**.

The second number in an ordered pair is called the **y-coordinate**.

For example, in (3, 5), the *x*-coordinate is 3 and the *y*-coordinate is 5.

Example 1

Nina ran 6 miles each hour she ran in a long-distance race. She ran for 4 hours. Make a graph that shows the pattern.

Strategy　　**Translate the pattern into a graph.**

　Write the relationship between hours and miles run.

　　　　　　　She ran 6 miles each hour.

　　　　　　　1 hour = 6 miles

　　　　　　　2 hours = 12 miles

　　　　　　　3 hours = 18 miles

　　　　　　　4 hours = 24 miles

Step 2   Make a table of values. List the ordered pairs.

Number of Hours (x)	Number of Miles (y)	Ordered pairs (x, y)
1	6	(1, 6)
2	12	(2, 12)
3	18	(3, 18)
4	24	(4, 24)

Step 3   Graph the ordered pairs on a coordinate plane.

Draw a straight line that connects the points.

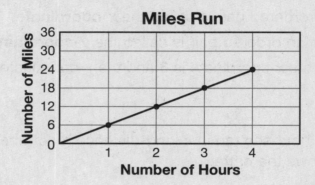

Solution   **The graph in Step 3 shows the pattern.**

You can make ordered pairs of corresponding terms from two patterns and then graph the ordered pairs.

Example 2

Create two patterns with 5 terms that both start with 0. Use two different rules: add 3 and add 6. Form ordered pairs of corresponding terms from the two patterns and graph them. How do the terms in the two patterns seem to be related?

Strategy   **Use the rules to write two new patterns.**
Write ordered pairs of corresponding terms, then graph.

Step 1   Write the pattern for the x terms.

Use the rule add 3. Start with 0.

0, 3, 6, 9, 12

Step 2   Write the pattern for the *y* terms.

Use the rule add 6. Start with 0.

0, 6, 12, 18, 24

Step 3   Write (*x*, *y*) ordered pairs using the corresponding terms from each pattern.

(0, 0)

(3, 6)

(6, 12)

(9, 18)

(12, 24)

Step 4   Graph the ordered pairs on a coordinate plane.

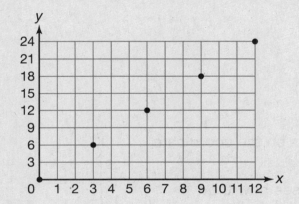

Step 5   Compare the terms to see how they are related.

$y = x \times 2$

$6 = 3 \times 2$

$12 = 6 \times 2$

$18 = 9 \times 2$

$24 = 12 \times 2$

The value of the *y*-coordinate is always 2 times the value of the *x*-coordinate.

Solution   **The graph is shown in Step 4. The value of the *y*-coordinate is 2 times the value of the *x*-coordinate.**

Coached Example

Create two patterns with 5 terms that both start at 0. Use two different rules: add 1 and add 4. Form ordered pairs of corresponding terms from the two patterns and graph them. How do the terms in the two patterns seem to be related?

Write the first 5 terms for the *x*-coordinate.

0, _____, _____, _____, _____

Write the first 5 terms for the *y*-coordinate.

0, _____, _____, _____, _____

Write ordered pairs of corresponding terms.

(0, 0)

(1, _____)

(2, _____)

(_____, _____)

(_____, _____)

Graph the ordered pairs on the coordinate plane below.

Compare the terms to see how they are related.

$y = x \times 4$

$4 = 1 \times 4$

$8 = 2 \times$ _____

$12 = 3 \times$ _____

$16 =$ _____ $\times$ _____

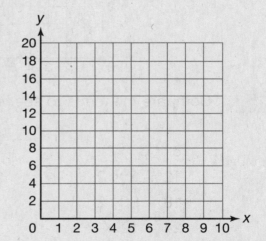

The value of the *y*-coordinate is _____ times the value of the *x*-coordinate.

Lesson Practice • Part 1

Choose the correct answer.

Use this information for questions 1–4.

Two patterns start at 0. The first pattern uses the rule add 1 and the second pattern uses the rule add 5.

1. Which shows the first five terms for the *x*-coordinates?

   A. 0, 1, 2, 3, 4

   B. 0, 2, 4, 6, 8

   C. 1, 2, 3, 4, 5

   D. 5, 6, 7, 8, 9

2. Which shows the first five terms for the *y*-coordinates?

   A. 0, 1, 2, 3, 4

   B. 0, 5, 10, 15, 20

   C. 1, 2, 3, 4, 5

   D. 5, 10, 15, 20, 25

3. Which shows the ordered pairs of corresponding terms of the patterns?

   A. (0, 0), (1, 0), (2, 0), (3, 0), (4, 0)

   B. (0, 0), (1, 2), (2, 3), (3, 4), (4, 5)

   C. (0, 0), (1, 5), (2, 10), (3, 15), (4, 20)

   D. (0, 0), (5, 1), (10, 2), (15, 3), (20, 4)

4. Which best describes how the corresponding terms are related?

   A. The value of the *y*-coordinate is 2 times the value of the corresponding *x*-coordinate.

   B. The value of the *y*-coordinates is 3 times the value of the corresponding *x*-coordinate.

   C. The value of the *y*-coordinates is 4 times the value of the corresponding *x*-coordinate.

   D. The value of the *y*-coordinates is 5 times the value of the corresponding *x*-coordinate.

5. Keisha planted a plant with seeds inside the ground. The plant's growth can be described by two rules. The first rule is that Keisha checked the plant height once a week. The second rule is the plant grew 2 centimeters each week. Which table matches the patterns?

A. **Plant Height**

Week	1	2	3	4
Height (cm)	1	2	3	4

C. **Plant Height**

Week	2	4	6	8
Height (cm)	1	2	3	4

B. **Plant Height**

Week	1	2	3	4
Height (cm)	2	4	6	8

D. **Plant Height**

Week	1	2	3	4
Height (cm)	4	8	12	16

6. Jerry wrote two patterns that both start with 0. The first pattern uses the rule add 3. The second pattern uses the rule add 12.

A. Write ordered pairs using the corresponding terms from each pattern. Then graph the ordered pairs.

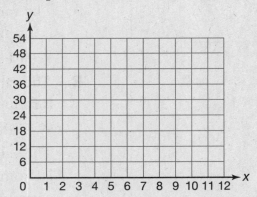

B. Explain how the corresponding terms in the patterns are related.

_____

_____

Lesson Practice • Part 2

Choose the correct answer.

1. Two patterns start at 0. The rule for the first pattern is to add 2. The rule for the second pattern is to add 5. Which is an ordered pair from the patterns?

   A. (0, 2)   **C.** (5, 2)

   B. (4, 25)   **D.** (6, 15)

2. Gina created two patterns. The first pattern starts at 0 and uses the rule add 4. The second pattern starts at 5 and uses the rule add 2. Which table shows Gina's patterns?

   A.

x	0	4	8	12	16
y	0	2	4	6	8

   B.

x	0	4	8	12	16
y	5	7	9	11	13

   C.

x	0	2	4	6	8
y	0	4	8	12	16

   D.

x	5	7	9	11	13
y	0	4	8	12	16

3. Two patterns start at 0. The rule for the first pattern is to add 4. The rule for the second pattern is to add 3. Which is an ordered pair from the patterns?

   A. (3, 4)

   B. (7, 7)

   C. (16, 12)

   D. (20, 16)

4. One pattern starts at 0 and has a rule to add 2. The second pattern starts at 2 and has a rule to add 2. Which is an ordered pair from the patterns?

   A. (2, 4)

   B. (4, 8)

   C. (6, 10)

   D. (8, 16)

5. Jorge wrote two patterns. His first pattern starts at 0 and has the rule add 1. His second pattern starts at 2 and has the rule add 1. Which graph shows Jorge's patterns?

A.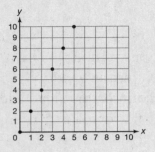

C.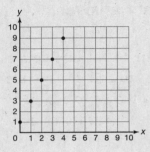

B.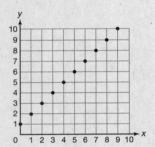

D.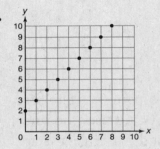

6. One pattern starts at 0 and uses the rule add 2. The second pattern starts at 10 and uses the rule subtract 1.

A. Write the ordered pairs formed by the first 5 terms of each pattern.

_____

_____

B. Graph the ordered pairs.

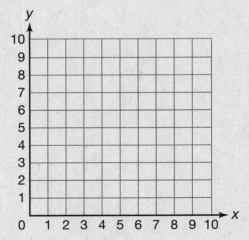

7. Look at the patterns. Select True or False for each statement.

    x-coordinates: 0, 3, 6, 9

    y-coordinates: 0, 12, 24, 36

    A. The pattern rule used to create the   ○ True   ○ False
        y-coordinates is add 9.

    B. The pattern rule used to create the   ○ True   ○ False
        x-coordinates is add 3.

    C. The value of the y-coordinate is 4 times the   ○ True   ○ False
        value of the corresponding x-coordinate.

    D. The ordered pairs of corresponding terms of the   ○ True   ○ False
        patterns are (0, 0), (3, 12), (6, 9), (24, 36).

8. Circle the ordered pair that is the next term in the pattern.

    (4, 32)

    (1, 7), (2, 14), (3, 21),   (5, 35)

    (4, 28)

9. Select the sets of ordered pairs in which the value of the y-coordinate is 3 times the
    value of the corresponding x-coordinate. Circle all that apply.

    A. (0, 0), (1, 4), (2, 8), (3, 12)

    B. (1, 3), (2, 6), (3, 9), (4, 12)

    C. (5, 15), (10, 30), (15, 45), (20, 60)

    D. (1, 4), (2, 5), (3, 6), (4, 7)

10. Draw a line from each graph to the pair of rules that describe the pattern.

A.

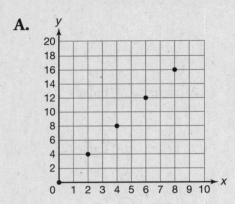

B.

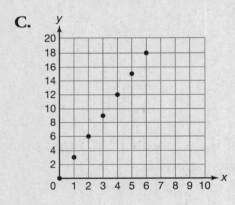

C.

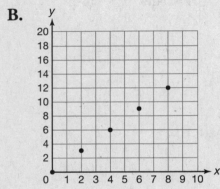

D.

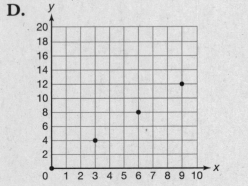

Rule 1: Add 2.
Rule 2: Add 3.

Rule 1: Add 1.
Rule 2: Add 3.

Rule 1: Add 3.
Rule 2: Add 4.

Rule 1: Add 2.
Rule 2: Add 4.

Domain 1: Cumulative Assessment for Lessons 1–5

1. Evaluate: $7 \times (7 - 2)$

   A. 35
   B. 39
   C. 47
   D. 52

2. Evaluate: $6 \times [(5 - 3) + 2]$

   A. 37
   B. 35
   C. 29
   D. 24

3. What is the next term in the pattern below?

   42, 35, 28, 21, <u>?</u>

   A. 15
   B. 14
   C. 12
   D. 9

4. Which represents the expression below?

   $(18,943 - 4,016) \times 20$

   A. the difference of 18,943 and 4,016, divided by 20
   B. the quotient of 18,943 and 4,016, multiplied by 20
   C. the difference of 18,943 and 4,016, multiplied by 20
   D. the sum of 18,943 and 4,016, multiplied by 20

5. Evaluate: $48 + [5 \times (12 - 4)] + 19$

   A. 69
   B. 107
   C. 443
   D. 651

6. Which represents the description below?

   21 fewer than 9 times 6

   A. $21 - (9 \times 6)$
   B. $(9 \times 6) + 21$
   C. $(9 + 6) - 21$
   D. $(9 \times 6) - 21$

7. Two patterns start at 0. The rule for the first pattern is add 2. The rule for the second pattern is add 3. Which ordered pairs show the corresponding terms from the patterns?

   A. (0, 0), (2, 3), (4, 6), (6, 9)

   B. (0, 0), (2, 3), (3, 6), (6, 8)

   C. (0, 0), (3, 2), (6, 4), (6, 9)

   D. (0, 0), (2, 4), (4, 6), (6, 8)

8. What is the rule for the pattern below?

   31, 37, 43, 49, …

   A. add 7

   B. subtract 7

   C. add 6

   D. subtract 6

9. Evaluate: $[(3 \times 15) + 10] \times (9 - 4)$

_____

10. Two patterns start at 0. The rule for the first pattern is add 1. The rule for the second pattern is add 8.

   A. Write ordered pairs using the first 5 corresponding terms from each pattern. Then graph the ordered pairs.

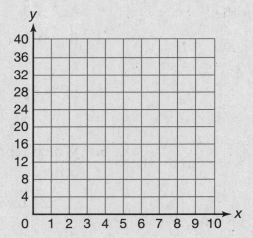

   B. Explain how the corresponding terms in the patterns are related.

_____

_____

Domain 2

Number and Operations in Base Ten

Domain 2: Diagnostic Assessment for Lessons 6–16

Domain 2: Cumulative Assessment for Lessons 6–16

Domain 2: Diagnostic Assessment for Lessons 6–16

1. Find the product.

$$7{,}352 \times 48 = \square$$

   A. 7,400

   B. 88,224

   C. 352,886

   D. 352,896

2. Find the quotient.

$$9{,}207 \div 27 = \square$$

   A. 339

   B. 340

   C. 341

   D. 342

3. Find the difference.

$$9.6 - 3.854 = \square$$

   A. 5.746

   B. 5.756

   C. 6.746

   D. 6.656

4. What is 9.482 rounded to the nearest hundredth?

   A. 9.40

   B. 9.48

   C. 9.49

   D. 9.5

5. Which is true?

   A. $5.864 > 5.846$

   B. $5.864 > 5.864$

   C. $5.846 > 5.864$

   D. $5.846 = 5.864$

6. Find the quotient.

$$0.56 \div 8 = \square$$

   A. 0.007

   B. 0.07

   C. 0.7

   D. 7

7. Find the product.

$$0.78 \times 10^3 = \boxed{}$$

A.   0.0078

B.   7.8

C.   78

D. 780

8. Which represents a value 10 times as much as 0.8?

A.   0.008

B.   0.08

C.   8

D. 80

9. What is four and fifteen thousandths using base-ten numerals?

_____

10. Roast beef is on sale at the deli for $6.78 per pound.

A. How much will it cost to buy 1.5 pounds of roast beef? Show your work.

B. Explain how you found your answer for Part A.

_____

_____

_____

Multiply Whole Numbers

Getting the Idea

In a multiplication problem, the numbers you multiply are called **factors**, and the result is called the **product**. When multiplying two- or three-digit numbers, multiply by the ones and then the tens to find the partial products. Then add the partial products to find the product.

Example 1

Find the product.

$523 \times 18 = \boxed{}$

Strategy   **Multiply by the ones and then the tens. Add the partial products.**

Step 1   Rewrite the problem vertically. Multiply 523 by the 8 ones in 18.

$$
\begin{array}{r}
12 \\
523 \\
\times\ 18 \\
\hline
4184 \\
\end{array}
\quad \leftarrow 8 \times 523
$$

Step 2   Multiply 523 by the 1 ten in 18.

Write a 0 in the ones place before multiplying.

$$
\begin{array}{r}
523 \\
\times\ 18 \\
\hline
4184 \\
5230 \\
\end{array}
\quad \leftarrow 10 \times 523
$$

Step 3   Add the partial products.

$$
\begin{array}{r}
523 \\
\times\ 18 \\
\hline
4184 \\
+\ 5230 \\
\hline
9,414 \\
\end{array}
$$

Solution $523 \times 18 = 9,414$

You can write an **equation** to solve a real-world problem. Use a **variable** to represent the unknown value.

Example 2

Mrs. Robinson is the principal of a school with 465 students. The librarian told Mrs. Robinson that there are 16 times as many books in the library as there are students in the school. How many books are in the library?

Strategy   **Write an equation for the problem, then solve.**

Step 1   Write an equation for the problem.

Let b represent the total number of books in the library.

$465 \times 16 = b$

Step 2   Rewrite the problem. Multiply 465 by the ones digit in 16.

$$
\begin{array}{r}
3\,3 \\
465 \\
\times\ 16 \\
\hline
2790 \\
\end{array}
$$
$\leftarrow 6 \times 465$

Step 3   Multiply 465 by the tens digit in 16.

Use a 0 as a placeholder in the partial product.

$$
\begin{array}{r}
465 \\
\times\ 16 \\
\hline
2790 \\
4650 \\
\end{array}
$$
$\leftarrow 10 \times 465$

Step 4   Add the partial products.

$$
\begin{array}{r}
465 \\
\times\ 16 \\
\hline
2790 \\
+\ 4650 \\
\hline
7{,}440 \\
\end{array}
$$

Solution   **There are 7,440 books in the library.**

Example 3

The new A5 computer sells for $1,499. Yesterday, Electronic World sold 23 of the A5 computers. How much money did Electronic World make from the sale of the A5 computers yesterday?

Strategy **Write an equation for the problem, then solve.**

Step 1   Write an equation for the problem.

Let m represent the total amount of money earned.

$1,499 \times 23 = m$

Step 2   Rewrite the problem vertically and multiply.

$$
\begin{array}{r}
11 \\
1\ 22 \\
1,499 \\
\times\ \ \ 23 \\
\hline
4497 \\
29980 \\
\hline
34,477
\end{array}
$$

Solution **Electronic World made $34,477 from the sale of the A5 computers yesterday.**

You can use the **distributive property** to multiply numbers. To use the distributive property, rewrite one of the factors as a sum of two or more numbers. Then multiply each of the **addends** by the other factor and add the products.

For example, this array model shows how to multiply 12×28.

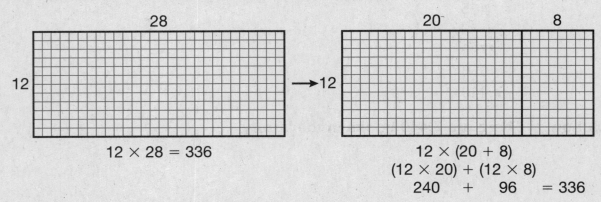

$$12 \times 28 = 336$$

$$
\begin{array}{c}
12 \times (20 + 8) \\
(12 \times 20) + (12 \times 8) \\
240\ \ +\ \ \ 96\ \ = 336
\end{array}
$$

Example 4

Use the distributive property to find 65 × 128.

Strategy   **Use the distributive property.**

Step 1   Write the second factor as a sum of each place value.

128 = 100 + 20 + 8

Step 2   Multiply each addend by 65.

65 × 128

65 × (100 + 20 + 8) = (65 × 100) + (65 × 20) + (65 × 8)

= 6,500 + 1,300 + 520

Step 3   Add the products.

6,500 + 1,300 + 520 = 8,320

Solution   **65 × 128 = 8,320**

Example 5

A rug buyer bought 15 rugs that each cost $462. How much did the rugs cost in all?

Strategy   **Write an equation for the problem. Use the distributive property.**

Step 1   Write an equation for the problem.

Let c represent the total cost of the rugs.

15 × $462 = c

Step 2   Write the second factor as the sum of each place value.

462 = 400 + 60 + 2

Step 3   Multiply each addend by 15.

15 × 462

15 × (400 + 60 + 2) = (15 × 400) + (15 × 60) + (15 × 2)

= 6,000 + 900 + 30

Step 4   Add the products.

6,000 + 900 + 30 = 6,930

Solution   **The rugs cost $6,930 in all.**

Coached Example

A theater sold 329 tickets to an afternoon performance for $26 each. How much money did the theater take in for this performance?

Write an equation for the problem.

Let *m* represent the total amount of money.

_____ × _____ = *m*

Rewrite the problem.

Multiply 329 by the ones digit in 26.

What is the partial product? _____

Use a _____ as a placeholder in the ones place of the second partial product.

Multiply 329 by the tens digit in 26.

What is the partial product? _____

Add the _____ _____ to find the product.

What is the product? _____

The theater took in _____ for this performance.

Lesson Practice • Part 1

Choose the correct answer.

1. What is the product?

   651
   × 22

   A. 2,604

   B. 5,874

   C. 13,222

   D. 14,322

2. $2,543 \times 56 = \boxed{}$

   A. 27,973

   B. 142,408

   C. 143,679

   D. 144,951

3. Which expression has the greatest product?

   A. 65 × 14

   B. 43 × 16

   C. 55 × 15

   D. 70 × 12

4. A restaurant has seating for 165 people. The restaurant offers a $15 buffet. If the restaurant is full and everyone orders the buffet, how much money will the restaurant earn?

   A. $990

   B. $2,475

   C. $2,525

   D. $2,575

5. Malik answered 121 math questions last week. If he completes 121 math questions each week for 36 weeks, how many math questions will Malik complete in all?

   A. 157

   B. 4,356

   C. 6,747

   D. 8,832

6. A bus line has 64 buses in its fleet. Each of the buses can seat 84 passengers. How many passengers can the fleet of buses seat at one time?

   A. 5,166

   B. 5,366

   C. 5,376

   D. 5,476

7. Which expression **cannot** be used to find 237×12?

   A. $(12 \times 200) + (12 \times 30) + (12 \times 7)$

   B. $(12 \times 100) + (12 \times 100) + (12 \times 37)$

   C. $(12 + 200) \times (12 + 37)$

   D. $(237 \times 10) + (237 \times 2)$

8. There are 1,452 seats in each of the 48 sections of an arena. How many seats are there in all?

   A. 17,424

   B. 67,286

   C. 69,696

   D. 69,746

9. Henry works 140 hours each month and earns $12 per hour.

   A. Show how to use the distributive property to find how much Henry earns each month.

   B. If Henry earns the same amount each month, how much will he earn in 12 months? Show your work.

Lesson Practice • Part 2

Choose the correct answer.

1. What is the product?

    827
    × 48

   A. 38,696

   B. 39,346

   C. 39,496

   D. 39,696

2. Silvertown has an area of 36 square miles. The population density of Silvertown is 1,425 people. How many people live in Silvertown?

   A. 52,200

   B. 51,300

   C. 49,300

   D. 41,070

3. Sam is going to multiply a 3-digit whole number times a 2-digit whole number. He will make the greatest product he can make and the least product he can make. What is the difference between products?

   A. 80,011

   B. 87,901

   C. 97,901

   D. 99,901

4. Multiply: $639 \times 74 = \boxed{}$

   A. 46,556

   B. 46,586

   C. 47,286

   D. 48,286

5. Each day Mia spends 45 minutes on the treadmill. There are 365 days in a year. How many minutes will Mia spend on the treadmill in a year?

   A. 16,425 minutes

   B. 16,225 minutes

   C. 16,125 minutes

   D. 15,425 minutes

6. Each ticket for a concert costs $88. There are 7,250 available tickets. If each ticket is sold, how much money will be earned in ticket sales?

   A. $616,000

   B. $621,600

   C. $633,600

   D. $638,000

7. During an event, 92 T-shirts and 38 sweatshirts were purchased. The T-shirts cost $24 each and the sweatshirts cost $42 each. How much money was earned in shirt sales during the event?

   A. $3,494

   B. $3,804

   C. $4,290

   D. $4,776

8. Multiply: 607 × 34 = ☐

   A. 20,418

   B. 20,438

   C. 20,638

   D. 22,780

9. Each person who buys a monthly pass at Park Here pays $27. There were 324 people that bought monthly passes. If 324 parking passes are bought each month, how much money is earned in 12 months?

   A. $104,976

   B. $92,526

   C. $8,748

   D. $3,888

10. Multiply: 7,036 × 52 = ☐

   A. 364,562

   B. 364,872

   C. 365,562

   D. 365,872

11. For each event in an auditorium, tickets on the first floor cost $65 each. Tickets for the second floor cost $45 each. There are 375 seats on the first floor and 284 tickets on the second floor.

   A. If the event is a sell out, how much money is earned? Show your work.

   B. The auditorium hosts 64 events each year. If each is a sell out, how much money will be earned? Show your work.

12. The students in a group photo are arranged in 12 rows. There are 30 students in each row. Use numbers from the box to complete the equation to find the number of students in the photo.

$$12 \times \underline{\hspace{1.5cm}} = \underline{\hspace{1.5cm}}$$

30
42
300
360

13. A car wash charges $12 for a car and $14 for a truck. Select True or False for each statement.

   A. The car wash earns $312 for 26 cars.   ○ True   ○ False

   B. The car wash earns $528 for 37 trucks.   ○ True   ○ False

   C. The car wash earns $146 for 13 cars.   ○ True   ○ False

   D. The car wash earns $406 for 29 trucks.   ○ True   ○ False

14. Draw a line from each expression to its value.

   A. 34×224 •   • 31,070

   B. 501×42 •   • 44,172

   C. $18 \times 2,454$ •   • 7,616

   D. 65×478 •   • 21,042

15. Find each product. Write the expression in the correct box.

21 × 565	421 × 17	121 × 62
48 × 352	22 × 227	72 × 364

Product is less than 10,000.	Product is greater than 10,000.

16. Which expressions can be used to find 354 × 14? Circle all that apply.

A. (300 × 14) + (50 × 14) + 4

B. (300 × 14) + (54 × 14)

C. (300 × 14) + (50 × 14) + (4 × 14)

D. (300 + 14) × (54 + 14)

E. (354 × 10) + (354 × 4)

17. Which expressions can be used to find 468 × 26? Circle all that apply.

A. (468 × 10) + (468 × 10) + (468 × 6)

B. (400 + 26) × (60 + 26) × (8 + 26)

C. (400 × 26) + (6 × 26) + (8 × 26)

D. (100 × 26) + (100 × 26) + (100 × 26) + (100 × 26) + (68 × 26)

E. (400 × 26) + (60 × 26) + (8 × 26)

Divide Whole Numbers

Getting the Idea

In a division problem, the number that is being divided is the **dividend**. The number that divides the dividend is the **divisor**. The answer to a division problem is the **quotient**. If there is a number left over after the division is complete, then the quotient has a **remainder**.

Example 1

There are 851 seats in an auditorium. Each of the 23 rows in the auditorium has the same number of seats. How many seats are in each row?

Strategy   **Write an equation for the problem. Then divide.**

Step 1   Write an equation for the problem.

Let s represent the number of seats in each row.

$851 \div 23 = s$

Step 2   Set up the division problem.

$23\overline{)851}$

Step 3   Decide where to place the first digit in the quotient.

The first digit of the quotient will be in the tens place.

Step 4   Divide 85 tens.

$$
\begin{array}{r}
3 \\
23\overline{)851} \\
-\ 69 \\
\hline
16
\end{array}
$$
  ← 3 × 23 = 69
  ← 85 − 69 = 16

Step 5   Bring down the 1 one. Divide 161 ones.

$$
\begin{array}{r}
37 \\
23\overline{)851} \\
-\ 69\!\downarrow \\
\hline
161 \\
-\ 161 \\
\hline
0
\end{array}
$$
  ← 7 × 23 = 161
  ← 161 − 161 = 0

Solution   **There are 37 seats in each row.**

Since multiplication and division are **inverse operations**, you can check division by using multiplication. Multiply the quotient by the divisor. If the product equals the dividend, the quotient is correct.

$$
\begin{array}{r}
37 \\
\times\ 23 \\
\hline
111 \\
+\ 740 \\
\hline
851
\end{array}
$$

⟵ The product equals the dividend, so the quotient is correct.

When solving a division word problem with a remainder, you need to interpret the remainder. You may ignore the remainder, add 1 to the quotient, or the remainder may be the answer.

Example 2

Tina has 426 stickers. She divides them equally among 15 friends. How many stickers will each friend get?

Strategy   **Write an equation for the problem. Then divide.**

Step 1   Write an equation for the problem.

Let s represent the number of stickers each friend will get.

$426 \div 15 = s$

Step 2   Set up the problem. The first digit of the quotient will be in the tens place.

Divide 42 tens.

$$
\begin{array}{r}
2 \\
15\overline{)426} \\
-\ 30 \\
\hline
12
\end{array}
$$

⟵ $2 \times 15 = 30$
⟵ $42 - 30 = 12$

Step 3   Bring down the 6 ones. Divide 126 ones.

$$
\begin{array}{r}
28\ R6 \\
15\overline{)426} \\
-\ 30\downarrow \\
\hline
126 \\
-\ 120 \\
\hline
6
\end{array}
$$

⟵ $8 \times 15 = 120$
⟵ $126 - 120 = 6$

Step 4   Interpret the remainder.

There are 6 stickers left over. There is no way to divide 6 stickers among 15 friends, so drop the remainder.

Solution   **Each friend will get 28 stickers.**

You can also check a quotient with a remainder. Multiply the quotient by the divisor and add the remainder to the product.

$28 \times 15 = 420$ $420 + 6 = 426$ ← The sum equals the dividend.

Example 3

Spencer wants to put his 2,188 stamps in a binder. Each page in the binder holds 24 stamps. How many stamps will be on the last page in the binder?

Strategy   **Divide each place from left to right.**

Step 1   Set up the division problem.

$$24\overline{)2{,}188}$$

Step 2   Divide each place from left to right.

```
        91 R4
   24)2188
     − 216↓
         28
       − 24
          4
```

Step 3   Interpret the remainder.

The quotient is 91. That means 91 pages are full with 24 stickers on each page.

The remainder is 4. That means there are 4 stickers left over.

The question asks how many stamps will be on the last page of the binder, so the remainder is the answer.

Solution   **There will be 4 stamps on the last page in the binder.**

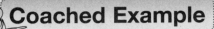

Coached Example

Katie has 568 oranges to put into bags. Each bag can hold 12 oranges. How many bags does Katie need for all the oranges?

Write the problem below that you can use to help answer the question. Then solve it.

The quotient is _____.

The remainder is _____.

The quotient means that _____ bags can be filled with 12 oranges.

The remainder means that there will be _____ oranges left over.

Interpret the remainder. The question asks how many bags Katie needs for all the oranges, so _____.

You can check your answer by multiplying _____ times _____ and adding _____.

Katie needs _____ bags for all the oranges.

Lesson Practice • Part 1

Choose the correct answer.

1. 17)‾323‾

   A. 18

   B. 19

   C. 20

   D. 21

2. 31)‾496‾

   A. 14 R2

   B. 15

   C. 15 R8

   D. 16

3. 72)‾9,234‾

   A. 100 R34

   B. 121 R22

   C. 128 R18

   D. 129 R46

4. In which problem will the quotient be greater than 100?

   A. 5,982 ÷ 54

   B. 6,348 ÷ 67

   C. 7,204 ÷ 73

   D. 8,423 ÷ 87

5. Guy is reading a science fiction book that is 558 pages long. If he reads 28 pages each day, how many days will it take him to read the book?

   A. 19 days

   B. 20 days

   C. 26 days

   D. 28 days

6. Jorge saved $115 to spend on CDs. How many CDs can he buy if each one costs $12?

   A. 12

   B. 10

   C. 9

   D. 7

7. A maximum of 24 people can ride the Jackrabbit roller coaster at one time. If 761 people are in line for the coaster, how many trips will the coaster have to make for all to ride?

A. 32

B. 31

C. 30

D. 17

8. An arena has 5,744 seats. The seats are divided into 16 sections with the same number of seats in each section. How many seats are in each section?

A. 349

B. 359

C. 369

D. 379

9. Simone collects refrigerator magnets. She has 756 magnets in her collection.

A. If each box can hold 22 magnets, how many boxes can Simone fill completely with her magnets? Show your work.

B. How many boxes will Simone need to hold all of her magnets? Explain how you interpreted the remainder to answer parts A and B.

_____

_____

_____

Lesson Practice • Part 2

Choose the correct answer.

1. What is the quotient?

   28)2,128

   A. 61

   B. 66

   C. 71

   D. 76

2. The book that Santiago is reading is 1,127 pages. He plans on reading 36 pages each day. How many days will it take Santiago to complete the book?

   A. 32 days

   B. 31 days

   C. 30 days

   D. 11 days

3. During his vacation Doug took 3,145 photos with his digital camera. His vacation lasted 17 days. How many photos did Doug take per day?

   A. 125

   B. 185

   C. 187

   D. 197

4. What is the quotient?

   46)3,691

   A. 80 R11

   B. 82 R19

   C. 84 R37

   D. 86 R35

5. There are 732 students trying out for baseball teams. There will be exactly 15 players on each team. How many students will not make a baseball team?

   A. 2

   B. 3

   C. 12

   D. 48

6. Genesis now has 1,404 stamps in her U.S. collection. That is 18 times as many stamps as she has in her foreign collection. How many stamps does Genesis have in her foreign collection?

   A. 72

   B. 73

   C. 77

   D. 78

7. Victoria divided 1,694 ÷ 47 and got a quotient of 36. Without performing the entire division, Daleyza said that Victoria made an error. Which sentence is true?

   A. Daleyza is incorrect because Victoria is correct.

   B. Daleyza is correct because if Victoria were correct the ones place in the dividend would have to be 2.

   C. Daleyza is correct because an estimate would show that the quotient is less than 30 because 1,500 ÷ 50 = 30.

   D. Daleyza is correct because an estimate would show that the quotient is greater than 40 because 1,600 ÷ 40 = 40.

8. For which situation should a remainder be ignored?

   A. when finding the part of a number that is not included in a group

   B. when finding the number of items of a type that are needed when there are extra

   C. when finding the number of complete groups when some are left after division

   D. when finding the number of complete groups when none are left after division

9. Zeke has a total of 9,840 baseball cards. He keeps the cards in 42 boxes that each have the same number of cards.

   A. How many cards are in each box? Show your work.

   B. What does the remainder represent?

   _____

   _____

10. Which expressions have a remainder in the quotient? Circle all that apply.

    A. $364 \div 16$

    B. $1,768 \div 68$

    C. $4,569 \div 23$

    D. $3,240 \div 24$

11. A hotel must set up tables for 2,654 people. Select True or False for each statement about how many tables are needed.

    A. If each table seats 12 people, 221 tables are needed.   ○ True   ○ False

    B. If each table seats 14 people, 189 tables are needed.   ○ True   ○ False

    C. If each table seats 15 people, 177 tables are needed.   ○ True   ○ False

    D. If each table seats 16 people, 166 tables are needed.   ○ True   ○ False

12. Find each quotient. Write the division problem in the correct box.

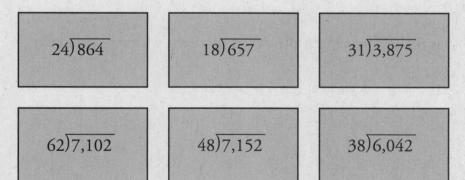

Quotient has a remainder.	Quotient has no remainder.

13. Draw a line from each expression to its value.

A. 6,732 ÷ 34   •   • 138

B. 5,778 ÷ 27   •   • 154

C. 6,348 ÷ 46   •   • 198

D. 2,002 ÷ 13   •   • 214

14. Which expressions have a quotient greater than 100? Circle all that apply.

A. 2,765 ÷ 24

B. 1,627 ÷ 17

C. 8,820 ÷ 86

D. 4,991 ÷ 49

E. 9,201 ÷ 90

F. 7,321 ÷ 75

G. 6,822 ÷ 69

15. Circle the number that makes the expression have a quotient with no remainder.

6,622 ÷ | 27 |
        | 43 |
        | 51 |

Quotients as Equations

Getting the Idea

In Lesson 7, you learned that to check a division problem, you multiply the quotient by the divisor and add the remainder to the product. If the result is equal to the dividend, the quotient is correct. You can use this idea to write an equation.

$$
\begin{array}{r}
13 \text{ R2} \\
18\overline{)236} \\
-18 \\
\hline
56 \\
-54 \\
\hline
2
\end{array}
$$

dividend	=	quotient	×	divisor	+	remainder
236	=	13	×	18	+	2

Example 1

Divide: 785 ÷ 25. Write the result as an equation.

Strategy **Divide. Identify the dividend, quotient, divisor, and remainder to write an equation.**

Step 1 Divide.

$$
\begin{array}{r}
31 \text{ R10} \\
25\overline{)785} \\
-75 \\
\hline
35 \\
-25 \\
\hline
10
\end{array}
$$

Step 2 Write an equation.

dividend	=	quotient	×	divisor	+	remainder
785	=	31	×	25	+	10

Solution **The equation is 785 = 31 × 25 + 10.**

When the result of division has a remainder, the result can be written as a mixed number. A **mixed number** is a number that has a whole-number part and a fraction part.

$$\begin{array}{r} 15\ R2 \\ 9\overline{)137} \\ -9\downarrow \\ \hline 47 \\ -45 \\ \hline 2 \end{array}$$

quotient $+$ $\dfrac{\text{remainder}}{\text{divisor}}$ $=$ mixed number

15 $+$ $\dfrac{2}{9}$ $=$ $15\dfrac{2}{9}$

Example 2

What is the result of $1{,}190 \div 13$ written as a mixed number?

Strategy   **Divide. Then write the mixed number.**

Step 1   Divide.

$$\begin{array}{r} 91\ R7 \\ 13\overline{)1190} \\ -117\downarrow \\ \hline 20 \\ -13 \\ \hline 7 \end{array}$$

Step 2   Write a mixed number.

quotient $+$ $\dfrac{\text{remainder}}{\text{divisor}}$ $=$ mixed number

91 $+$ $\dfrac{7}{13}$ $=$ $91\dfrac{7}{13}$

Solution   The mixed number is $91\dfrac{7}{13}$.

Coached Example

Divide: 963 ÷ 34. Write the result as an equation and as a mixed number.

Write the problem below. Then solve it.

What is the dividend? _____

What is the quotient? _____

What is the divisor? _____

What is the remainder? _____

Write the equation as dividend = quotient × divisor + remainder.

963 = _____ × _____ + _____

Write the mixed number as quotient + $\frac{\text{remainder}}{\text{divisor}}$ = mixed number.

_____ + _____ = _____

The equation for 963 ÷ 34 is _____ = _____ and the mixed number is _____.

Lesson Practice • Part 1

Choose the correct answer.

1. Which equation shows the result of 42 ÷ 15?

   A. $42 = 2 \times 15 + 12$

   B. $42 = 20 \times 2 + 4$

   C. $42 = 10 \times 4 + 2$

   D. $42 = 5 \times 3 + 27$

2. Which mixed number shows the result of 89 ÷ 35?

   A. $1\frac{54}{35}$

   B. $2\frac{19}{35}$

   C. $2\frac{35}{19}$

   D. $19\frac{2}{35}$

3. Which equation shows the result of 302 ÷ 21?

   A. $50 \times 6 + 2 = 302$

   B. $42 \times 7 + 8 = 302$

   C. $14 \times 21 + 8 = 302$

   D. $4 \times 75 + 2 = 302$

4. Which mixed number shows the result of 671 ÷ 83?

   A. $7\frac{8}{83}$

   B. $8\frac{7}{83}$

   C. $8\frac{13}{83}$

   D. $83\frac{7}{8}$

5. Which equation shows the result of 2,501 ÷ 67?

   A. $2{,}501 = 47 \times 53 + 10$

   B. $2{,}501 = 100 \times 25 + 1$

   C. $2{,}501 = 50 \times 50 + 1$

   D. $2{,}501 = 37 \times 67 + 22$

6. Which mixed number shows the result of 4,683 ÷ 29?

   A. $14\frac{29}{161}$

   B. $29\frac{14}{161}$

   C. $161\frac{14}{29}$

   D. $161\frac{29}{14}$

7. There are 355 students in the auditorium. They are sitting in rows with 24 seats in each row. Which mixed number represents the rows that the students are sitting in?

A. $14\frac{11}{24}$

B. $14\frac{19}{24}$

C. $19\frac{14}{24}$

D. $24\frac{14}{19}$

8. A florist had 215 flowers. He used 12 flowers to make each bouquet and had some flowers left over. Which equation shows the result of $215 \div 12$?

A. $215 = 17 \times 12 + 11$

B. $215 = 29 \times 7 + 12$

C. $215 = 15 \times 14 + 5$

D. $215 = 10 \times 20 + 15$

9. Kaleigh has 288 inches of ribbon. She wants to cut the ribbon into 25-inch pieces.

A. Write an equation that shows how many 25-inch pieces of ribbon Kaleigh will have and how much will be left over. Show your work.

B. Write a mixed number that represents the ribbon after Kaleigh cuts it. Explain what each part of the mixed number represents.

_____

_____

_____

Lesson Practice • Part 2

Choose the correct answer.

1. Which equation shows the result of 138 ÷ 17?

   A. $138 = 17 \times 8 + 2$

   B. $138 = 24 \times 5 + 17$

   C. $138 = 30 \times 4 + 17$

   D. $138 = 40 \times 3 + 17$

2. Roman divided two numbers that resulted in a remainder that he wrote as a mixed number that was not put into simplest form. Which sentence about the fraction part of the mixed number is **not** true?

   A. The denominator in the remainder is equal to the divisor.

   B. The numerator in the remainder can be less than the divisor.

   C. The denominator is greater than the numerator in the remainder.

   D. The numerator in the remainder can be equal to the divisor.

3. Which mixed number shows the result of 4,193 ÷ 38?

   A. $107\frac{27}{38}$

   B. $110\frac{13}{38}$

   C. $120\frac{33}{38}$

   D. $136\frac{25}{38}$

4. Which equation shows the result of 6,274 ÷ 86?

   A. $6,274 = 72 \times 86 + 82$

   B. $6,274 = 100 \times 62 + 74$

   C. $6,274 = 80 \times 78 + 34$

   D. $6,274 = 90 \times 69 + 64$

5. Which mixed number shows the result of 5,639 ÷ 45?

   A. $103\frac{3}{45}$

   B. $122\frac{28}{45}$

   C. $125\frac{14}{45}$

   D. $127\frac{23}{45}$

6. Which equation shows the result of $3{,}275 \div 23$?

A. $3{,}275 = 100 \times 32 + 75$

B. $3{,}275 = 110 \times 29 + 85$

C. $3{,}275 = 136 \times 24 + 11$

D. $3{,}275 = 142 \times 23 + 9$

7. Each CD shelf holds 54 CDs. Melanie's family has 688 CDs in their collection. They are going to put the maximum number of CDs on each shelf. Which mixed number represents the number of shelves that are filled?

A. $13\frac{14}{54}$

B. $12\frac{40}{54}$

C. $12\frac{30}{54}$

D. $10\frac{48}{54}$

8. Which describes how to write an equation to check a quotient that has a remainder?

A. Multiply the quotient times the dividend and add the remainder. If the sum is equal to the divisor, the quotient is correct.

B. Multiply the quotient times the divisor and add the remainder. If the sum is equal to the dividend, the quotient is correct.

C. Multiply the remainder times the dividend and add the quotient. If the sum is equal to the divisor, the quotient is correct.

D. Multiply the remainder times the divisor and add the quotient. If the sum is equal to the dividend, the quotient is correct.

9. Eliana has collected 842 pennies. She wants to organize them into groups of 35 pennies.

A. Write an equation that shows how many 35-penny groups Eliana can make and how much will be left over.

_____

B. Write a mixed number that represents the number of 35-penny groups. Explain what each part of the mixed number represents.

_____

_____

_____

10. Find each quotient. Write the expression in the correct box based on the fraction part of the quotient.

243 ÷ 19	283 ÷ 19	986 ÷ 19

815 ÷ 19	870 ÷ 19	718 ÷ 19

Fraction part is $\frac{15}{19}$.	Fraction part is $\frac{17}{19}$.

11. Circle the fraction that completes the mixed number of the quotient.

$9{,}576 \div 62 = 154$

$$\frac{62}{28}$$

$$\frac{28}{9{,}576}$$

$$\frac{28}{62}$$

12. Draw a line from each division problem to its quotient as a mixed number.

A. $9,496 \div 49$ •   • $135\frac{15}{49}$

B. $8,602 \div 49$ •   • $167\frac{22}{49}$

C. $6,630 \div 49$ •   • $175\frac{27}{49}$

D. $8,205 \div 49$ •   • $193\frac{39}{49}$

13. Select True or False for each statement.

A. The result of $1,506 \div 29$ is $51\frac{27}{29}$.   ○ True   ○ False

B. The result of $2,589 \div 37$ is $69\frac{36}{37}$.   ○ True   ○ False

C. The result of $4,183 \div 17$ is $246\frac{3}{17}$.   ○ True   ○ False

D. The result of $3,759 \div 23$ is $163\frac{9}{23}$.   ○ True   ○ False

14. Write an equation that can be used to check the result of $6,742 \div 41$. Use the numbers in the box to complete the equation.

_____ = _____ × _____ + _____

| 18 |
| 41 |
| 164 |
| 6,742 |

Read and Write Decimals

Getting the Idea

A **decimal** is a number with a decimal point. A **decimal point (.)** separates the ones place from the tenths place.

The grids below represent one tenth, one hundredth, and one thousandth.

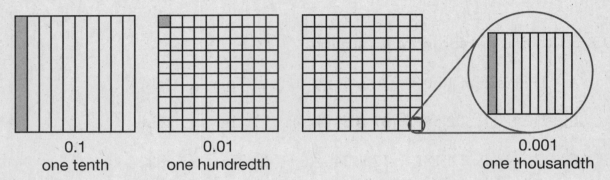

0.1	0.01	0.001
one tenth	one hundredth	one thousandth

To read or write a decimal number less than one, read the number to the right of the decimal point. Then read the least place value. For example, 0.7 is *seven tenths*, and 0.36 is *thirty-six hundredths*.

To read or write a decimal number greater than 1, use the word *and* to separate the whole-number part from the decimal part. For example, 2.003 is *two and three thousandths.*

There are different ways to read and write decimals.

Hundreds	Tens	Ones	.	Tenths	Hundredths	Thousandths
1	9	6	.	7	4	8

base-ten numeral: 196.748

number name: one hundred ninety-six and seven hundred forty-eight thousandths

expanded form: 100 + 90 + 6 + 0.7 + 0.04 + 0.008

Each place in a decimal has a value that is 10 times the value of the place to its right.

For example, in 6.666, the 6 in the hundredths place has a value of 0.06. That is 10 times the value of the 6 in the thousandths place.

$0.006 \times 10 = 0.06$

Each place in a decimal has a value that is $\frac{1}{10}$ the value of the place to its left.

For example, in 6.666, the 6 in the thousandths place has a value of 0.006. That is $\frac{1}{10}$ the value of the 6 in the hundredths place.

Example 1

A lab sample has a mass of 0.222 gram. What is the value of the 2 in the thousandths place in relation to the 2 in the hundredths place?

Strategy   **Use a place-value chart.**

Step 1   Write each digit of the number in a chart.

Ones	.	Tenths	Hundredths	Thousandths
0	.	2	2	2

Step 2   Find the value of the 2 in the thousandths place: 0.002.

The digit to its left is in the hundredths place: 0.02.

$0.002 \div 0.02 = \frac{1}{10}$

The value of the 2 in the thousandths place is $\frac{1}{10}$ the value of the 2 in the hundredths place.

Solution   **The value of the 2 in the thousandths place is $\frac{1}{10}$ the value of the 2 in the hundredths place.**

Example 2

What decimal describes the shaded part of the grids?

Strategy   **Count the number of small shaded squares in each grid.**

Step 1   There are 100 small squares in the grid on the left and all are shaded.

Each small square is one hundredth, or 0.01.

So the entire grid is equal to 100 × 0.01 or 1.

Step 2 There are 100 small squares in the grid on the right and 64 are shaded.

Each small square is one hundredth, or 0.01.

So the shaded squares are equal to 64 × 0.01 or 0.64.

Step 3 Write the decimal for each grid and combine them.

1 + 0.64 = 1.64

Solution **The decimal 1.64, or one and sixty-four hundredths, describes the shaded part of the grids.**

Example 3

The winning speed in a car race was 125.044 miles per hour. How do you write that speed in expanded form?

Strategy **Make a place-value chart to find the value of each digit.**

Step 1 Write the decimal in a place-value chart.

Hundreds	Tens	Ones	.	Tenths	Hundredths	Thousandths
1	2	5	.	0	4	4

Step 2 Find the value of each digit.

1 hundred = 1 × 100 = 100

2 tens = 2 × 10 = 20

5 ones = 5 × 1 = 5

4 hundredths = 4 × 0.01 = 0.04

4 thousandths = 4 × 0.001 = 0.004

Step 3 Write the expanded form of the number.

125.044 = 100 + 20 + 5 + 0.04 + 0.004

Solution **In expanded form, 125.044 is written as 100 + 20 + 5 + 0.04 + 0.004.**

Another way to write expanded form is with multiplication.

For example, write 347.392 in expanded form.

347.392 = 300 + 40 + 7 + 0.3 + 0.09 + 0.002

Then write 347.392 in expanded form with multiplication.

Multiply each digit in the number by the value its place represents. You can use fractions or decimals to write a number in expanded form. The fraction $\frac{1}{10}$ is equivalent to the decimal 0.1.

$$347.392 = 3 \times 100 + 4 \times 10 + 7 \times 1 + 3 \times \frac{1}{10} + 9 \times \frac{1}{100} + 2 \times \frac{1}{1000}$$

Example 4

Write the decimal 468.721 in expanded form with multiplication.

Strategy   **Use a place-value chart.**

Step 1   Write the decimal in a place value chart.

Hundreds	Tens	Ones	.	Tenths	Hundredths	Thousandths
4	6	8	.	7	2	1

Step 2   Show each digit as a multiplication expression.

4 hundreds ⟶ 4×100

6 tens ⟶ 6×10

8 ones ⟶ 8×1

7 tenths ⟶ $7 \times \frac{1}{10}$

2 hundredths ⟶ $2 \times \frac{1}{100}$

1 thousandth ⟶ $1 \times \frac{1}{1000}$

Step 3   Write the expanded form with multiplication.

$$4 \times 100 + 6 \times 10 + 8 \times 1 + 7 \times \frac{1}{10} + 2 \times \frac{1}{100} + 1 \times \frac{1}{1000}$$

Solution $\mathbf{468.721 = 4 \times 100 + 6 \times 10 + 8 \times 1 + 7 \times \frac{1}{10} + 2 \times \frac{1}{100} + 1 \times \frac{1}{1000}}$

Coached Example

The currency of China is the yuan. When Alana went to China, $1 was worth about 6.837 yuan. What is the number name and the expanded form with multiplication for 6.837?

To write the number name, first write the decimal in a place-value chart.

Ones	.	Tenths	Hundredths	Thousandths

Separate the decimal into two parts: the whole-number part and the decimal part.

Write the number name for 6. _____

Write the word that separates the whole-number part from the decimal part. _____

Write the decimal part as you would a whole number. _____

What is the least place value of the decimal part? _____

The number name for 6.837 is _____.

Write the expanded form with multiplication.

Find the value of each digit.

6 ones = _____

8 tenths = _____

3 hundredths = _____

7 thousandths = _____

Write the expanded form. 6.837 = _____

Write the expanded form with multiplication.

6.837 = _____

Lesson Practice • Part 1

Choose the correct answer.

1. What decimal represents the part of the grids that is shaded?

   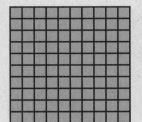 

   A. 1.04

   B. 1.06

   C. 1.4

   D. 1.6

2. Which shows two and twelve thousandths written using base-ten numerals?

   A. 2.012

   B. 2.102

   C. 2.12

   D. 2.201

3. In the decimal 99.999, which is $\frac{1}{10}$ the value of the 9 in the tenths place?

   A. The 9 in the tens place.

   B. The 9 in the ones place.

   C. The 9 in the hundredths place.

   D. The 9 in the thousandths place.

4. Which has a value 10 times greater than 0.008?

   A. 0.08

   B. 0.8

   C. 8

   D. 80

5. The land speed record for one mile is seven hundred sixty-three and thirty-five thousandths miles per hour. Which shows the decimal in expanded form?

   A. 700 + 60 + 3 + 0.3 + 0.05

   B. 700 + 60 + 3 + 0.03 + 0.005

   C. 700 + 60 + 3 + 30 + 5

   D. 700 + 30 + 5 + 0.6 + 0.03

6. If the mass of Earth is equal to 1, the mass of Mercury is 0.055. Which is the number name for Mercury's mass?

   A. fifty-five

   B. fifty-five tenths

   C. fifty-five hundredths

   D. fifty-five thousandths

7. Which has $\frac{1}{10}$ the value of 0.01?

   A.　　0.001

   B.　　0.1

   C.　　10

   D. 1,000

8. Which is the expanded form with multiplication for 836.205?

   A. $8 \times 1{,}000 + 3 \times 100 + 60 \times 1 + 2 \times \frac{1}{10} + 5 \times \frac{1}{1000}$

   B. $8 \times 1{,}000 + 3 \times 100 + 6 \times 1 + 2 \times \frac{1}{10} + 5 \times \frac{1}{1000}$

   C. $8 \times 100 + 3 \times 10 + 6 \times 1 + 2 \times \frac{1}{10} + 5 \times \frac{1}{1000}$

   D. $8 \times 100 + 3 \times 10 + 6 \times 1 + 2 \times \frac{1}{100} + 5 \times \frac{1}{1000}$

9. Randy said that the number 0.03 has a value 10 times greater than 0.003.

   A. Is he correct? Explain your answer.

   _____

   _____

   _____

   _____

   _____

   B. What number is ten times greater than 0.3? Explain your answer.

   _____

   _____

   _____

   _____

   _____

   _____

Lesson Practice • Part 2

Choose the correct answer.

1. The gold medal winning time in the women's 100-meter backstroke in the 2012 Summer Olympics was 58.33 seconds. Which shows the number name for the number of seconds?

   A. five and eight hundred thirty-three thousandths

   B. fifty-eight and thirty-three thousandths

   C. fifty-eight and thirty-three hundredths

   D. five thousand, eight hundred thirty-three

2. Which describes the relationship between the 4 in 26.492 and the 4 in 4.15?

   A. The 4 is 26.492 has $\frac{1}{100}$ the value of the 4 in 4.15.

   B. The 4 is 26.492 has $\frac{1}{10}$ the value of the 4 in 4.15.

   C. The 4 is 26.492 has 10 times the value of the 4 in 4.15.

   D. The 4 is 26.492 has 100 times the value of the 4 in 4.15.

3. Jupiter has a rotational inclination of one and three hundred four thousandths degrees. Which shows the number of degrees written in expanded form?

   A. $1 + \frac{3}{100} + \frac{4}{1,000}$

   B. $1 + \frac{3}{10} + \frac{4}{1,000}$

   C. $1 + \frac{3}{10} + \frac{4}{100}$

   D. $10 + 3 + \frac{4}{1,000}$

4. The winning speed at the 2014 Brickyard 400 was one hundred fifty and two hundred ninety-seven thousandths miles per hour. Which shows that number of miles per hour using base-ten numerals?

   A. 152.907

   B. 152.097

   C. 150.297

   D. 105.297

5. Which decimal represents the shaded part of the grid using a number name?

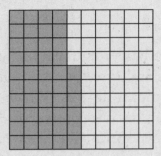

   A. forty-six hundredths

   B. forty-six thousandths

   C. forty-six hundreds

   D. forty-six thousands

6. Which decimal has 2 fewer tens and 4 more thousandths than 2,638.172?

   A. 6,618.172

   B. 2,638.212

   C. 2,638.152

   D. 2,618.176

7. The winner of a computer game is the person who finishes in the least amount of time. Jade finished a game in 40.056 seconds. Which shows Jade's time in seconds in expanded form?

   A. 40 + 0.05 + 0.006

   B. 40 + 0.5 + 0.006

   C. 40 + 0.5 + 0.06

   D. 40 + 5 + 0.6

8. Which describes the relationship between the 7 in 386.742 and the 7 in 4,028.173?

   A. The 7 is 386.742 has $\frac{1}{100}$ the value of the 7 in 4,028.173.

   B. The 7 is 386.742 has $\frac{1}{10}$ the value of the 7 in 4,028.173.

   C. The 7 is 386.742 has 10 times the value of the 7 in 4,028.173.

   D. The 7 is 386.742 has 100 times the value of the 7 in 4,028.173.

9. On a recent trip to Mexico, Mr. Gomez received an exchange rate of 13.026 pesos for each dollar.

   A. Write 13.026 in expanded form using fractions for the decimal places.

   _____

   B. Write 13.026 in expanded form using decimals for the decimal places.

   _____

   C. Write the number name for 13.026.

   _____

10. Draw a line from each pair of grids to the decimal that describes the shaded part of the grids.

A.  • • 1.2

B.  • • 1.47

C. 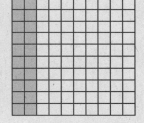 • • 1.5

D. 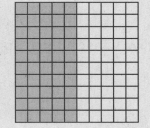 • • 1.74

11. Draw a line from each number name to the correct base-ten numeral.

A. thirty-two and two hundredths • • 3.22

B. three hundred twenty and two thousandths • • 30.202

C. three and twenty-two hundredths • • 32.02

D. thirty and two hundred two thousandths • • 320.002

12. Complete the expanded form of 256.17. Use the numbers from the box.

200 + 50 + _____ + _____ + 0.07

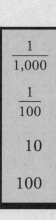

0.1

0.6

1

6

13. Use numbers from the box to complete the expanded form for 126.987.

$1 \times$ ____ $+ 2 \times$ ____ $+ 6 \times 1 + 9 \times \frac{1}{10} + 8 \times$ ____ $+ 7 \times$ ____

$\frac{1}{1,000}$

$\frac{1}{100}$

10

100

14. Select the correct ways to write 638.257. Circle all that apply.

A. six hundred thirty-eight and two hundred fifty-seven hundredths

B. $600 \times 30 \times 8 \times 0.2 \times 0.05 \times 0.007$

C. $6 \times 100 + 3 \times 10 + 8 \times 1 + 2 \times \frac{1}{10} + 5 \times \frac{1}{100} + 7 \times \frac{1}{1000}$

D. six hundred thirty-eight and two hundred fifty-seven thousandths

Compare Decimals

Getting the Idea

Comparing decimals is similar to comparing whole numbers. When comparing decimals, start by comparing the numbers in the greatest place. If they are the same, compare the digits in the next place to the right. Do this until you can determine which digit is greater.

Decimals can be compared using the following symbols.

= means **is equal to.**

< means **is less than.**

> means **is greater than.**

Example 1

Which symbol makes this number sentence true? Use >, <, or =.

32.135 ◯ 32.035

Strategy   **Line up the numbers on the decimal point. Compare the digits, starting with the greatest place value.**

Step 1   Line up the digits on the decimal point.

32.135

32.035

Step 2   Look for the greatest place where the digits are different.

The digits in the tenths place are different.

Step 3   Compare the digits in the tenths place.

1 > 0, so 32.135 > 32.035

Solution   **32.135 ⊵ 32.035**

Example 2

Which symbol makes this number sentence true? Use >, <, or =.

47.085 ◯ 47.09

Strategy	**Line up the numbers on the decimal point. Compare the digits starting with the greatest place value.**
Step 1	Line up the digits on the decimal point.
	47.085
	47.09
Step 2	Look for the greatest place where the digits are different.
	The digits in the hundredths place are different.
Step 3	Compare the digits in the hundredths place.
	8 < 9, so 47.085 < 47.09

Solution   **47.085 ◯< 47.09**

Example 3

Which of these numbers is the least? Which is the greatest?

7.35   6.989   7.038

Strategy	**Compare the decimals.**
Step 1	Compare the whole-number parts.
	Since 6 < 7, the least number is 6.989.
	The other two numbers have 7 as the whole-number part.
Step 2	Compare the tenths for the other two numbers.
	The tenths place of 7.35 is 3.
	The tenths place of 7.038 is 0.
	Since 3 > 0, 7.35 > 7.038.

Solution   **The least number is 6.989. The greatest number is 7.35.**

Example 4

Emma is mailing some packages. The weights of the packages, in pounds, are shown below. Order the weights from least to greatest.

9.42   3.201   4.083   11.2

Strategy   **Compare the decimals.**

Step 1   Compare the whole-number parts.

They are all different.

Step 2   Order the whole-number parts.

3, 4, 9, 11

Step 3   Since the whole-number parts are all different, order the decimals the same way.

3.201, 4.083, 9.42, 11.2

Solution   **The weights of the packages in order from least to greatest are 3.201 pounds, 4.083 pounds, 9.42 pounds, and 11.2 pounds.**

Coached Example

Which represents the lesser distance: 4.295 kilometers or 4.3 kilometers?

Compare the _____-number parts first.

The whole-number parts are _____.

Next compare the digits in the _____ place.

Use >, <, or = to compare.

_____ ◯ _____, so 4.295 ◯ 4.3.

The lesser distance is _____ kilometers.

Lesson Practice • Part 1

Choose the correct answer.

1. Which symbol makes this number sentence true?

   38.21 $\bigcirc$ 38.023

   A. >

   B. <

   C. =

   D. +

2. Which decimal makes this sentence true?

   17.2 > _____

   A. 17.3

   B. 17.212

   C. 17.25

   D. 17.025

3. Which decimal is greater than 24.07 and less than 24.075?

   A. 24.007

   B. 24.070

   C. 24.071

   D. 24.08

4. Which number sentence is true?

   A. 6.73 > 6.728

   B. 4.32 < 4.320

   C. 5.039 = 5.390

   D. 3.154 > 3.16

5. Which decimal is between 4.1 and 4.3?

   A. 4.34

   B. 4.17

   C. 4.06

   D. 4.02

6. Which shows the decimals in the correct order?

   A. 5.271 > 5.217 > 5.38

   B. 5.38 > 5.217 > 5.271

   C. 5.271 > 5.38 > 5.217

   D. 5.38 > 5.271 > 5.217

Use the following information for questions 7 and 8.

The table shows the number of miles Tyra ran each day last week.

Tyra's Running Distances

Day	Number of Miles
Monday	4.35
Tuesday	5.714
Wednesday	3.73
Thursday	3.51
Friday	4.161

7. On which day did Tyra run the least number of miles?

   A. Monday

   B. Tuesday

   C. Wednesday

   D. Thursday

8. On which day did Tyra run the greatest number of miles?

   A. Monday

   B. Tuesday

   C. Wednesday

   D. Thursday

9. The table shows the capacities of four different containers.

Container Capacity

Container	Number of Liters
A	1.73
B	2.061
C	1.59
D	2.1

A. List the containers from least to greatest capacity.

_____

B. Explain or show why your answer to part A is correct.

_____

_____

_____

Lesson Practice • Part 2

Choose the correct answer.

1. Which decimal is greater than 7.26 and less than 7.27?

   A. 7.026

   B. 7.258

   C. 7.263

   D. 7.271

2. Which sentence is true?

   A. 8.342 < 8.35

   B. 7.62 = 7.602

   C. 6.174 > 6.18

   D. 5.09 > 5.092

3. Which decimal makes this sentence true?

   28.349 < _____

   A. 28.34

   B. 28.35

   C. 28.347

   D. 28.3

4. Which symbol makes this number sentence true?

   4.027 ◯ 4.1

   A. >   C. =

   B. <   D. +

5. Which sentence about comparing two decimals greater than 0 and less than 1 is true?

   A. The decimal with the greater number of decimal places is greater.

   B. The decimal with the lesser number of decimal places is greater.

   C. The decimal that has the greater digit in its least place value is greater.

   D. The decimal that has the greater digit in the place closest to the decimal point is greater.

6. Usian Bolt won two gold medals in the 200-meter run in the Summer Olympics. In 2008, he won with a time of 19.3 seconds. In 2012, he won with a time of 19.32 seconds. Which sentence is true?

   A. 19.3 > 19.32

   B. 19.3 = 19.32

   C. 19.32 < 19.3

   D. 19.32 > 19.3

7. The table shows the number of dollars that were worth 1 euro in recent years.

Dollars Per Euro

Year	Dollars Worth 1 Euro
2010	0.754
2011	0.718
2012	0.778
2013	0.753

In which year was the dollar worth the most?

A. 2010

B. 2011

C. 2012

D. 2013

8. The table shows the gold medal winning times in the women's 100-meter hurdles in the Summer Olympics.

100-Meter Hurdle Times

Year	Time (in seconds)
2000	12.65
2004	12.37
2008	12.54
2012	12.35

Which gold medal winning time was the least?

A. 12.65 seconds

B. 12.37 seconds

C. 12.54 seconds

D. 12.35 seconds

9. Mr. Brickman put these numbers and decimal point on the board.

0 1 2 3 .

He provided these rules.

• Each digit and the decimal point must be used for each number.

• The decimal cannot be equivalent to a whole number.

• The 0 cannot be the first or last digit.

A. What is the least number that can be made?

_____

B. What is the greatest number that can be made?

_____

10. Circle the symbol that makes the number sentence true.

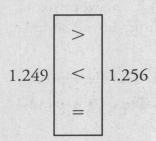

1.249   [>   <   =]   1.256

11. The table shows the masses of four different rocks. Select True or False for each statement.

Rock Masses

Rock	Mass (in grams)
A	24.560
B	23.189
C	24.509
D	23.302

A. Rock A has a greater mass than rock C.   ○ True ○ False

B. Rock B has a greater mass than rock D.   ○ True ○ False

C. Rock C has a greater mass than rock B.   ○ True ○ False

D. Rock D has less mass than rock C.   ○ True ○ False

12. Draw a line from each number sentence to the symbol that makes it true.

A. 17.401 ◯ 17.389 •   • <

B. 17.183 ◯ 17.185 •   • =

C. 17.236 ◯ 17.236 •   • >

13. Circle the number that makes the statement true.

2.485 >

    2.489

    2.476

    2.510

14. Which decimals are greater than 32.071? Circle all that apply.

   A. 32.12

   B. 32.07

   C. 32.076

   D. 31.999

   E. 32.069

   F. 32.09

15. Compare each decimal to 12.505. Write the decimal in the correct box.

| 12.5 | 12.503 | 12.507 | 12.7 | 12.601 | 13.112 |

Less than 12.505	Greater than 12.505

Round Decimals

Getting the Idea

Rounding decimals is similar to rounding whole numbers.

To **round** a decimal, look at the digit to the right of the place you are rounding to.

- If the digit is 5 or greater, round up.
- If the digit is 4 or less, round down.

Example 1

What is 32.86 rounded to the nearest tenth?

Strategy　　**Use rounding rules to round to the nearest tenth.**

　　Step 1　　Look at the digit to the right of the place you are rounding to.

　　　　　　The digit to the right of the tenths place is in the hundredths place.

　　　　　　32.8**6**

　　　　　　The digit is 6.

　　Step 2　　Use the rounding rules to decide if you should round up or down.

　　　　　　Since 6 > 5, round up.

　　　　　　32.86 rounds to 32.9.

Solution　　**Rounded to the nearest tenth, 32.86 is 32.9.**

Example 2

In her physical education class, Jenny ran 1 mile in 7.38 minutes. What is Jenny's time rounded to the nearest minute?

Strategy   **Use a number line to round.**

Step 1   Locate 7.38 between 7 and 8 on a number line.

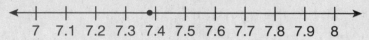

Step 2   Decide if 7.38 is closer to 7 or 8 on the number line.

7.38 is closer to 7 than to 8.

So 7.38 rounded to the nearest minute is 7.

Solution   **Jenny's time rounded to the nearest minute is 7 minutes.**

Example 3

Sean has 23.69 meters of string. How many meters of string, rounded to the nearest tenth of a meter, does Sean have?

Strategy   **Use rounding rules.**

Step 1   Look at the digit to the right of the place that you are rounding to.

The digit to the right of the tenths place is 9.

23.6**9**

Step 2   Use rounding rules to decide if you should round up or down.

9 > 5, so round up.

23.69 rounded to the nearest tenth is 23.7.

Solution   **Sean has 23.7 meters of string, rounded to the nearest tenth of a meter.**

Example 4

Dwayne ran 11.374 kilometers. Rounded to the nearest hundredth, how many kilometers did he run?

Strategy   **Use rounding rules.**

Step 1   Look at the digit to the right of the place that you are rounding to.

The digit to the right of the hundredths place is 4.

11.37**4**

Step 2   Use rounding rules to decide if you should round up or down.

4 < 5, so round down.

11.374 rounded to the nearest hundredth is 11.37.

Solution   **Rounded to the nearest hundredth, Dwayne ran 11.37 kilometers.**

Coached Example

In his swim class, Alan swam 1 lap in 18.27 seconds. What is Alan's time, rounded to the nearest whole second?

Round 18.27 to the nearest _____.

Look at the digit to the _____ of the place you are rounding to.

The digit in that place is _____, which means you round _____.

Rounded to the nearest whole second, 18.27 is _____.

Lesson Practice • Part 1

Choose the correct answer.

1. It takes 686.98 days for Mars to revolve around the sun. To the nearest whole number, how many days does it take for Mars to revolve around the sun?

   A. 686 days

   B. 686.9 days

   C. 687 days

   D. 688 days

2. What is 8.14 rounded to the nearest tenth?

   A. 8

   B. 8.1

   C. 8.2

   D. 9

3. What is 14.999 rounded to the nearest hundredth?

   A. 10

   B. 14

   C. 15

   D. 20

4. Lionel's bedroom is 3.37 meters wide. What is the width of Lionel's bedroom to the nearest tenth of a meter?

   A. 4 meters

   B. 3.4 meters

   C. 3.3 meters

   D. 3 meters

5. Hannah exercised on a stationary bike for 19.55 minutes. For how many minutes did Hannah exercise, to the nearest tenth?

   A. 20 minutes

   B. 19.6 minutes

   C. 19.5 minutes

   D. 19 minutes

6. What is 6.493 rounded to the nearest hundredth?

   A. 6

   B. 6.48

   C. 6.49

   D. 6.5

7. A caterpillar is 2.83 centimeters long. How long is the caterpillar to the nearest whole centimeter?

    A. 2 centimeters

    B. 2.8 centimeters

    C. 2.9 centimeters

    D. 3 centimeters

8. An apple has a mass of 32.01 grams. What is the mass of the apple rounded to the nearest tenth of a gram?

    A. 32 grams

    B. 32.1 grams

    C. 32.11 grams

    D. 32.2 grams

9. Teresa's dog weighs 9.25 pounds. Her cat weighs 8.75 pounds.

    A. Round the weight of each pet to the nearest whole pound.

    _____

    _____

    B. What do you notice about the rounded weights? Explain your answer.

    _____

    _____

    _____

Lesson Practice • Part 2

Choose the correct answer.

1. The women's world record for the 100-meter run is 10.49 seconds. What is 10.49 seconds rounded to the nearest second?

   A. 10 seconds

   B. 10.4 seconds

   C. 10.5 seconds

   D. 11 seconds

2. In 2013, $1 was worth 30.696 Thailand baht. What is 30.696 rounded to the nearest hundredth?

   A. 30.6

   B. 30.69

   C. 30.7

   D. 31

3. Levi said that 26.247 rounds to 26.3 to the nearest tenth. Amaya said that 26.247 rounds to 26.25 to the nearest hundredth. Who is correct?

   A. Levi only

   B. Amaya only

   C. They are both correct.

   D. Neither is correct.

4. In 2013, New York City had 66.37 inches of precipitation. What is that amount of precipitation to the nearest inch?

   A. 67 inches

   B. 66.4 inches

   C. 66.3 inches

   D. 66 inches

5. A greyhound can reach a top speed of 39.35 miles per hour. Lucia said that 39.35 rounds to 40 to the nearest whole number. Elias said that 39.35 rounds to 39.3 to the nearest tenth. Who is correct?

   A. Lucia only

   B. Elias only

   C. They are both correct.

   D. Neither is correct.

6. Which number does **not** round to 17.8 to the nearest tenth?

   A. 17.76

   B. 17.749

   C. 17.841

   D. 17.751

7. The greatest gain in the history of the Dow Jones was 936.42 points in 2008. Which sentence about 936.42 is true?

   A. It rounds to 936.4 to the nearest tenth.

   B. It rounds to 937 to the nearest whole.

   C. It rounds to 930 to the nearest ten.

   D. It rounds to 1,000 to the nearest hundred.

8. It is a major league baseball player's goal to hit 0.300. Batting averages are rounded to the nearest thousandth. Which is the least actual batting average that a baseball player can have and still hit 0.300?

   A. 0.2991

   B. 0.2994

   C. 0.2995

   D. 0.2999

9. Rounded to the nearest ten-thousandth, a centimeter has a length of 0.3937 inch.

   A. What is the length of a centimeter to the nearest thousandth inch?

   _____

   B. What is the length of a centimeter to the nearest hundredth inch?

   _____

   C. For 0.3937 inch, is it better to round to the nearest inch or to the nearest tenth inch? Explain.

   _____

   _____

   _____

10. Circle the hundredths digit that makes the decimal round to 65.7.

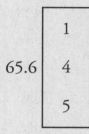

11. Round each decimal to the nearest tenth. Write the decimal in the correct box.

| 15.26 | 15.36 | 15.329 | 15.349 | 15.35 | 15.384 |

Rounds to 15.3	**Rounds to 15.4**

12. Draw a line from each decimal to its value when rounded to the nearest hundredth.

A.	12.518	●		●	12.48
B.	12.485	●		●	12.49
C.	12.514	●		●	12.51
D.	12.483	●		●	12.52

13. Select True or False for each statement.

A. To the nearest hundredth, 125.647 rounds to 125.6.	○ True ○ False
B. To the nearest tenth, 36.429 rounds to 36.4.	○ True ○ False
C. To the nearest whole number, 8.721 rounds to 9.	○ True ○ False
D. To the nearest tenth, 84.482 rounds to 84.5.	○ True ○ False
E. To the nearest hundredth, 78.157 rounds to 78.15.	○ True ○ False
F. To the nearest tenth, 1.148 rounds to 1.1.	○ True ○ False

14. Which decimals have a value of 3.7 when rounded to the nearest tenth? Circle all that apply.

A. 3.71 **D.** 3.649

B. 3.692 **E.** 3.791

C. 3.75 **F.** 3.65

15. A corn plant is 5.267 feet tall. Select True or False for each statement.

A. It is 5.26 feet tall to the nearest hundredth.	○ True ○ False
B. It is 5.3 feet tall to the nearest whole foot.	○ True ○ False
C. It is 5.27 feet tall to the nearest hundredth.	○ True ○ False
D. It is 5.3 feet tall to the nearest tenth.	○ True ○ False

16. Draw a line from each decimal to its value when rounded to the nearest tenth.

A. 8.457 •   • 8.3

B. 8.371 •   • 8.4

C. 8.567 •   • 8.5

D. 8.999 •   • 8.6

E. 8.809 •   • 8.7

F. 8.661 •   • 8.8

G. 8.858 •   • 8.9

H. 8.329 •   • 9

Multiply and Divide by Powers of Ten

Getting the Idea

To multiply a whole number by a **power of 10**, add on zeros at the end of the whole number.

To multiply a whole number by 10, put one zero at the end of the number.

For example, 12 × 10 = 12**0**

To multiply a whole number by 100, put two zeros at the end of the number.

For example, 12 × 100 = 1,2**00**

To multiply a whole number by 1,000, put three zeros at the end of the number.

For example, 12 × 1,000 = 12,**000**

Each place in a number has a value that is 10 times the value of the place to its right. For example, in 3.37 the 3 before the decimal point has a value that is 10 times the 3 after the decimal point.

Likewise, each place in a number has a value that is $\frac{1}{10}$ the value of the place to its left. For example, in 3.37 the 3 after the decimal point has a value that is $\frac{1}{10}$ the value of the 3 before the decimal point.

Example 1

What is the product?

53 × 10 = ☐

Strategy   **Use mental math.**

Any whole number multiplied by 10 is the number with one zero at the end of the number.

53 × 10 = 53**0**

Solution   **53 × 10 × 530**

Example 2

Jackie rides her bicycle for 13 miles a day. If she does this for 100 days, how many miles will she ride in all?

Strategy   **Use mental math.**

Step 1   Write an equation for the problem.

Let m represent the number of miles she will ride in all.

$13 \times 100 = m$

Step 2   Multiply.

Any whole number multiplied by 100 is the number with two zeros at the end.

$13 \times 100 = m$

$13 \times 100 = 1{,}300$

Solution   **Jackie will ride 1,300 miles in all.**

You can write a power of 10 with an **exponent**. The exponent tells how many times 10 is used as a factor.

For example, 100 is a power of 10 since $10 \times 10 = 100$. The number 10 is used as a factor 2 times. This is written as 10^2 and read as *ten to the second power* or *ten squared*.

Example 3

What is the value of 10^6? When it is written using base-ten numerals, how many zeros does 10^6 have?

Strategy   **Use a pattern.**

Step 1   Use a pattern.

$10^1 = 10$

$10^2 = 10 \times 10 = 100$

$10^3 = 100 \times 10 = 1{,}000$

$10^4 = 1{,}000 \times 10 = 10{,}000$

$10^5 = 10{,}000 \times 10 = 100{,}000$

$10^6 = 100{,}000 \times 10 = 1{,}000{,}000$

Step 2	Identify the pattern.

10^1 evaluates to an answer with 1 zero.

10^2 evaluates to an answer with 2 zeros.

10^3 evaluates to an answer with 3 zeros.

10^4 evaluates to an answer with 4 zeros.

10^5 evaluates to an answer with 5 zeros.

10^6 will have an answer with 6 zeros.

1,000,000

Solution   **The value of 10^6 is 1,000,000. Using base-ten numerals, 10^6 has 6 zeros.**

When multiplying or dividing a decimal by a power of 10, use the exponent to decide how many places to move the decimal point.

When you multiply by a power of 10, use the exponent to decide how many places to move the decimal point to the right.

For example,

$6.32 \times 10^1 = 63.2$ ← move the decimal point one place to the right

$6.32 \times 10^2 = 632$ ← move the decimal point two places to the right

$6.32 \times 10^3 = 6,320$ ← move the decimal point three places to the right

When you divide a decimal by a power of 10, use the exponent to decide how many places to move the decimal point to the left.

For example,

$6.32 \div 10^1 = 0.632$ ← move the decimal point one place to the left

$6.32 \div 10^2 = 0.0632$ ← move the decimal point two places to the left

$6.32 \div 10^3 = 0.00632$ ← move the decimal point three places to the left

Example 4

What is the product?

$$0.3 \times 10^2 = \boxed{}$$

Strategy   **Multiply by a power of 10.**

Step 1   Decide in which direction to move the decimal point.

You are multiplying by a power of 10, so move the decimal point to the right.

Step 2   Find the number of places to move the decimal point in the product.

The exponent tells how many places to move to the right.

The exponent is 2, so move the decimal point 2 places.

Step 3   Write the product.

Move the decimal point in 0.3 two places to the right.
Fill the empty places with zeros.

0.30.

Solution $0.3 \times 10^2 = 30$

Example 5

What is the quotient?

$$627.4 \div 10^3 = \boxed{}$$

Strategy   **Divide by a power of 10.**

Step 1   Decide in which direction to move the decimal point.

You are dividing by a power of 10, so move the decimal point to the left.

Step 2   Find the number of places to move the decimal point in the quotient.

The exponent tells how many places to move to the left.

The exponent is 3, so move the decimal point 3 places.

Step 3   Write the quotient.

Move the decimal point in 627.4 three places to the left.
Write a leading zero.

0.627.4

Solution $627.4 \div 10^3 = 0.6274$

Coached Example

What is the quotient?

$0.9 \div 10^3 = \boxed{}$

Will you multiply or divide 0.9 by a power of 10? _____

When you divide by a power of 10, do you move the decimal point to the right
or to the left? _____

The _____ tells how many places to move the decimal point.

What is the exponent, or the power of 10? _____

Move the decimal point in 0.9 _____ places to the
_____ to find the quotient.

Fill the empty places with _____.

$0.9 \div 10^3 =$ _____

$0.9 \div 10^3 =$ _____

Lesson Practice • Part 1

Choose the correct answer.

1. Find the product.

$$84 \times 10 = \boxed{}$$

   A.   0.84
   B.   84
   C.   840
   D. 8,400

2. Find the product.

$$152 \times 100 = \boxed{}$$

   A.   1.52
   B.   152
   C.   1,520
   D. 15,200

3. Find the product.

$$7.69 \times 10^2 = \boxed{}$$

   A. 7,690
   B.   769
   C.   0.769
   D.   0.0769

4. Find the product.

$$2.5 \times 10^3 = \boxed{}$$

   A.   0.25
   B.   25
   C.   250
   D.   2,500

5. Find the quotient.

$$47 \div 10 = \boxed{}$$

   A.   0.047
   B.   0.47
   C.   4.7
   D.   470

6. Find the quotient.

$$2.34 \div 10^2 = \boxed{}$$

   A.   234
   B.   0.234
   C.   0.0234
   D.   0.00234

7. Find the quotient.

$$9.5 \div 10^3 = \boxed{}$$

A.   0.0095

B.   0.095

C.   0.95

D.   9,500

8. Find the product.

$$47.62 \times 10^4 = \boxed{}$$

A.   0.4762

B.   4,762

C.   47,620

D.   476,200

9. Ms. Clarkson wrote two expressions on the board.

$$4.325 \times 10^3 \qquad 4.325 \div 10^2$$

A. Find the value of the expression 4.325×10^3. Explain how you found your answer.

_____

_____

_____

B. Find the value of the expression $4.325 \div 10^2$. Explain how you found your answer.

_____

_____

_____

Lesson Practice • Part 2

Choose the correct answer.

1. What is the relationship between the left 5 and the right 5 in 4,553.72?

   A. The left 5 is $\frac{1}{100}$ the value of the right 5.

   B. The left 5 is $\frac{1}{10}$ the value of the right 5.

   C. The left 5 is 10 times the value of the right 5.

   D. The left 5 is 100 times the value of the right 5.

2. Find the product.

   $272 \times 10^3 = \boxed{}$

   A. 2,720

   B. 27,200

   C. 272,000

   D. 2,720,000

3. Find the quotient.

   $68,342 \div 10^2 = \boxed{}$

   A. 6,834.2

   B. 683.42

   C. 68.342

   D. 6.8342

4. A one-digit whole number greater than 0 is multiplied by 10^5. How many zeros will the product have?

   A. 4

   B. 5

   C. 6

   D. 10

5. A one-digit whole number greater than 0 is divided by 10^4. How many zeros will be to the right of the decimal point before the first non-zero digit?

   A. 3

   B. 4

   C. 5

   D. 10

6. Which will have the greatest quotient?

   A. $15 \div 10^6$

   B. $15 \div 10^5$

   C. $15 \div 10^4$

   D. $15 \div 10^3$

7. Which power of 10 makes this sentence true?

$$7.4 \times \boxed{} = 740{,}000$$

A. 10^3

B. 10^4

C. 10^5

D. 10^6

8. Which power of 10 makes this sentence true?

$$63{,}000 \div \boxed{} = 6.3$$

A. 10^3

B. 10^4

C. 10^5

D. 10^6

9. Savannah wrote this problem on the board for her classmates to solve.

$$0.85 \times 10^4$$

A. What is Savannah's product? Explain how you found your answer.

_____

_____

B. What happens to Savannah's product if the exponent is increased by 1?

_____

_____

C. What happens to Savannah's product if the exponent is decreased by 1?

_____

_____

10. Circle the power of 10 that makes the equation true.

$$6.5 \times \boxed{\begin{array}{c} 10^2 \\ 10^3 \\ 10^4 \end{array}} = 6{,}500$$

11. Draw a line from each expression to its quotient.

A. $320 \div 10^2$ •   • 0.32

B. $3{,}200 \div 10$ •   • 3.2

C. $32 \div 10^2$ •   • 32

D. $320 \div 10$ •   • 320

12. Evaluate each expression. Write the expression in the correct box.

0.015×10^4	$1.5 \div 10$	$1{,}500 \div 10^4$
0.15×10^3	$15{,}000 \div 10^2$	0.015×10

Equal to 150	Equal to 0.15

13. Draw a line from each expression to its product.

A. 0.156×10^2 •   • 1.56

B. 15.6×10 •   • 15.6

C. 0.156×10 •   • 156

D. 1.56×10^3 •   • 1,560

14. Which expressions have a value of 8,500? Circle all that apply.

  A. $0.85 \times 1{,}000$

  B. 8.5×10^2

  C. 85×100

  D. 0.85×10^4

  E. 8.5×10^4

15. Look at each expression. Is it equivalent to 0.78? Select Yes or No.

  A. 0.078×10^2 ○ Yes   ○ No

  B. $78 \div 10^2$ ○ Yes   ○ No

  C. $7.8 \div 10$ ○ Yes   ○ No

  D. 0.78×100 ○ Yes   ○ No

  E. 0.078×10 ○ Yes   ○ No

  F. $7{,}800 \div 10^3$ ○ Yes   ○ No

16. Which expressions have a value of 0.91? Circle all that apply.

  A. $0.091 \div 10$

  B. $910 \div 10^3$

  C. 0.091×10

  D. 91×10^2

  E. $9.1 \div 10$

Domain 2 • Lesson 13

Add Decimals

Getting the Idea

You can add decimals the same way you add whole numbers. Just align the numbers on the decimal points and write a decimal point in the sum. Remember, when the sum of a column is 10 or greater, you will have to **regroup** 10 of that unit as 1 of the next greater unit. For example, 12 hundredths can be regrouped as 1 tenth and 2 hundredths.

$$\begin{array}{r} 1 \\ 1.53 \\ + 2.09 \\ \hline 3.6\mathbf{2} \end{array}$$

Example 1

Find the sum: $5.6 + 0.1 = \boxed{}$.

Strategy **Use mental math.**

Think: What is 6 tenths plus 1 tenth? 7 tenths

$5.6 + 0.1 = 5.7$

Solution **$5.6 + 0.1 = 5.7$**

Example 2

Find the sum: $1.26 + 0.65 = \boxed{}$.

Strategy **Use models.**

Step 1 Model the greater decimal using grids.

Use two grids and shade the first one completely.

1.26 is one and twenty-six hundredths. So, shade 26 squares in the second grid.

Step 2 Use the same model to add 0.65.

0.65 is sixty-five hundredths, so shade 65 more squares in the second grid.

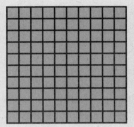 

Step 3 Write the total number of shaded squares as a decimal.

One grid is completely shaded, so it represents 1.

The other grid has 91 squares shaded, so it represents 0.91.

Together, the grids show the decimal 1.91.

Solution **1.26 + 0.65 = 1.91**

Example 3

Amir recorded the snowfall during the first week of February. On Monday he recorded 12.78 inches, and on Thursday he recorded another 13.65 inches. How much snow did Amir record for the first week of February?

Strategy **Write an equation for the problem. Then add each place from right to left.**

Step 1 Write an equation for the problem.

Let *s* represent the number of inches of snow for the first week of February.

12.78 + 13.65 = *s*

Step 2 Rewrite the problem vertically.

Align the numbers on the decimal point.
Write the decimal point in the sum.

```
  12.78
+ 13.65
      .
```

Step 3   Add the hundredths: $8 + 5 = 13$ hundredths.

Regroup 13 hundredths as 1 tenth 3 hundredths.

$$
\begin{array}{r}
1 \quad\quad\ \\
12.7\mathbf{8} \\
+\ 13.6\mathbf{5} \\
\hline
.\ \mathbf{3}
\end{array}
$$

Step 4   Add the tenths: $1 + 7 + 6 = 14$ tenths.

Regroup 14 tenths as 1 one 4 tenths.

$$
\begin{array}{r}
1\ 1\quad\ \\
12.\mathbf{7}8 \\
+\ 13.\mathbf{6}5 \\
\hline
.\mathbf{43}
\end{array}
$$

Step 5   Add the ones: $1 + 2 + 3 = 6$ ones.

$$
\begin{array}{r}
1\ 1\quad\ \\
1\mathbf{2}.78 \\
+\ 1\mathbf{3}.65 \\
\hline
\mathbf{6}.43
\end{array}
$$

Step 6   Add the tens: $1 + 1 = 2$ tens.

$$
\begin{array}{r}
1\ 1\quad\ \\
\mathbf{1}2.78 \\
+\ \mathbf{1}3.65 \\
\hline
\mathbf{2}6.43
\end{array}
$$

Solution   **Amir recorded 26.43 inches of snow for the first week in February.**

Sometimes it may be necessary to write an equivalent decimal before computing. Inserting a 0 at the right end of a decimal does not change its value.

Example 4

Find the sum: $2.45 + 6.7 = \boxed{}$.

Strategy   **Add each place from right to left.**

Step 1   Align the numbers on the decimal point.

Insert a 0 to the right of 6.7.
Now both addends have the same number of places.

$$
\begin{array}{r}
2.45 \\
+\ 6.7\mathbf{0}
\end{array}
$$

| Step 2 | Write the decimal point in the sum. Add from right to left. |

5 + 0 = 5 hundredths

4 + 7 = 11 tenths

Regroup 11 tenths as 1 one 1 tenth.

1 + 2 + 6 = 9 ones

$$\begin{array}{r} 1 \\ 2.45 \\ +\ 6.70 \\ \hline 9.15 \end{array}$$

Solution   2.45 + 6.7 = 9.15

You can use the properties of operations to make computation easier.

Additive identity property of 0 The sum of any number and 0 is that number.	$a + 0 = 0 + a = a$	$8.7 + 0 = 0 + 8.7 = 8.7$
Commutative property of addition The order of addends can be changed. The sum does not change.	$a + b = b + a$	$4.2 + 3.6 = 3.6 + 4.2$ $7.8 = 7.8$
Associative property of addition Addends can be grouped in different ways. The sum will be the same.	$(a + b) + c =$ $a + (b + c)$	$3.4 + (2.6 + 6.5) =$ $(3.4 + 2.6) + 6.5$ $3.4 + (2.6 + 6.5) =$ $3.4 + \quad 9.1 \quad = 12.5$ $(3.4 + 2.6) + 6.5 =$ $6 \quad + 6.5 = 12.5$

Example 5

What number is missing from the equation below?

$5.39 + \boxed{} = 2.47 + 5.39$

Strategy　**Use the commutative property of addition.**

The commutative property of addition states that changing the order of the addends does not change the sum.

$5.39 + 2.47 = 2.47 + 5.39$

Solution　**The missing number is 2.47.**

You can use an **estimate** to check if answers are reasonable. If an estimate is not close to the actual answer, an error was made in finding the answer. You can estimate by rounding to the nearest whole number or nearest dollar.

Example 6

Robert bought a sandwich for $2.29, a drink for $0.99, and a cookie for $1.59. How much did Robert spend in all?

Strategy　**Estimate the amount spent. Then find the actual cost.**

Step 1　Round each amount to the nearest dollar. Then add.

$2.29 rounds down to $2.00

$0.99 rounds up to $1.00

$1.59 rounds up to $2.00

$2.00 + $1.00 + $2.00 = $5.00

The total should be about $5.00.

Step 2　Add the costs of the items.

Align the numbers on the decimal point.

$$
\begin{array}{r}
{\scriptstyle 1\ 2} \\
\$2.29 \\
0.99 \\
+\ 1.59 \\
\hline
\$4.87
\end{array}
$$

Step 3	Compare the actual answer to the estimate.

$4.87 is close to $5.00.

$4.87 is a reasonable answer.

Solution   Robert spent $4.87.

Coached Example

Harrison weighed three samples during science class. The samples had masses of 5.64 grams, 9.5 grams, and 2.07 grams. Estimate the total mass of the three samples. Then find the actual total mass of the samples.

Find the estimated total mass. Round each mass to the nearest whole number.

5.64 rounds _____ to _____.

9.5 rounds _____ to _____.

2.07 rounds _____ to _____.

Add the rounded numbers: _____ + _____ + _____ = _____

The estimated mass of the three samples is _____ grams.

Find the actual total mass. Write and solve the addition problem.

Do all the digits have the same number of places to the right of the decimal point? _____

To write the problem, you need to insert a 0 to the right of _____.

Make sure the decimal points are _____.

Find the actual mass.

The actual mass of the 3 samples is _____ grams.

Is the actual answer close to the estimate? _____

The total mass of the samples is _____ grams.

Lesson Practice • Part 1

Choose the correct answer.

1. Find the sum.

    28.65
    + 14.93

    A. 32.58

    B. 42.58

    C. 43.58

    D. 43.68

2. Find the sum.

    5.82 + 9.7 = ☐

    A. 15.89

    B. 15.52

    C. 14.89

    D. 14.52

3. Find the sum.

    7.09 + 0.01 = ☐

    A. 7.01

    B. 7.1

    C. 7.19

    D. 7.91

4. Which shows the additive identity property of 0?

    A. 4.5 + 0.8 = 0.8 + 4.5

    B. 3.8 + (1.2 + 8.9) = (3.8 + 1.2) + 8.9

    C. 6.7 + 3.3 = 10.0

    D. 7.2 + 0 = 7.2

5. Bruce bought a movie ticket for $7.50, popcorn for $3.95, and a drink for $2.25. How much money did Bruce spend in all?

    A. $12.60

    B. $12.70

    C. $13.60

    D. $13.70

6. Eva drove 9.8 miles to visit her brother and then drove 2.5 miles to visit her sister. How many miles did Eva drive in all?

    A. 11.3 miles

    B. 11.8 miles

    C. 12.3 miles

    D. 12.8 miles

7. One year, a city had 21.65 inches of rain. The next year the city had 28.7 inches of rain. How many inches of rain fell during the two years?

    A. 50.35 inches

    B. 49.72 inches

    C. 49.35 inches

    D. 40.35 inches

8. Last year Kelvin was 56.5 inches tall. Since then he has grown 3.75 inches. How tall is Kelvin now?

    A. 59.25 inches

    B. 59.8 inches

    C. 60.25 inches

    D. 60.8 inches

9. Maya mailed three packages. Their weights were 4.5 pounds, 2.75 pounds, and 3.4 pounds.

    A. What was the total weight of the three packages?

    _____

    B. Explain how you found your answer for part A.

    _____

    _____

    _____

Lesson Practice • Part 2

Choose the correct answer.

1. Which number makes this sentence true?

$$9.25 + \boxed{} = 9.25$$

   A. 0

   B. 1

   C. 8.25

   D. 9.25

2. Find the sum.

$$4.72 + 8.67 + 3.28 = \boxed{}$$

   A. 15.57

   B. 15.67

   C. 16.57

   D. 16.67

3. Destiny bought a skirt for $27.92 and a matching top for $18.79. How much money did Destiny spend in all?

   A. $45.61

   B. $45.71

   C. $46.61

   D. $46.71

4. Find the sum.

$$5,167.38 + 392.4 = \boxed{}$$

   A. 5,579.78

   B. 5,559.78

   C. 5,559.42

   D. 5,206.62

5. Which number makes this sentence true?

$$36.48 + \boxed{} = 87.29 + 36.48$$

   A. 36.48

   B. 40.81

   C. 87.29

   D. 126.77

6. It takes Mercury 87.97 days to revolve around the Sun. It takes Venus 136.73 more days than Mercury to revolve around the Sun. How many days does it take Venus to revolve around the Sun?

   A. 224.7 days

   B. 223.7 days

   C. 214.6 days

   D. 213.6 days

7. The women's world record for the triple jump is 15.5 meters. The men's world record in the triple jump is 2.79 meters greater than the women's record. What is the men's world record in the triple jump?

   A.   4.34 meters

   B. 17.29 meters

   C. 17.84 meters

   D. 18.29 meters

8. Three friends want to buy a pizza. Zach has $6.29, Ian has $3.65, and Emilio has $2.35. How much money do the three boys have altogether?

   A. $13.29

   B. $13.19

   C. $12.29

   D. $12.19

9. At a bookstore, Bailey bought a book for $12.59, a magazine for $3.79, and a poster for $8.99. After buying the items, she had $17.86 left.

   A. How much did Bailey spend at the bookstore? Show your work.

   B. How much money did Bailey have before shopping? Show your work.

10. Which number sentences show the commutative property of addition? Circle all that apply.

   A. 2.58 + 1.72 = 1.72 + 2.58

   B. 25.89 + (2.48 + 12.5) = (25.89 + 2.48) + 12.5

   C. (2.78 + 5.8) + 9.84 = (5.8 + 2.78) + 9.84

   D. 45.1 + 0 = 45.1

   E. 3.77 + 2 = 2 + 3.77

11. Draw a line from each expression to its sum.

A. $8.5 + 5.19$ •   • 12.56

B. $7.18 + 6.95$ •   • 13.21

C. $3.66 + 8.9$ •   • 13.69

D. $5.49 + 7.72$ •   • 14.13

12. Use decimals from the box to write a true number sentence.

_____ + 2.56 = _____

| 1.23 |
| 3.59 |
| 6.15 |
| 8.21 |

13. The table shows the prices of some school supplies. Select True or False for each statement.

School Supplies

Item	Cost
Pencil	$0.25
Eraser	$0.85
Notebook	$1.65
Index cards	$2.10

A. The cost of a notebook and a pencil is $1.85.   ○ True   ○ False

B. The cost of index cards and a notebook is $3.75.   ○ True   ○ False

C. The cost of an eraser, a pencil, and index cards is $3.30.   ○ True   ○ False

D. The cost of an eraser, a notebook, and a pencil is $2.75.   ○ True   ○ False

14. Which expressions have a value of 12.67? Circle all that apply.

A. 6.58 + 6.19

B. 7.97 + 4.7

C. 3.81 + 8.86

D. 10.18 + 2.69

E. 2.2 + 10.47

15. Draw a line from each expression to its sum.

A. 7.26 + 2.78 •   • 9.84

B. 3.33 + 6.51 •   • 9.96

C. 5.46 + 4.5 •   • 10.04

D. 2.63 + 7.53 •   • 10.16

16. Which expressions have a value of 18.95? Circle all that apply.

A. 7.58 + 11.37

B. 14.25 + 4.7

C. 3.81 + 9.24 + 5.3

D. 2.7 + 7.25 + 9

E. 8.28 + 10.47

Subtract Decimals

Getting the Idea

You can subtract decimals the same way you subtract whole numbers. Just align the numbers on the decimal points and write a decimal point in the difference. Remember, when there are not enough units to subtract from, you will have to regroup 1 of the next greater unit as 10 of the lesser unit. For example, you can regroup 7 tenths 3 hundredths as 6 tenths 13 hundredths.

$$
\begin{array}{r}
{\scriptstyle 6\ 13} \\
1.\cancel{7}\,\cancel{3} \\
-\ 0.2\ 9 \\
\hline
1.4\ 4
\end{array}
$$

Example 1

Find the difference.

4.29 − 0.01 = ☐

Strategy **Use mental math.**

Think: What is 9 hundredths minus 1 hundredth?

4.29 − 0.01 = 4.28

Solution **4.29 − 0.01 = 4.28**

Example 2

Find the difference.

1.7 − 0.93 = ☐

Strategy   **Use models.**

Step 1   Model the greater decimal using grids.

1.7 is one and seven tenths, or one and seventy hundredths.

Use two grids and shade the first one completely.

Shade 70 squares in the second grid.

Step 2   Cross out squares to represent the number being subtracted.

0.93 is ninety-three hundredths, so cross out 93 of the shaded squares.

Cross out 70 shaded squares in the second grid.

Cross out 23 more in the first grid.

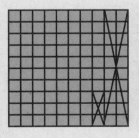 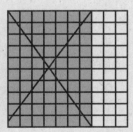

Step 3   Count the number of shaded squares that are not crossed out.

77 squares are shaded and not crossed out.

77 hundredths = 0.77

Solution   **1.7 − 0.93 = 0.77**

Example 3

In 2010, Ms. Clark earned $528.56 per week. In 2000, she earned $390.73 per week. How much more did Ms. Clark earn per week in 2010 than in 2000?

Strategy   **Write an equation for the problem. Then solve.**

Step 1   Write an equation for the problem.

Let n represent how much more was earned per week in 2010.

$528.56 - $390.73 = n$

Step 2   Rewrite the problem.

Align the numbers on the decimal point.

Write the decimal point in the difference.

Subtract the hundredths.

6 hundredths − 3 hundredths = 3 hundredths

$$
\begin{array}{r}
\$528.5\mathbf{6} \\
-\ 390.7\mathbf{3} \\
\hline
.\ \mathbf{3}
\end{array}
$$

Step 3   Subtract the tenths.

Because 7 is greater than 5, regroup from the ones.

15 tenths − 7 tenths = 8 tenths

$$
\begin{array}{r}
{}^{7\ 15} \\
\$52\not{8}.\not{5}6 \\
-\ 390.73 \\
\hline
.\mathbf{8}3
\end{array}
$$

Step 4   Subtract the ones.

7 ones − 0 ones = 7 ones

$$
\begin{array}{r}
{}^{7\ 15} \\
\$52\not{8}.\not{5}6 \\
-\ 390.73 \\
\hline
\mathbf{7}.83
\end{array}
$$

Step 5   Subtract the tens.

Because 9 is greater than 2, regroup from the hundreds.

12 tens − 9 tens = 3 tens

$$
\begin{array}{r}
\scriptstyle 4\,12\,7\ 15 \\
\$\cancel{5}\cancel{2}8.\cancel{5}6 \\
-\ 390.73 \\
\hline
37.83
\end{array}
$$

Step 6   Subtract the hundreds.

4 hundreds − 3 hundreds = 1 hundred

Write the dollar sign in the difference.

$$
\begin{array}{r}
\scriptstyle 4\,12\,7\ 15 \\
\$\cancel{5}\cancel{2}8.\cancel{5}6 \\
-\ 390.73 \\
\hline
\$137.83
\end{array}
$$

Solution   **Ms. Clark earned $137.83 more per week in 2010 than in 2000.**

You can check the answer to a subtraction problem by using addition.

Since $137.83 + $390.73 = $528.56, the answer is correct.

Remember, you can estimate to check if answers are reasonable. If an estimate is not close to the actual answer, an error was made in finding the answer. You can estimate by rounding to the nearest whole number or nearest dollar.

Example 4

A bike trail is 36.25 miles long. Andrew stopped to rest after he had biked 13.8 miles of the trail. How many more miles must he ride to finish the trail?

Strategy   **Estimate the distance. Then find the actual distance left.**

Step 1   Round each number to the nearest whole number. Then subtract.

36.25 rounds down to 36.

13.8 rounds up to 14.

36 miles − 14 miles = 22 miles

The difference should be about 22 miles.

Step 2   Find the actual distance.

Align the numbers on the decimal point. Insert a 0 to the right of 13.8 so that both decimals have the same number of places.

$$
\begin{array}{r}
{\scriptstyle 5\,12} \\
3\cancel{6}.25 \\
-\ 13.80 \\
\hline
22.45
\end{array}
$$

Step 3   Compare the actual answer to the estimate.

22.45 is close to 22.

22.45 is a reasonable answer.

Solution   **Andrew must ride 22.45 miles to finish the trail.**

Coached Example

In all, Kobe ran 15.5 miles on Friday, Saturday, and Sunday. He ran 3.75 miles on Friday and 5.6 miles on Saturday. How many miles did Kobe run on Sunday?

Do all the digits have the same number of places to the right of the decimal point? _____

To write the problem, you need to insert a 0 to the right of _____ and _____.

First, _____ to find the total number of miles Kobe ran on Friday and Saturday.

Compute.

Kobe ran _____ miles on Friday and Saturday.

Next, _____ the sum of those two days from the number of miles that Kobe ran in all.

Compute.

What is the result? _____

Kobe ran _____ miles on Sunday.

Lesson Practice • Part 1

Choose the correct answer.

1. Find the difference.

$$\begin{aligned} 45.37 \\ -\ 27.63 \end{aligned}$$

  A. 22.34

  B. 18.74

  C. 18.34

  D. 17.74

2. Find the difference.

$$8.6 - 3.71 = \boxed{}$$

  A. 4.11

  B. 4.35

  C. 4.89

  D. 5.11

3. Find the difference.

$$56.23 - 0.01 = \boxed{}$$

  A. 46.23

  B. 55.23

  C. 56.13

  D. 56.22

4. Find the difference.

$$62.16 - 43.7 = \boxed{}$$

  A. 18.09

  B. 18.46

  C. 18.66

  D. 19.09

5. Tyler walked 10.4 kilometers and ran 4.6 kilometers yesterday. How much farther did he walk than run?

  A. 5.8 kilometers

  B. 5.9 kilometers

  C. 6.8 kilometers

  D. 15 kilometers

6. The distance from Chloe's home to Sandy's home is 92.6 miles. After one hour, Chloe has driven 57.8 miles. How many more miles does Chloe need to drive to reach Sandy's home?

  A. 34.8 miles

  B. 44.8 miles

  C. 45.2 miles

  D. 150.4 miles

7. The Olympic record for men's discus throw is 69.89 meters. The women's record is 72.3 meters. How much greater is the women's record than the men's record?

   A. 3.59 meters

   B. 2.59 meters

   C. 2.41 meters

   D. 2.14 meters

8. Melissa worked 37.25 hours this week. She worked 29.5 hours last week. How many more hours did Melissa work this week than last week?

   A. 8.75 hours

   B. 8.65 hours

   C. 8.25 hours

   D. 7.75 hours

9. Nick bought a sweater for $16.75 and a pair of pants for $28.92.

   A. Estimate how much Nick spent on the sweater and pants. Show your work.

   B. If Nick paid with a $50 bill, about how much money will he receive in change? Show your work.

   C. Find the actual amount that Nick will receive in change. Show your work.

Lesson Practice • Part 2

Choose the correct answer.

1. Find the difference.

   $$\begin{array}{r} 95.7 \\ -\ 28.64 \\ \hline \end{array}$$

   A. 67.16
   B. 67.14
   C. 67.06
   D. 67.04

2. At Ho's Wok, the sesame chicken costs $12.45 on the regular menu. The cost for a smaller portion on the combination platter is $8.79. How much less money is the sesame chicken on the combination platter?

   A. $3.66
   B. $3.76
   C. $4.66
   D. $4.76

3. Which number makes both sentences true?

   $75.3 - \boxed{} = 36.84$

   $36.84 + \boxed{} = 75.3$

   A. 38.44
   B. 38.46
   C. 38.54
   D. 39.56

4. Ryan bought two CDs for $13.79 each. He paid with two $20 bills. How much change did Ryan receive?

   A. $6.21
   B. $7.31
   C. $12.42
   D. $14.62

5. It takes Uranus 84.01 years to revolve around the Sun. It takes Saturn 29.46 years to revolve around the Sun. How many years fewer does it take Saturn than Uranus to revolve around the Sun?

   A. 55.65 years
   B. 55.55 years
   C. 54.65 years
   D. 54.55 years

6. It is Luna's goal to jog 27.5 kilometers this week. She jogged 5.75 kilometers on Sunday and 3.5 kilometers on Monday. How many more kilometers does she need to jog to reach her goal this week?

   A. 9.25 kilometers
   B. 18.25 kilometers
   C. 21.75 kilometers
   D. 36.75 kilometers

7. Find the difference.

$$7{,}097.42$$
$$- \quad 634.8$$

A. 6,362.52   **C.** 6,462.58

B. 6,453.62   **D.** 6,462.62

8. The playlist that Brandon made lasted 76.04 minutes. That was 12.57 minutes longer than his prior playlist. What was the length of Brandon's prior playlist?

A. 63.47 minutes

B. 63.83 minutes

C. 88.61 minutes

D. 88.97 minutes

9. Find the difference.

$$872.3 - 46.76 = \boxed{}$$

A. 40.47

B. 825.54

C. 826.56

D. 836.54

10. Diego spent $5.25 at an arcade and $4.69 buying lunch. If he had $20, how much money does he have left?

A. $9.84   **C.** $10.06

B. $9.94   **D.** $10.16

11. The special breakfast menu at Dan's Diner is shown.

Breakfast Menu

Item	Cost
Egg Sandwich	$2.79
French Toast	$5.62
Oatmeal	$4.25
Pancakes	$3.89

A. How much more money does the French toast cost than the pancakes? Show your work.

B. If a pair of people bought one order of pancakes and one egg sandwich and paid with a $10 bill, how much change would they receive? Show your work.

C. If a family bought one of each item and paid with a $20 bill, how much change would they receive? Show your work.

12. Which expressions have a value of 6.78? Circle all that apply.

    A. $12.5 - 5.62$

    B. $13.67 - 6.89$

    C. $23.81 - 17.23$

    D. $10.58 - 3.8$

    E. $22.2 - 15.42$

13. Draw a line from each expression to its difference.

    A. $18.5 - 11.4$ •   • 6.7

    B. $17.1 - 10.4$ •   • 6.9

    C. $9.6 - 2.3$ •   • 7.1

    D. $10.4 - 3.5$ •   • 7.3

14. Use decimals from the box to write a true number sentence.

$16.2 - \underline{\hspace{2cm}} = \underline{\hspace{2cm}}$

| 7.39 |
| 7.59 |
| 8.31 |
| 8.81 |

15. The table shows the weights of four dogs. Select True or False for each statement.

Weights of Dogs

Dog	Weight (in pounds)
Fido	26.51
Fifi	15.98
Rex	18.75
Zoe	20.62

A. Fifi weighs 4.64 pounds less than Zoe.   ○ True ○ False

B. Rex weighs 2.77 pounds more than Fifi.   ○ True ○ False

C. Fido weighs 5.79 pounds more than Zoe.   ○ True ○ False

D. Rex weighs 7.76 pounds less than Fido.   ○ True ○ False

16. Draw a line from each expression to its difference.

A. 27.68 − 14.46 •   • 12.62

B. 16.8 − 4.14 •   • 12.66

C. 26.42 − 13.16 •   • 13.22

D. 19.1 − 6.48 •   • 13.26

17. Which expressions have a value of 35.48? Circle all that apply.

A. 97.56 − 61.28

B. 66.48 − 31

C. 58 − 22.52

D. 71.58 − 36.1

E. 81.5 − 16.22

Multiply Decimals

Getting the Idea

Multiplying decimals is similar to multiplying whole numbers. When you multiply decimals, remember to write the decimal point in the product. Where you place the decimal point depends on the decimal points in the factors.

Example 1

Find the product.

$0.7 \times 0.4 = \boxed{}$

Strategy   **Use a model.**

Step 1   Use a 10-by-10 grid.

Shade 0.7 of the columns of squares.

Step 2   Shade 0.4 of the rows of squares.

The part that overlaps is the product.

There are 28 out of 100 squares, or 0.28, in the overlap.

Solution   **$0.7 \times 0.4 = 0.28$**

When you multiply a decimal by a decimal, the product will have the same number of decimal places as the sum of the decimal places in the factors.

Example 2

Find the product.

0.28 × 0.4 = ☐

Strategy   **Multiply as you would with whole numbers. Write the decimal point in the product.**

Step 1   Rewrite the problem. Multiply.

$$
\begin{array}{r}
3 \\
0.28 \\
\times\ 0.4 \\
\hline
112
\end{array}
$$

Step 2   Write the decimal point in the product.

There are 3 decimal places in the factors, so there will be 3 decimal places in the product.

$$
\begin{array}{r}
3 \\
0.28 \\
\times\ 0.4 \\
\hline
0.112
\end{array}
$$

← 2 decimal places
← 1 decimal place
← 3 decimal places

Solution   **0.28 × 0.4 = 0.112**

Example 3

A jeweler bought 4.8 ounces of silver at $17.35 per ounce. How much did the jeweler pay for the silver?

Strategy   **Write an equation for the problem. Then solve.**

Step 1   Write an equation for the problem.

Let n represent how much the jeweler paid for the silver.

$17.35 × 4.8 = n$

Step 2   Rewrite the problem. Multiply the tenths.

        5 2 4
        $17.35
      × 4.8
        13880

Step 3   Multiply the ones. Write a 0 in the ones place of the second partial product.

        2 1 2
        5̶2̶4̶
        $17.35
      × 4.8
        13880
        69400

Step 4   Add the partial products.

        Write the $ sign and the decimal point in the product.

        $17.35   ← 2 decimal places
      × 4.8   ← 1 decimal place
        13880
    + 69400
        $83.280   ← 3 decimal places

Solution   **The jeweler paid $83.28 for the silver.**

Sometimes when you multiply with decimals, you will need to put zeros in the product.

Example 4

Find the product.

   0.09 × 0.7 = ☐

Strategy   **Multiply as you would with whole numbers.**
Write the decimal point in the product.

Step 1   Multiply.

          6
        0.09
      × 0.7
          63

| Step 2 | Write the decimal point in the product.

$$\begin{array}{r} 6 \\ 0.09 \\ \times\ 0.7 \\ \hline 0.063 \end{array}$$

0.09 ← 2 decimal places
× 0.7 ← 1 decimal place
0.063 ← 3 decimal places

Since 3 decimal places are needed in the product, write a zero in the tenths place.

Solution $0.09 \times 0.7 = 0.063$

You can use the properties of operations to make computation easier.

Multiplicative identity property of 1 The product of any number and 1 is that number.	$a \times 1 = 1 \times a = a$	$9.3 \times 1 = 1 \times 9.3 = 9.3$
Commutative property of multiplication The order of factors can be changed. The product does not change.	$a \times b = b \times a$	$2.8 \times 1.7 = 1.7 \times 2.8$ $4.76 = 4.76$
Associative property of multiplication Factors can be grouped in different ways. The product will be the same.	$(a \times b) \times c =$ $a \times (b \times c)$	$3.2 \times (4.5 \times 8.1) =$ $(3.2 \times 4.5) \times 8.1$ $3.2 \times (4.5 \times 8.1) =$ $3.2 \times\ \ \ \ \ 36.45\ \ \ \ \ = 116.64$ $(3.2 \times 4.5) \times 8.1 =$ $14.4\ \ \ \ \times 8.1 = 116.64$

Example 5

What number is missing from the equation below?

$$5.3 \times (7.9 \times 6.2) = (5.3 \times \boxed{}) \times 6.2$$

Strategy   Use the associative property of multiplication.

Changing the grouping of the factors does not change the product.

$$5.3 \times (7.9 \times 6.2) = (5.3 \times 7.9) \times 6.2$$

Solution   The missing number is 7.9.

Coached Example

Mr. Starr's class is taking a field trip to a museum. Tickets cost $13.95 each. If Mr. Starr buys 27 tickets, what is the total cost of the tickets?

Write the problem in vertical form.

$$\begin{array}{r} 13.95 \\ \times\ 27 \\ \hline \end{array}$$

Multiply by the ones: _____

Write the first partial product.

Multiply by the tens: _____

Write the second partial product.

Add the partial products: _____ + _____ = _____

There are _____ decimal places in the factors, so the product will have _____ decimal places.

Write the decimal point and the $ in the product: _____

The total cost of the tickets is _____.

Lesson Practice • Part 1

Choose the correct answer.

1. Find the product. Use the grid to help you multiply.

$0.9 \times 0.5 = \boxed{}$

A. 0.05

B. 0.4

C. 0.45

D. 0.5

2. Which shows the commutative property of multiplication?

A. $4.1 \times (6.2 \times 3.9) =$ $(4.1 \times 6.2) \times 3.9$

B. $2.7 \times 1 = 2.7$

C. $7.2 \times 0 = 0$

D. $8.5 \times 0.4 = 0.4 \times 8.5$

3. Find the product.

$5.95 \times 12 = \boxed{}$

A. 71.4   **C.** 70.4

B. 71.04   **D.** 70.14

4. Find the product.

$0.72 \times 1.6 = \boxed{}$

A. 0.494

B. 1.142

C. 1.152

D. 4.932

5. Find the product.

$0.13 \times 0.4 = \boxed{}$

A. 0.0052

B. 0.052

C. 0.52

D. 5.2

6. Monica is 4.5 feet tall. Her mother is 1.2 times as tall as Monica. How tall is Monica's mother?

A. 5.7 feet

B. 5.4 feet

C. 5.3 feet

D. 5.04 feet

7. Tom worked 5.5 hours on Saturday. He earns $7.20 per hour. How much did he earn on Saturday?

   A. $39.60

   B. $39.06

   C. $36.90

   D. $12.70

8. Pablo went to Mexico City to visit relatives. He exchanged $82 for Mexican pesos. When he was there, $1 was worth 13.36 Mexican pesos. How many pesos did Pablo receive?

   A.   995.52

   B. 1,071.42

   C. 1,084.52

   D. 1,095.52

9. For a barbecue, Mrs. Charles bought 12.5 pounds of hamburger meat for $2.89 per pound.

   A. How much did the hamburger meat cost? Show your work.

   B. Was it necessary to round the product in part A? Explain your answer.

   _____

   _____

   _____

Lesson Practice • Part 2

Choose the correct answer.

1. Find the product.

$$0.27 \times 0.06 = \boxed{}$$

A. 0.0122 **C.** 0.122

B. 0.0162 **D.** 0.162

2. Mr. Fraioli bought 12 ounces of smoked salmon for $1.49 per ounce. How much did Mr. Fraioli spend on the smoked salmon?

A. $16.78 **C.** $17.78

B. $16.88 **D.** $17.88

3. Each lap around a walking trail is 2.4 kilometers. Angel and Jose walked 2.75 laps before leaving the trail. What was the distance that they walked on the trail?

A. 6.6 kilometers

B. 6.58 kilometers

C. 6.5 kilometers

D. 6.3 kilometers

4. Which number makes this sentence true?

$$7.8 \times 3.6 \times 1 = 7.8 \times \boxed{}$$

A. 1 **C.** 4.6

B. 3.6 **D.** 7.8

5. A skateboard that normally costs $72.80 is on sale for 0.75 of the cost. What is the discount?

A. $18.20

B. $19.84

C. $52.96

D. $54.60

6. When traveling back from Europe, Morgan exchanged 85 euros for dollars. She received $1.30 for each euro. How much did Morgan receive?

A. $109.40

B. $109.50

C. $110.40

D. $110.50

7. Carlos's garden last year had an area of 28.88 square meters. This year his garden will be 2.5 times the area of last year's garden. What will be the area of this year's garden?

A. 56.66 square meters

B. 62.76 square meters

C. 71.1 square meters

D. 72.2 square meters

8. Find the product.

$$3.5 \times 6.7 \times 4.2 = \boxed{}$$

A. 98.49

B. 98.29

C. 97.82

D. 88.83

9. Which number makes this sentence true?

$$(5.2 \times 2.7) \times 4.5 =$$
$$(5.2 \times \boxed{}) \times 2.7$$

A. 0.7

B. 2.7

C. 4.5

D. 5.2

10. Two decimals are going to be multiplied. Which sentence about the number of decimal places the product will have is true?

A. It is equal to the number of decimal places in the factor with the greater number of decimal places.

B. It is equal to the sum of the number of decimal places in the factors.

C. It is equal to the number of decimal places in the factor with the lesser number of decimal places.

D. There is no relationship between the number of decimal places in the factors and the number of decimal places in the product.

11. The table shows the amount of time and the speed at which Aubree was walking on her treadmill each day for three days.

Treadmill Walking

Day	Time (in hours)	Speed (in miles per hour)
Monday	0.55	3.6
Tuesday	0.75	3.8
Wednesday	0.6	4.2

A. How many more miles did Aubree walk on Tuesday than on Monday? Show your work.

B. How many miles did Aubree walk in all? Show your work.

12. Use decimals from the box to write a true number sentence.

$0.04 \times$ _____ $=$ _____

0.032
0.32
0.08
0.8

13. Which expressions have a value of 0.96? Circle all that apply.

A. 0.4×0.12

B. 8×0.12

C. 0.2×4.8

D. 0.16×0.06

E. 0.03×32

14. Draw a line from each expression to its product.

A. 0.6×0.7 •   •   0.042

B. 0.8×0.06 •   •   0.048

C. 0.3×1.6 •   •   0.42

D. 0.14×0.3 •   •   0.48

15. Which number sentences show the associative property of multiplication? Circle all that apply.

A. $21.86 \times (2.48 \times 12.5) = (21.86 \times 2.48) \times 12.5$

B. $2.8 \times 0.72 = 0.72 \times 2.8$

C. $45.1 \times 1 = 45.1$

D. $(12.78 \times 4.8) \times 6.83 = 12.78 \times (4.8 \times 6.83)$

E. $8.34 \times 0 = 0$

16. The table shows the costs per pound of different fruits. Select True or False for each statement.

Fruit Prices

Fruit	Cost (per pound)
Apples	$0.84
Bananas	$0.45
Grapes	$1.74
Pears	$0.95

A. 4.5 pounds of apples cost $3.88.　　○ True　○ False

B. 7.2 pounds of pears cost $6.84.　　○ True　○ False

C. 5 pounds of bananas cost $2.25.　　○ True　○ False

D. 3.8 pounds of grapes cost $6.42.　　○ True　○ False

17. Which expressions have a value of 0.064? Circle all that apply.

A. 0.2×0.32

B. 4×0.16

C. 3.2×0.2

D. 1.6×0.04

E. 0.8×0.08

Divide Decimals

Getting the Idea

You can use a model to divide decimals.

Example 1

Find the quotient: $0.2 \div 5 = \boxed{}$.

Strategy   **Use a model.**

Step 1   Use a 10-by-10 grid.

Shade 0.2 of the model.

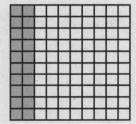

Step 2   Use circles to separate the shaded area into 5 equal groups.

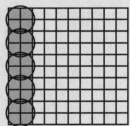

Step 3   Count the number of squares in each group.

There are 4 squares in each group.

Four squares represents 4 hundredths, or 0.04.

Solution $0.2 \div 5 = 0.04$

When using paper and pencil, write the decimal point in the quotient above the decimal point of the dividend. Then divide just as you would with whole numbers.

Example 2

Mrs. Collins bought 8 towels for $66.24. Each towel was the same price.
What was the price of one towel?

Strategy   **Write an equation for the problem. Then divide from left to right.**

Step 1   Write an equation for the problem.

Let p represent the price of one towel.

$66.24 ÷ 8 = p$

Step 2   Write the decimal point in the quotient. Divide 66 ones.

$$
\begin{array}{r}
8. \\
8\overline{)66.24} \\
-64 \\
\hline
2
\end{array}
$$

    ← $8 \times 8 = 64$
    ← $66 - 64 = 2$

Step 3   Bring down the 2 tenths. Divide the tenths.

$$
\begin{array}{r}
8.2 \\
8\overline{)66.24} \\
-64 \\
\hline
2\,2 \\
-1\,6 \\
\hline
6
\end{array}
$$

    ← $8 \times 2 = 16$
    ← $22 - 16 = 6$

Step 4   Bring down the 4 hundredths. Divide the hundredths.

$$
\begin{array}{r}
8.28 \\
8\overline{)66.24} \\
-64 \\
\hline
2\,2 \\
-1\,6 \\
\hline
64 \\
-64 \\
\hline
0
\end{array}
$$

    ← $8 \times 8 = 64$
    ← $64 - 64 = 0$

Step 5   Write the dollar sign in the quotient.

$8.28 = p$

Solution   **The price of one towel is $8.28.**

Sometimes you may need to insert zeros in the quotient as placeholders.

Example 3

Find the quotient: $0.42 \div 6 = \boxed{}$.

Strategy   **Divide each place, going from left to right.**

Step 1   Rewrite the problem.

Write the decimal point in the quotient. Since the dividend is less than 1, write a 0 in the ones place.

$$\begin{array}{r} 0. \\ 6\overline{)0.42} \end{array}$$

Step 2   Divide the tenths.

$$\begin{array}{r} 0.0 \\ 6\overline{)0.42} \\ \underline{-0} \\ 4 \end{array}$$ ← 6 × 0 = 0
← 4 − 0 = 4

Step 3   Bring down the 2 hundredths. Divide the hundredths.

$$\begin{array}{r} 0.07 \\ 6\overline{)0.42} \\ \underline{-0}\downarrow \\ 42 \\ \underline{-42} \\ 0 \end{array}$$ ← 6 × 7 = 42
← 42 − 42 = 0

Solution   **$0.42 \div 6 = 0.07$**

When dividing a decimal by a decimal divisor, you can multiply the divisor by a power of 10 to form a whole number. Use the same power of 10 to multiply the dividend. Then use the new divisor and dividend to divide.

For example, divide $1.5 \div 0.3$. Multiply the divisor and dividend by 10:

$(1.5 \times 10) \div (0.3 \times 10) =$

$15 \div 3 = 5$

To find a decimal remainder, you can annex zeroes at the end of the dividend. Annexing a 0 to the right of a decimal does not change its value.

Example 4

Find the quotient: $82.6 \div 0.4 = \boxed{}$.

Strategy   **Multiply by 10 to create a whole-number divisor. Then divide.**

Step 1   There is one decimal place in the divisor, so multiply the divisor and the dividend by 10.

$$0.4 \times 10 = 4$$
$$82.6 \times 10 = 826$$

Step 2   Write the problem with the new divisor and dividend. Divide each place from left to right.

```
      206
  4)826
   − 8
    ‾‾‾
     02
    − 0
    ‾‾‾
     26
   − 24
   ‾‾‾‾
      2
```

Step 3   Annex a 0 and continue dividing.

```
      206.5
  4)826.0
   − 8
    ‾‾‾
     02
    − 0
    ‾‾‾
     26
   − 24
   ‾‾‾‾
      20
    − 20
    ‾‾‾‾
       0
```

Solution $82.6 \div 0.4 = 206.5$

Remember to check the answer by multiplying the quotient by the divisor.

Since $206.3 \times 0.4 = 82.6$, the answer is correct.

Coached Example

Madison paid $28.12 for 9.5 gallons of gas. What was the price of each gallon of gas?

Write an equation for the problem. _____

What is the dividend? _____

What is the divisor? _____

How many decimal places are after the decimal point in the divisor? _____

By what number should you multiply both the divisor and dividend? _____

_____ × 28.12 = _____

_____ × 9.5 = _____

Write the problem with the new dividend and divisor. Write the decimal point in the quotient. Then divide each place.

Madison paid _____ for each gallon of gas.

Lesson Practice • Part 1

Choose the correct answer.

1. Find the quotient. Use the grid to help you divide.

$$0.4 \div 5 = \boxed{}$$

A. 8

B. 0.8

C. 0.08

D. 0.008

2. Find the quotient.

$$175.8 \div 6 = \boxed{}$$

A. 293

B. 29.3

C. 2.93

D. 0.293

3. Find the quotient.

$$0.65 \div 0.25 = \boxed{}$$

A. 0.026

B. 0.26

C. 2.6

D. 26

4. A restaurant bill totaled $70.40. If 4 friends split the bill equally, how much did each contribute toward the bill?

A. $16.60

B. $17.60

C. $18.60

D. $19.60

5. Laurie is running in a 20-kilometer race. After the starting point, there are water stations every 0.8 kilometer. How many water stations are there?

A. 25

B. 16

C. 8

D. 4

6. It took Neal 2.4 hours to run 19.8 miles last Sunday while training for a marathon. What was his average speed?

A. 7.5 miles per hour

B. 7.75 miles per hour

C. 8.25 miles per hour

D. 8.5 miles per hour

7. Sergio bought 1.2 pounds of turkey breast at the deli counter. He paid $8.34 for the turkey. What was the price per pound of the turkey?

   A. $6.24

   B. $6.31

   C. $6.90

   D. $6.95

8. Ana spent $10.92 on ribbon that cost $0.84 per yard. How many yards of ribbon did Ana buy?

   A. 0.13 yard

   B. 1.3 yards

   C. 3.1 yards

   D. 13 yards

9. The Rivera family drove 267.9 miles from their home to Cape Cod, Massachusetts. They used 9.5 gallons of gas.

   A. How many miles per gallon of gas did they get on the trip? Show your work.

   B. Use the division problem from part A to explain how dividing decimals is similar to dividing whole numbers.

_____

_____

_____

Lesson Practice • Part 2

Choose the correct answer.

1. Find the quotient.

$$46.08 \div 0.8 = \boxed{}$$

A. 5.71

B. 5.76

C. 57.1

D. 57.6

2. To divide $175.78 \div 9.4$, what should you do before dividing?

A. multiply the dividend by 100 and the divisor by 10 so both are whole numbers

B. multiply the dividend and divisor by 10 so the divisor is a whole number

C. divide the dividend by 100 and the divisor by 10 so both are whole numbers

D. divide the dividend and divisor by 10 so the divisor is a whole number

3. Serenity spent $13.68 to buy as many pencils as she could. Each pencil cost $0.76. How many pencils did she buy?

A. 18

B. 19

C. 180

D. 181

4. Main Street is 4.8 kilometers long. There are 4 traffic lights every 0.6 kilometer after the start of the street. How many traffic lights are there on Main Street?

A. 8

B. 32

C. 80

D. 320

5. Cooper jogged 2.48 miles at an average speed of 6.2 miles per hour. How long did Cooper jog?

A. 0.4 hour

B. 2.5 hours

C. 3.72 hours

D. 15.376 hours

6. Vince worked 7.5 hours at his mother's office. He was paid $94.50 for his work. How much money did Vince earn per hour?

A. $11.27

B. $12.00

C. $12.60

D. $12.87

7. Ms. Jefferson spent $15 to buy 12.8 ounces of smoked trout. What was the cost per pound? Hint: There are 16 ounces in a pound.

A. $13.65

B. $18.20

C. $18.75

D. $19.20

8. Find the quotient.

$$147.2 \div 3.2 = \boxed{}$$

A. 46

C. 460

B. 49.125

D. 491.25

9. Sophie plays third base for her softball team. She has 8 hits in 25 at bats. What is her batting average (hits ÷ at bats)?

A. 0.302

C. 3.125

B. 0.320

D. 3.18

10. Miles was given 63.2 ÷ 0.25 to divide. He said he could multiply the dividend and divisor by 4 to find the quotient without dividing. Which sentence is true?

A. Miles is correct because if he multiplies the dividend and divisor by 4, the divisor becomes 1 and he can use the multiplicative identity for the quotient.

B. Miles is incorrect because he must multiply the dividend by 10 and the divisor by 100, so both are whole numbers.

C. Miles is incorrect because he must multiply the dividend and divisor by 100, so both are whole numbers.

D. Miles is incorrect because if he multiplies the dividend and divisor by 4, the divisor is still a decimal less than 1.

11. Lydia has $20 to buy school supplies. Each pencil cost $0.59 and each notebook cost $3.50. She decides that she will buy as many notebooks as she can for $12 and then buy as many pencils as she can?

A. How many notebooks can Lydia buy for $12 or less? How much did she spend on the notebooks? Explain your reasoning.

_____

_____

_____

B. How many pencils can Lydia buy with the money that remains after she pays for the notebooks? Explain your reasoning.

_____

_____

_____

12. Which expressions have a value of 4.8? Circle all that apply.

- **A.** $1.44 \div 0.3$
- **B.** $18.24 \div 3.8$
- **C.** $31.85 \div 6.5$
- **D.** $4.23 \div 0.9$
- **E.** $32.4 \div 6.75$

13. Draw a line from each expression to its quotient.

A. $6.63 \div 1.5$ •	• 4.25
B. $18.7 \div 4.4$ •	• 4.36
C. $11.64 \div 2.4$ •	• 4.42
D. $54.5 \div 12.5$ •	• 4.85

14. Which expressions have a value of 0.82? Circle all that apply.

- **A.** $7.48 \div 9$
- **B.** $4.1 \div 5$
- **C.** $3.32 \div 4$
- **D.** $6.56 \div 8$
- **E.** $4.68 \div 6$

15. The table shows the miles driven and the gas used by four cars. Select True or False for each statement.

Gas Mileage Data

Car	Gas Used (in gallons)	Distance (in miles)
A	8.6	178.88
B	6.2	140.74
C	7.5	140.25
D	9.4	184.24

A. Car A gets 20.5 miles per gallon. ○ True ○ False

B. Car B gets 22.7 miles per gallon. ○ True ○ False

C. Car C gets 18.7 miles per gallon. ○ True ○ False

D. Car D gets 19.8 miles per gallon. ○ True ○ False

16. Which expressions have a value of 12.4? Circle all that apply.

A. $104.16 \div 8.4$

B. $82.96 \div 6.8$

C. $59.22 \div 4.7$

D. $39.68 \div 3.2$

E. $65.19 \div 5.3$

17. Use decimals from the box to write a true number sentence.

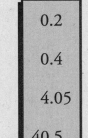

$16.2 \div$ _____ = _____

0.2

0.4

4.05

40.5

Domain 2: Cumulative Assessment for Lessons 6–16

1. Find the product.

   $$4{,}578 \times 29 = \boxed{}$$

   A. 50,358
   B. 91,560
   C. 128,092
   D. 132,762

2. Find the quotient.

   $$8{,}352 \div 32 = \boxed{}$$

   A. 258
   B. 260
   C. 261
   D. 263

3. Find the sum.

   $$7.52 + 4.836 = \boxed{}$$

   A. 11.356
   B. 12.356
   C. 12.456
   D. 13.356

4. Elena bought 6.39 pounds of apples. What is 6.39 rounded to the nearest whole number?

   A. 6
   B. 6.3
   C. 6.4
   D. 7

5. Which is true?

   A. $8.659 = 8.651$
   B. $8.659 > 8.651$
   C. $8.651 = 8.659$
   D. $8.651 > 8.659$

6. Find the quotient.

   $$9.54 \div 1.8 = \boxed{}$$

   A. 0.53
   B. 5.03
   C. 5.3
   D. 53

7. Find the quotient.

$$6.2 \div 10^3 = \boxed{}$$

A.   0.00062

B.   0.0062

C.   0.062

D. 6,200

8. Which represents a value $\frac{1}{10}$ of 0.7?

A.   0.007

B.   0.07

C.   7

D. 70

9. Write 95.417 in expanded form with multiplication.

_____

10. Chicken cutlets are on sale for $3.48 per pound.

A. How much will it cost to buy 3.5 pounds of chicken cutlets? Show your work.

B. Explain how you found your answer for Part A.

_____

_____

_____

Domain 3

Number and Operations—Fractions

Domain 3: Diagnostic Assessment for Lessons 17–24

Lesson 17 Equivalent Fractions

Lesson 18 Improper Fractions and Mixed Numbers

Lesson 19 Add Fractions

Lesson 20 Subtract Fractions

Lesson 21 Understand Multiplication of Fractions

Lesson 22 Multiply Fractions

Lesson 23 Fractions as Division

Lesson 24 Divide Fractions

Domain 3: Cumulative Assessment for Lessons 17–24

Domain 3: Diagnostic Assessment for Lessons 17–24

1. Imani has $\frac{2}{3}$ yard of fabric. Which fraction is equivalent to $\frac{2}{3}$?

   A. $\frac{8}{12}$

   B. $\frac{9}{12}$

   C. $\frac{12}{15}$

   D. $\frac{5}{6}$

2. Find the difference.

   $$\frac{4}{5} - \frac{2}{3} = \boxed{}$$

   A. $\frac{2}{15}$

   B. $\frac{8}{15}$

   C. $\frac{1}{2}$

   D. $1\frac{7}{15}$

3. Paul has shaded $\frac{31}{100}$ of a grid. Then he shades another $\frac{3}{5}$ of the grid. What fraction of the grid is shaded?

   A. $\frac{29}{100}$

   B. $\frac{91}{100}$

   C. $\frac{34}{105}$

   D. $\frac{93}{500}$

4. A rectangle has a length of $\frac{3}{4}$ foot and a width of $\frac{1}{2}$ foot. What is the area of the rectangle?

   A. $\frac{3}{8}$ square foot

   B. $\frac{4}{6}$ square foot

   C. 1 square foot

   D. $1\frac{1}{4}$ square feet

5. The fraction $\frac{5}{8}$ is a factor in a multiplication expression. When $\frac{5}{8}$ is multiplied by the other factor, the product is less than $\frac{5}{8}$. Which could be the other factor?

   A. $\frac{3}{1}$

   B. $\frac{7}{6}$

   C. $\frac{9}{10}$

   D. $\frac{10}{5}$

6. Andrea went on a $\frac{3}{5}$-mile walk through a park. After she had walked $\frac{1}{3}$ of the distance, she stopped to take some pictures. How far did she walk before stopping?

   A. $\frac{1}{5}$ mile   C. $\frac{1}{2}$ mile

   B. $\frac{4}{15}$ mile   D. 1 mile

7. Find the quotient.

$$\frac{1}{4} \div 3 = \boxed{}$$

A. 12

B. $\frac{1}{6}$

C. $\frac{1}{7}$

D. $\frac{1}{12}$

8. How much cheese will each friend get if 4 friends share $\frac{1}{2}$ pound equally?

A. 2 pounds

B. $\frac{1}{4}$ pound

C. $\frac{2}{8}$ pound

D. $\frac{1}{8}$ pound

9. Find the sum. $3\frac{5}{8} + 4\frac{1}{3} = \boxed{}$

10. If 5 friends want to share 18 ounces of chocolate equally by weight, how many ounces should each friend get?

A. Write an equation for the problem.

B. Solve the problem. Show your work.

Equivalent Fractions

Getting the Idea

A **fraction** names part of a whole or a group. The number above the fraction bar is called the **numerator**. It shows the number of parts being considered. The number below the fraction bar is called the **denominator**. It shows the total number of equal parts in the whole or in the group. The fraction bar means *divided by*. So if *a* and *b* are whole numbers, $\frac{a}{b}$ means $a \div b$.

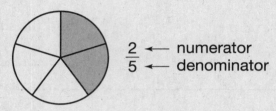

$$\frac{2}{5} \begin{array}{l} \leftarrow \text{ numerator} \\ \leftarrow \text{ denominator} \end{array}$$

Example 1

What fraction of the rectangle is shaded?

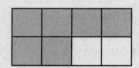

Strategy **Find the denominator. Then find the numerator.**

Step 1 Count the number of equal parts in the rectangle.

There are 8 parts. This is the denominator.

Step 2 Count the number of parts that are shaded.

There are 6 parts shaded. This is the numerator.

Step 3 Write the fraction.

$$\frac{\text{numerator}}{\text{denominator}} = \frac{6}{8}$$

Solution $\frac{6}{8}$ **of the rectangle is shaded.**

Two fractions are **equivalent fractions** if they represent the same part of a whole. For example, the model below shows that $\frac{1}{2}$ is equivalent to $\frac{4}{8}$.

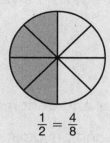

$$\frac{1}{2} = \frac{4}{8}$$

The fraction $\frac{1}{2}$ is in **simplest form** because the numerator and denominator do not have any common factors except 1. To simplify a fraction, divide the numerator and denominator by the **greatest common factor (GCF)**.

Example 2

What is $\frac{6}{8}$ in simplest form?

Strategy   **Write an equivalent fraction in simplest form.**

Step 1   Identify the common factors of 6 and 8.

The factors of 6 are 1, 2, 3, and 6.

The factors of 8 are 1, 2, 4, and 8.

2 is the GCF.

Step 2   Divide the numerator and denominator by 2.

$$\frac{6}{8} = \frac{6 \div 2}{8 \div 2} = \frac{3}{4}$$

Solution $\frac{6}{8}$ **written in simplest form is** $\frac{3}{4}$**.**

You can use number lines to find equivalent fractions. On the number lines below, the fractions $\frac{3}{4}$ and $\frac{6}{8}$ are equivalent fractions, since both $\frac{3}{4}$ and $\frac{6}{8}$ are the same distance from 0.

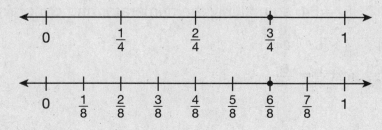

You can also find equivalent fractions by multiplying the numerator and denominator by the same number. Multiplying the numerator and denominator by the same number is the same as multiplying by 1, so the value of the fraction is unchanged.

Example 3

Write two equivalent fractions for $\frac{2}{3}$.

Strategy   **Multiply the numerator and denominator by the same number.**

Step 1   Multiply the numerator and denominator by 2.

$$\frac{2}{3} = \frac{2 \times 2}{3 \times 2} = \frac{4}{6}$$

Step 2   Multiply the numerator and denominator by 3.

$$\frac{2}{3} = \frac{2 \times 3}{3 \times 3} = \frac{6}{9}$$

Solution   **Two equivalent fractions for $\frac{2}{3}$ are $\frac{4}{6}$ and $\frac{6}{9}$.**

An important use for equivalent fractions is to create pairs of fractions with the same denominator. One way to find fractions with the same denominator is to multiply the denominators of the fractions.

Example 4

Write equivalent fractions for $\frac{5}{6}$ and $\frac{1}{4}$ that have the same denominator.

Strategy   **Multiply the two denominators to write equivalent fractions.**

Step 1   Multiply the denominators.

$$6 \times 4 = 24$$

Step 2   Write an equivalent fraction for $\frac{5}{6}$ that has a denominator of 24.

$6 \times 4 = 24$, so multiply the numerator and denominator by 4.

$$\frac{5}{6} = \frac{5 \times 4}{6 \times 4} = \frac{20}{24}$$

Step 3   Write an equivalent fraction for $\frac{1}{4}$ that has a denominator of 24.

$4 \times 6 = 24$, so multiply the numerator and denominator by 6.

$$\frac{1}{4} = \frac{1 \times 6}{4 \times 6} = \frac{6}{24}$$

Solution $\frac{5}{6} = \frac{20}{24}$ and $\frac{1}{4} = \frac{6}{24}$

One way to determine if two fractions are equivalent is to rename one or both fractions using a common denominator. It is not necessary to use the least common multiple to find the least common denominator. You can multiply the denominators to find a common denominator.

Example 5

Determine if $\frac{2}{6}$ and $\frac{3}{9}$ are equivalent.

Strategy   **Rename each fraction using a common denominator.**

Step 1   Multiply the denominators.

$6 \times 9 = 54$

Rename the fractions using 54 as the denominator.

Step 2   Write equivalent fractions.

$$\frac{2}{6} \times \frac{9}{9} = \frac{18}{54}$$

$$\frac{3}{9} \times \frac{6}{6} = \frac{18}{54}$$

Solution   **The fractions $\frac{2}{6}$ and $\frac{3}{9}$ are equivalent.**

Another method to determine if two fractions are equivalent is to write each in simplest form.

Example 6

Determine if $\frac{8}{10}$ and $\frac{12}{15}$ are equivalent.

Strategy   **Write each fraction in simplest form.**

Step 1   Write $\frac{8}{10}$ in simplest form.

$$\frac{8}{10} \div \frac{2}{2} = \frac{4}{5}$$

Step 2   Write $\frac{12}{15}$ in simplest form.

$$\frac{12}{15} \div \frac{3}{3} = \frac{4}{5}$$

Solution   **The fractions $\frac{8}{10}$ and $\frac{12}{15}$ are equivalent.**

Coached Example

Write $\frac{8}{10}$ in simplest form. Then write another equivalent fraction for $\frac{8}{10}$.

First, write the fraction in simplest form.

The factors of 8 are _____, _____, _____, _____.

The factors of 10 are _____, _____, _____, _____.

The greatest common factor of 8 and 10 is _____.

Divide the numerator and denominator by _____.

$\frac{8}{10}$ = _____

Next, find another equivalent fraction.

Multiply the numerator and denominator of $\frac{8}{10}$ by _____.

Show your work.

In simplest form, $\frac{8}{10}$ is _____.

Another fraction equivalent to $\frac{8}{10}$ is _____.

Lesson Practice • Part 1

Choose the correct answer.

1. In simplest form, what fraction of the figure is shaded?

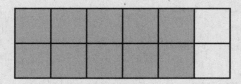

   A. $\frac{2}{3}$

   B. $\frac{3}{4}$

   C. $\frac{5}{6}$

   D. $\frac{7}{8}$

2. Which fraction is equivalent to $\frac{3}{9}$?

   A. $\frac{1}{4}$

   B. $\frac{1}{3}$

   C. $\frac{2}{5}$

   D. $\frac{1}{2}$

3. Which fraction is **not** equivalent to $\frac{5}{6}$?

   A. $\frac{25}{30}$

   B. $\frac{20}{24}$

   C. $\frac{15}{18}$

   D. $\frac{30}{42}$

4. Which can you use as a denominator to write equivalent fractions for $\frac{4}{7}$ and $\frac{5}{6}$?

   A. 24

   B. 30

   C. 35

   D. 42

5. Which pair of fractions is equivalent to $\frac{5}{6}$ and $\frac{3}{5}$?

   A. $\frac{25}{30}$ and $\frac{18}{30}$

   B. $\frac{30}{35}$ and $\frac{21}{35}$

   C. $\frac{10}{12}$ and $\frac{6}{12}$

   D. $\frac{15}{20}$ and $\frac{12}{20}$

6. Which fraction is in simplest form?

   A. $\frac{9}{21}$

   B. $\frac{6}{14}$

   C. $\frac{8}{18}$

   D. $\frac{5}{12}$

7. Which number sentence is **not** true?

   A. $\frac{15}{20} = \frac{3}{4}$

   B. $\frac{4}{12} = \frac{1}{3}$

   C. $\frac{2}{5} = \frac{6}{10}$

   D. $\frac{10}{15} = \frac{2}{3}$

8. Which fractions are **not** equivalent to each other?

   A. $\frac{1}{4}$ and $\frac{5}{20}$

   B. $\frac{3}{8}$ and $\frac{8}{24}$

   C. $\frac{2}{5}$ and $\frac{14}{35}$

   D. $\frac{9}{10}$ and $\frac{36}{40}$

9. Look at the figure below.

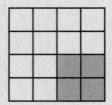

   A. In simplest form, what fraction of the figure is shaded? Show your work.

   B. Find two more fractions that are equivalent to the fraction you found in part A. Show your work.

Lesson Practice • Part 2

Choose the correct answer.

1. Which number completes the sentence?

$$\frac{6}{16} = \frac{9}{\boxed{}}$$

 A. 19   C. 27

 B. 24   D. 32

2. Which fraction is equivalent to $\frac{3}{5}$?

 A. $\frac{12}{20}$

 B. $\frac{16}{25}$

 C. $\frac{20}{30}$

 D. $\frac{26}{40}$

3. Which pair of fractions is equivalent?

 A. $\frac{9}{12}$ and $\frac{14}{20}$

 B. $\frac{6}{16}$ and $\frac{10}{25}$

 C. $\frac{12}{15}$ and $\frac{25}{35}$

 D. $\frac{10}{18}$ and $\frac{25}{45}$

4. Which fraction is in simplest form?

 A. $\frac{11}{15}$ C. $\frac{9}{21}$

 B. $\frac{12}{18}$ D. $\frac{14}{24}$

5. A fraction is greater than 0 and less than 1. How can you tell if such a fraction is in simplest form by knowing prime numbers?

 A. If the numerator is a prime number, the fraction is in simplest form.

 B. If the denominator is a prime number, the fraction is in simplest form.

 C. If the numerator is a prime number, the fraction can always be simplified further.

 D. If the denominator is a prime number, the fraction can always be simplified further.

6. Which pair of fractions has a common denominator that is less than the product of the two denominators?

 A. $\frac{2}{3}$ and $\frac{3}{8}$

 B. $\frac{5}{6}$ and $\frac{7}{11}$

 C. $\frac{7}{9}$ and $\frac{11}{12}$

 D. $\frac{7}{10}$ and $\frac{5}{7}$

7. Which pair of fractions is equivalent to $\frac{5}{8}$ and $\frac{7}{12}$?

   A. $\frac{20}{36}$ and $\frac{28}{36}$

   B. $\frac{25}{40}$ and $\frac{24}{36}$

   C. $\frac{25}{60}$ and $\frac{35}{60}$

   D. $\frac{60}{96}$ and $\frac{56}{96}$

8. Which number completes the sentence?

   $$\frac{12}{18} = \frac{\square}{30}$$

   A. 15

   B. 18

   C. 20

   D. 24

9. Which fraction is equivalent to $\frac{15}{24}$?

   A. $\frac{2}{3}$

   B. $\frac{3}{4}$

   C. $\frac{5}{8}$

   D. $\frac{7}{12}$

10. Which fraction is equivalent to $\frac{5}{12}$?

   A. $\frac{15}{36}$

   B. $\frac{18}{48}$

   C. $\frac{24}{60}$

   D. $\frac{35}{72}$

11. Each day Gianna practices penalty kicks with her older brother as the goalie. Yesterday she made $\frac{18}{24}$ of her penalty kicks. Today she plans on shooting 36 penalty kicks.

   A. How many penalty kicks would Gianna have to make to successfully shoot an equivalent fraction as yesterday? Show your work.

   B. In simplest form, what fraction of her penalty kicks did Gianna make yesterday? Show your work.

12. Look at each fraction. Is it equivalent to $\frac{9}{12}$? Select Yes or No.

  A. $\frac{3}{4}$ ◯ Yes   ◯ No

  B. $\frac{12}{9}$ ◯ Yes   ◯ No

  C. $\frac{4}{6}$ ◯ Yes   ◯ No

  D. $\frac{18}{24}$ ◯ Yes   ◯ No

13. Select True or False for each number sentence.

  A. $\frac{5}{15} = \frac{10}{20}$ ◯ True   ◯ False

  B. $\frac{6}{8} = \frac{3}{4}$ ◯ True   ◯ False

  C. $\frac{4}{16} = \frac{8}{20}$ ◯ True   ◯ False

  D. $\frac{3}{6} = \frac{15}{30}$ ◯ True   ◯ False

14. Which fraction of the figure is shaded? Circle all that apply.

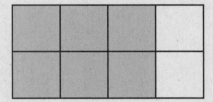

  A. $\frac{12}{16}$

  B. $\frac{10}{12}$

  C. $\frac{6}{8}$

  D. $\frac{3}{4}$

  E. $\frac{9}{11}$

15. Write each fraction in simplest form. Write the fraction in the correct box.

| $\dfrac{14}{35}$ | $\dfrac{8}{20}$ | $\dfrac{18}{30}$ | $\dfrac{24}{40}$ | $\dfrac{9}{15}$ | $\dfrac{10}{25}$ |

Equivalent to $\dfrac{2}{5}$	Equivalent to $\dfrac{3}{5}$

16. Which fractions are in simplest form? Circle all that apply.

A. $\dfrac{14}{21}$

B. $\dfrac{5}{7}$

C. $\dfrac{9}{16}$

D. $\dfrac{18}{20}$

E. $\dfrac{8}{19}$

17. Draw a line from each fraction to an equivalent fraction.

A. $\dfrac{2}{4}$ •   • $\dfrac{1}{6}$

B. $\dfrac{4}{12}$ •   • $\dfrac{1}{4}$

C. $\dfrac{3}{18}$ •   • $\dfrac{1}{3}$

D. $\dfrac{5}{20}$ •   • $\dfrac{1}{2}$

Improper Fractions and Mixed Numbers

Getting the Idea

A **mixed number** can be written as an **improper fraction**. In an improper fraction, the numerator is greater than the denominator. For example, the mixed number $1\frac{1}{4}$ can be written as an improper fraction. The model below shows that $1\frac{1}{4} = \frac{5}{4}$. Each rectangle is divided into 4 equal parts, which is the denominator. There are 5 parts shaded, so that is the numerator.

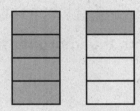

Example 1

In simplest form, what mixed number is modeled below?

Strategy   **Find the whole-number part. Then find the fraction part.**

| Step 1 | Count the number of completely shaded figures. |

There are 2 rectangles completely shaded.

The whole-number part is 2.

| Step 2 | Find the fraction of the figure that is partially shaded. |

$\frac{2}{4}$ of the figure is shaded.

| Step 3 | Write the fraction part in simplest form. |

The greatest common factor of 2 and 4 is 2.

$\frac{2}{4} = \frac{2 \div 2}{4 \div 2} = \frac{1}{2}$

| Step 4 | Add the whole-number part and the fraction part. |

$2 + \frac{1}{2} = 2\frac{1}{2}$

Solution   **The mixed number shown by the model is $2\frac{1}{2}$.**

Example 2

What improper fraction does the model represent?

Strategy   **Identify the numerator and the denominator.**

Step 1   To find the numerator, count the number of shaded parts.

There are 13 shaded parts.

Step 2   To find the denominator, count the number of equal parts in each rectangle.

Each rectangle is divided into 6 equal parts.

Solution   **The model represents the improper fraction $\frac{13}{6}$.**

Example 3

What mixed number and improper fraction does this model represent?

Strategy   **Identify the whole-number part and the fraction part.**

Step 1   Identify the whole-number part of the mixed number.

One circle is completely shaded. The whole-number part is 1.

Step 2   Identify the fraction part of the mixed number.

In the second circle, 3 parts are shaded out of 8 equal parts. The fraction part is $\frac{3}{8}$. The mixed number is $1\frac{3}{8}$.

Step 3   Identify the numerator of the improper fraction.

There are 11 shaded parts. The numerator is 11.

Step 4   Identify the denominator of the improper fraction.

Each circle is divided into 8 equal parts. The denominator is 8. The improper fraction is $\frac{11}{8}$.

Solution   **The model represents the mixed number $1\frac{3}{8}$ and the improper fraction $\frac{11}{8}$.**

You can convert a mixed number to an improper fraction. A mixed number represents the sum of a whole number and a fraction less than 1. Writing the whole-number part as an equivalent fraction can help you to write a mixed number as an improper fraction.

For example, convert $2\frac{1}{6}$ to an improper fraction.

Write the whole number as a fraction with a denominator of 1.

$$2\frac{1}{6} = \frac{2}{1} + \frac{1}{6}$$

Write an equivalent fraction for it with the same denominator as the fraction part of the mixed number.

$$\frac{2}{1} + \frac{1}{6} = \frac{12}{6} + \frac{1}{6}$$

Add the two fractions to represent the mixed number as an improper fraction.

$$\frac{12}{6} + \frac{1}{6} = \frac{13}{6}$$

So, $2\frac{1}{6}$ written as an improper fraction is $\frac{13}{6}$.

Example 4

Convert $3\frac{1}{2}$ to an improper fraction.

Strategy **Write the whole-number part as an equivalent fraction.**

Step 1 Write the whole number as a fraction with a denominator of 1.

$$3 = \frac{3}{1}$$

Step 2 Write $\frac{3}{1}$ as an equivalent fraction with a denominator of 2.

Multiply the numerator and the denominator by 2.

$$\frac{3}{1} = \frac{3 \times 2}{1 \times 2} = \frac{6}{2}$$

Step 3 Add the equivalent fraction and the fraction part of the mixed number.

$$\frac{6}{2} + \frac{1}{2} = \frac{7}{2}$$

Solution $3\frac{1}{2} = \frac{7}{2}$

You could also follow these steps to convert a mixed number to an improper fraction.

1. Multiply the whole number by the denominator of the fraction part.

2. Add the numerator of the fraction part to the product. This sum is the numerator of the improper fraction.

3. The denominator of the improper fraction is the same as the denominator of the fraction part in the mixed number.

Example 5

Write $4\frac{7}{10}$ as an improper fraction.

Strategy **Multiply the whole-number part by the denominator. Then add the numerator to the product.**

Step 1 Multiply the whole number by the denominator.

$$4 \times 10 = 40$$

Step 2 Add the numerator of the fraction part to the product.

$$40 + 7 = 47$$

Step 3 Write the improper fraction.

The numerator is 47.

The denominator remains 10.

Solution $4\frac{7}{10} = \frac{47}{10}$

To convert an improper fraction to a mixed number, divide the numerator by the denominator. The quotient (without the remainder) is the whole-number part of the mixed number. The remainder is the numerator of the fraction part. The denominator remains the same if the mixed number is in simplest form.

Example 6

Write $\frac{16}{6}$ as a mixed number in simplest form.

Strategy **Divide the numerator by the denominator.**

Step 1 Divide the numerator by the denominator.

$$\frac{16}{6} = 16 \div 6 = 2 \text{ R}4$$

Step 2   Write the mixed number.

The quotient, 2, is the whole-number part.

The remainder, 4, is the numerator of the fraction part.

The denominator, 6, stays the same.

The mixed number is $2\frac{4}{6}$.

Step 3   Write the fraction in simplest form.

The greatest common factor of 4 and 6 is 2.

$$\frac{4}{6} = \frac{4 \div 2}{6 \div 2} = \frac{2}{3}$$

Solution $\frac{16}{6}$ **written as a mixed number in simplest form is** $2\frac{2}{3}$**.**

Note: You can also use the fact that $\frac{6}{6} = 1$ to convert the improper fraction in Example 6 to a mixed number. $\frac{16}{6} = \frac{6}{6} + \frac{6}{6} + \frac{4}{6} = 1 + 1 + \frac{4}{6} = 2\frac{2}{3}$

Coached Example

Ms. Rossi's class had a pizza party. The shaded parts of the diagram show the amount of pizza that the class ate.

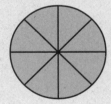 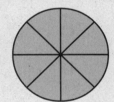 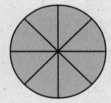 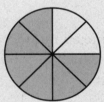

What mixed number in simplest form represents the amount of pizza the class ate?

How many pizzas are completely shaded? _____

Each pizza is divided into _____ equal parts.

How many parts are shaded in the partially shaded circle? _____

What fraction of the last circle is shaded? _____

Write the fraction in simplest form. _____

Add the whole-number part and the fraction part. _____ + _____ = _____

A total of _____ pizzas were eaten.

Lesson Practice • Part 1

Choose the correct answer.

Use the model for questions 1 and 2.

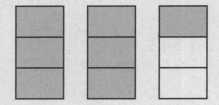

1. What improper fraction does the model show?

    A. $\frac{5}{3}$

    B. $\frac{3}{2}$

    C. $\frac{7}{3}$

    D. $\frac{7}{2}$

2. What mixed number does the model show?

    A. $2\frac{1}{3}$ C. $3\frac{1}{3}$

    B. $2\frac{2}{3}$ D. $3\frac{2}{3}$

3. Which shows $4\frac{2}{5}$ written as an improper fraction?

    A. $\frac{10}{4}$ C. $\frac{22}{5}$

    B. $\frac{14}{5}$ D. $\frac{42}{5}$

4. Which is $\frac{26}{4}$ written as a mixed number in simplest form?

    A. $6\frac{1}{4}$

    B. $6\frac{1}{2}$

    C. $6\frac{2}{4}$

    D. $6\frac{3}{4}$

5. Which shows $\frac{21}{12}$ written as a mixed number in simplest form?

    A. $1\frac{1}{2}$

    B. $1\frac{7}{12}$

    C. $1\frac{2}{3}$

    D. $1\frac{3}{4}$

6. What improper fraction is equivalent to $4\frac{7}{8}$?

    A. $\frac{31}{8}$

    B. $\frac{39}{8}$

    C. $\frac{41}{8}$

    D. $\frac{47}{8}$

7. Which mixed number and improper fraction are **not** equivalent?

   A. $\frac{9}{2}$ and $4\frac{1}{2}$

   B. $\frac{14}{4}$ and $3\frac{1}{2}$

   C. $\frac{16}{6}$ and $2\frac{2}{3}$

   D. $\frac{28}{8}$ and $3\frac{1}{4}$

8. Which is another way to write $2\frac{3}{5}$?

   A. $\frac{11}{5}$

   B. $\frac{13}{5}$

   C. $\frac{18}{5}$

   D. $\frac{33}{5}$

9. Rajeev put pieces of a puzzle together and made this figure.

  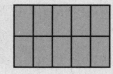

   A. What mixed number in simplest form represents the shaded part of the figure?

   _____

   B. What improper fraction represents the shaded part of the figure? Explain how you found your answer.

   _____

   _____

   _____

Lesson Practice • Part 2

Choose the correct answer.

1. Which improper fraction is equivalent to a whole number?

   A. $\frac{15}{4}$ C. $\frac{18}{6}$

   B. $\frac{17}{5}$ D. $\frac{22}{8}$

2. Which describes how to rename a mixed number as the numerator of an improper fraction?

   A. Multiply the whole number times the numerator. Then add the product to the numerator of the fraction, which is the numerator of the improper fraction.

   B. Multiply the whole number times the denominator. Then add the product to the denominator of the fraction, which is the denominator of the improper fraction.

   C. Multiply the whole number times the numerator. Then add the product to the denominator of the fraction, which is the denominator of the improper fraction.

   D. Multiply the whole number times the denominator. Then add the product to the numerator of the fraction, which is the numerator of the improper fraction.

3. Which shows $\frac{36}{16}$ as a mixed number in simplest form?

   A. $2\frac{1}{8}$ C. $2\frac{1}{2}$

   B. $2\frac{1}{4}$ D. $2\frac{3}{4}$

4. Which describes how to rename an improper fraction to a mixed number?

   A. Divide the numerator by the denominator. The quotient is the whole-number part and the remainder is the numerator of the fraction part of the mixed number. The denominator stays the same.

   B. Divide the denominator by the numerator. The quotient is the whole-number part and the remainder is the numerator of the fraction part of the mixed number. The denominator stays the same.

   C. Divide the numerator by the denominator. The quotient is the numerator of the fraction and the remainder is the whole-number part of the mixed number. The denominator stays the same.

   D. Divide the denominator by the numerator. The quotient is the numerator of the fraction and the remainder is the whole-number part of the mixed number. The denominator stays the same.

5. Which improper fraction is equivalent to $5\frac{5}{6}$?

    A. $\frac{25}{6}$ **C.** $\frac{35}{6}$

    B. $\frac{31}{6}$ **D.** $\frac{55}{6}$

6. Which number completes the sentence?

$$4\frac{5}{12} = \frac{\square}{12}$$

    A. 45   **C.** 55

    B. 53   **D.** 64

7. Which improper fraction completes the sentence?

$$\frac{37}{5} = \underline{\hspace{2cm}}$$

    A. $7\frac{2}{5}$ **C.** $8\frac{2}{5}$

    B. $7\frac{3}{5}$ **D.** $8\frac{3}{5}$

8. Which has a different value than the others?

    A. $\frac{14}{4}$ **C.** $3\frac{2}{4}$

    B. $3\frac{1}{2}$ **D.** $\frac{40}{12}$

9. Julian jogged $2\frac{3}{4}$ miles yesterday.

    A. What improper fraction is equivalent to $2\frac{3}{4}$?

    _____

    B. Write two more equivalent improper fractions for $2\frac{3}{4}$. Show your work.

    _____

10. Select True or False for each number sentence.

    A. $1\frac{1}{4} = \frac{5}{4}$ ○ True   ○ False

    B. $2\frac{6}{8} = \frac{26}{8}$ ○ True   ○ False

    C. $3\frac{2}{3} = \frac{9}{3}$ ○ True   ○ False

    D. $2\frac{3}{6} = \frac{15}{6}$ ○ True   ○ False

11. Is each improper fraction equivalent to $2\frac{8}{10}$? Select Yes or No.

A. $\frac{24}{5}$ ○ Yes ○ No

B. $\frac{28}{10}$ ○ Yes ○ No

C. $\frac{18}{10}$ ○ Yes ○ No

D. $\frac{14}{5}$ ○ Yes ○ No

E. $\frac{42}{15}$ ○ Yes ○ No

12. Draw a line from each improper fraction to the equivalent mixed number in simplest form.

A. $\frac{15}{6}$ •　　　　　• $1\frac{1}{3}$

B. $\frac{28}{12}$ •　　　　　• $1\frac{1}{4}$

C. $\frac{12}{9}$ •　　　　　• $2\frac{1}{2}$

D. $\frac{15}{12}$ •　　　　　• $2\frac{1}{3}$

13. Write each improper fraction as a mixed number in simplest form. Write the improper fraction in the correct box.

| $\frac{33}{12}$ | $\frac{27}{12}$ | $\frac{22}{8}$ | $\frac{9}{4}$ | $\frac{18}{8}$ | $\frac{11}{4}$ |

Equivalent to $2\frac{1}{4}$	Equivalent to $2\frac{3}{4}$

14. Select True or False for each number sentence.

A. $1\frac{7}{8} = \frac{15}{8}$ ○ True ○ False

B. $3\frac{3}{5} = \frac{18}{5}$ ○ True ○ False

C. $2\frac{2}{7} = \frac{22}{7}$ ○ True ○ False

D. $1\frac{5}{6} = \frac{11}{6}$ ○ True ○ False

15. What does the shaded part of the model show? Circle all that apply.

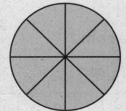 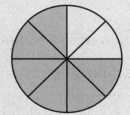

A. $\frac{13}{4}$

B. $1\frac{6}{8}$

C. $\frac{14}{8}$

D. $1\frac{3}{4}$

E. $\frac{14}{16}$

16. Draw a line from each mixed number to the equivalent improper fraction.

A. $2\frac{5}{12}$ •   • $\frac{35}{12}$

B. $3\frac{7}{12}$ •   • $\frac{29}{12}$

C. $2\frac{11}{12}$ •   • $\frac{43}{12}$

D. $1\frac{7}{12}$ •   • $\frac{19}{12}$

Add Fractions

To find the sum of fractions that have **like denominators**, add the numerators. The denominator remains the same. Write the sum in simplest form.

Example 1

Add.

$$\frac{5}{12} + \frac{9}{12} = \square$$

Strategy   **Use fraction strips to find the sum.**

Step 1   Shade fraction strips to show $\frac{5}{12}$ and $\frac{9}{12}$.

| $\frac{1}{12}$ | $\frac{1}{12}$ | $\frac{1}{12}$ | $\frac{1}{12}$ | $\frac{1}{12}$ | $\frac{1}{12}$ | $\frac{1}{12}$ | $\frac{1}{12}$ | $\frac{1}{12}$ | $\frac{1}{12}$ | $\frac{1}{12}$ | $\frac{1}{12}$ |

| $\frac{1}{12}$ | $\frac{1}{12}$ | $\frac{1}{12}$ | $\frac{1}{12}$ | $\frac{1}{12}$ | $\frac{1}{12}$ | $\frac{1}{12}$ | $\frac{1}{12}$ | $\frac{1}{12}$ | $\frac{1}{12}$ | $\frac{1}{12}$ | $\frac{1}{12}$ |

Step 2   Count the total number of shaded parts.

Write 14 as the numerator. The denominator stays the same.

$$\frac{5}{12} + \frac{9}{12} = \frac{5+9}{12} = \frac{14}{12}$$

Step 3   Convert the improper fraction to a mixed number.

$$\frac{14}{12} = \frac{12}{12} + \frac{2}{12} = 1\frac{2}{12}$$

Step 4   Write the mixed number in simplest form.

$$\frac{2}{12} = \frac{2 \div 2}{12 \div 2} = \frac{1}{6}$$

So $1\frac{2}{12} = 1\frac{1}{6}$.

Solution $\frac{5}{12} + \frac{9}{12} = 1\frac{1}{6}$

To add fractions with unlike denominators, you will need to find equivalent fractions for one or both fractions, so that they have a common denominator. One way to find a **common denominator** is to multiply the denominators of the fractions.

Example 2

In a science experiment, a plant grew $\frac{3}{4}$ inch one week and another $\frac{2}{3}$ inch the following week. How many inches did it grow during the two weeks?

Strategy **Write equivalent fractions with a common denominator. Then add.**

Step 1 Find a common denominator.

Multiply the two denominators.

$4 \times 3 = 12$

Step 2 Write equivalent fractions with 12 as the denominator.

$$\frac{3}{4} = \frac{3 \times 3}{4 \times 3} = \frac{9}{12}$$

$$\frac{2}{3} = \frac{2 \times 4}{3 \times 4} = \frac{8}{12}$$

Step 3 Add.

$$\frac{9}{12} + \frac{8}{12} = \frac{17}{12}$$

Step 4 Convert the improper fraction to a mixed number in simplest form.

$$\frac{17}{12} = 1\frac{5}{12}$$

Solution **The plant grew $1\frac{5}{12}$ inches.**

Add mixed numbers in the same way that fractions are added. First add the fraction parts and then add the whole-number parts.

When the denominator of one fraction is a factor of the other fraction, use the greater number as the common denominator.

Example 3

Robert hiked $3\frac{1}{5}$ miles Saturday and $4\frac{3}{10}$ miles Sunday. How many miles did he hike in all?

Strategy **Add the whole numbers and then add the fractions.**

Step 1 Find a common denominator.

Since 10 is a multiple of 5, a common denominator is 10.

Step 2   Find the fraction equivalent to $\frac{1}{5}$ with a denominator of 10.

$$\frac{1 \times 2}{5 \times 2} = \frac{2}{10}$$

$$3\frac{1}{5} = 3\frac{2}{10}$$

Step 3   Add the fractions in simplest form.

$$\frac{2}{10} + \frac{3}{10} = \frac{5}{10}$$

$$\frac{5}{10} \div \frac{5}{5} = \frac{1}{2}$$

Step 4   Add the whole numbers.

$$3 + 4 = 7$$

Step 5   Add the sums.

$$\frac{1}{2} + 7 = 7\frac{1}{2}$$

Solution   Robert hiked $7\frac{1}{2}$ miles in all.

You can use **benchmarks** to make an estimate. A benchmark is a common number that can be compared to another number.

> Use the benchmarks 0, $\frac{1}{2}$, and 1 to make an estimate.
>
> - If the fraction is less than $\frac{1}{4}$, round the fraction to 0.
> - Ilf the fraction is greater than or equal to $\frac{1}{4}$ and less than $\frac{3}{4}$, round to $\frac{1}{2}$.
> - Ilf the fraction is greater than or equal to $\frac{3}{4}$, round up to 1.

Example 4

Estimate the sum of $\frac{2}{3} + \frac{2}{5}$ to the nearest $\frac{1}{2}$.

Strategy   **Round each addend to the nearest $\frac{1}{2}$.**

> **Step 1**   Round $\frac{2}{3}$ to the nearest $\frac{1}{2}$.
>
> Since $\frac{1}{2} < \frac{2}{3} < \frac{3}{4}$, round $\frac{2}{3}$ to $\frac{1}{2}$.

> **Step 2**   Round $\frac{2}{5}$ to the nearest $\frac{1}{2}$.
>
> Since $\frac{1}{4} < \frac{2}{5} < \frac{1}{2}$, round $\frac{2}{5}$ to $\frac{1}{2}$.

> **Step 3**   Add the rounded numbers.
>
> $\frac{1}{2} + \frac{1}{2} = 1$

Solution   **The sum of $\frac{2}{3} + \frac{2}{5}$ is about 1.**

Another way to add fractions with unlike denominators is to write equivalent fractions with the **least common denominator (LCD)**. You can find the LCD by listing the multiples of the denominators and finding the least number that is a common multiple.

Example 5

Keira walked $\frac{5}{8}$ mile on Oak Avenue and then $\frac{7}{10}$ mile on Third Street to visit Cora. How far did Keira walk to visit Cora?

Strategy   **Write equivalent fractions using the LCD. Then add.**

> **Step 1**   Find the LCD of $\frac{5}{8}$ and $\frac{7}{10}$.
>
> List the multiples of 8: 8, 16, 24, 32, 40
>
> List the multiples of 10: 10, 20, 30, 40
>
> The LCD is 40.

> **Step 2**   Write equivalent fractions with 40 as the denominator.
>
> $\frac{5}{8} \times \frac{5}{5} = \frac{25}{40}$
>
> $\frac{7}{10} \times \frac{4}{4} = \frac{28}{40}$

Step 3 Add the equivalent fractions.

$$\frac{25}{40} + \frac{28}{40} = \frac{53}{40}$$

Step 4 Write the sum as a mixed number.

$$\frac{53}{40} = 1\frac{13}{40}$$

Solution Keira walked $1\frac{13}{40}$ miles to visit Cora.

You can add fractions with unlike denominators by multiplying the denominators to write a common denominator. For the numerators, you can multiply each numerator by the denominator of the other fraction and add the products.

Example 6

Add: $\frac{3}{4} + \frac{5}{6}$

Strategy **Use multiplication to add fractions.**

Step 1 Multiply the denominators to find a common denominator.

$4 \times 6 = 24$

Use 24 for the denominator.

Step 2 Multiply the numerator of one fraction by the denominator of the other fraction.

$$\frac{3}{4} + \frac{5}{6} = \frac{3 \times 6}{24} + \frac{5 \times 4}{24}$$

$$\frac{3 \times 6}{24} + \frac{5 \times 4}{24} = \frac{18}{24} + \frac{20}{24}$$

Step 3 Add.

$$\frac{18}{24} + \frac{20}{24} = \frac{38}{24}$$

Step 4 Write the sum as a mixed number in simplest form.

$$\frac{38}{24} = \frac{38 \div 2}{24 \div 2} = \frac{19}{12}$$

$$\frac{19}{12} = 1\frac{7}{12}$$

Solution $\frac{3}{4} + \frac{5}{6} = 1\frac{7}{12}$

Coached Example

Suki rides her bicycle $\frac{5}{6}$ mile before seeing a sign that reads "Tybee Island: $\frac{3}{4}$ mile." If Suki rides to Tybee Island, how many miles will she travel in all?

Add to find the total miles.

The denominators of the fractions are _____ and _____.

Multiples of 6: _____

Multiples of 4: _____

The least number that is a common multiple of 6 and 4 is _____.

Find equivalent fractions with _____ as the common denominator.

$$\frac{5}{6} = \frac{5 \times 2}{6 \times 2} = \frac{\boxed{}}{\boxed{}}$$

$$\frac{3}{4} = \frac{3 \times \boxed{}}{4 \times \boxed{}} = \frac{\boxed{}}{\boxed{}}$$

Add.

$$\frac{\boxed{}}{12} + \frac{\boxed{}}{12} = \frac{\boxed{}}{\boxed{}}$$

Write your answer in simplest form: _____

Suki will ride _____ miles in all to reach Tybee Island.

Lesson Practice • Part 1

Choose the correct answer.

1. What is $\frac{4}{9} + \frac{1}{9}$?

   A. $\frac{1}{3}$

   B. $\frac{3}{9}$

   C. $\frac{5}{9}$

   D. $\frac{2}{3}$

2. What is $1\frac{3}{4} + 3\frac{1}{8}$?

   A. $4\frac{1}{3}$

   B. $4\frac{1}{2}$

   C. $4\frac{7}{8}$

   D. 5

3. Paulo shaded $\frac{1}{3}$ of a grid. Then he shaded another $\frac{2}{5}$ of the grid. What fraction of the grid did he shade?

   A. $\frac{1}{5}$

   B. $\frac{3}{10}$

   C. $\frac{3}{5}$

   D. $\frac{11}{15}$

4. What is $3\frac{5}{6} + 2\frac{2}{3}$?

   A. $5\frac{1}{3}$

   B. $5\frac{1}{2}$

   C. 6

   D. $6\frac{1}{2}$

5. Sophie takes tap and ballet. Today she practiced tap for $\frac{3}{4}$ hour and ballet for $\frac{1}{2}$ hour. How many hours did Sophie spend practicing dance?

   A. $\frac{2}{3}$ hour

   B. $1\frac{1}{4}$ hours

   C. $1\frac{3}{8}$ hours

   D. $1\frac{1}{2}$ hours

6. Frances has $5\frac{1}{6}$ yards of red yarn and $2\frac{5}{6}$ yards of blue yarn. How many yards of yarn does she have in all?

   A. $3\frac{2}{3}$ yards

   B. $7\frac{2}{3}$ yards

   C. $7\frac{5}{6}$ yards

   D. 8 yards

7. What is $\frac{7}{9} + \frac{1}{6}$?

   A. $\frac{17}{18}$

   B. $\frac{8}{9}$

   C. $\frac{15}{18}$

   D. $\frac{5}{6}$

8. What is $1\frac{5}{8} + 2\frac{3}{16}$?

   A. 4

   B. $3\frac{13}{16}$

   C. $3\frac{1}{2}$

   D. $3\frac{7}{16}$

9. Blake bought $\frac{3}{8}$ pound of cashew nuts, $\frac{1}{8}$ pound of almonds, and $\frac{5}{6}$ pound of walnuts.

   A. What is the total weight of the nuts that Blake bought? Write the answer in simplest form. Show your work.

   B. Explain how you found your answer for Part A.

   _____

   _____

   _____

Lesson Practice • Part 2

Choose the correct answer.

1. Which sum is less than 1?

   A. $\frac{3}{8} + \frac{2}{5}$

   B. $\frac{3}{5} + \frac{1}{2}$

   C. $\frac{2}{3} + \frac{3}{4}$

   D. $\frac{5}{8} + \frac{2}{3}$

2. Sebastian added $\frac{2}{3} + \frac{3}{5}$ and computed a sum of $\frac{5}{8}$. Which sentence is true?

   A. Sebastian is correct because $2 + 3 = 5$ and $3 + 5 = 8$.

   B. Sebastian is incorrect because $\frac{5}{8}$ is less than $\frac{3}{5}$.

   C. Sebastian is incorrect because $\frac{5}{8}$ is less than $\frac{2}{3}$.

   D. Sebastian is correct because when the addends are simplified the sum is $\frac{5}{8}$.

3. Skylar read a book for $2\frac{1}{4}$ hours and then spoke on the phone for $1\frac{1}{2}$ hours. How much time did Skylar spend reading and talking on the phone?

   A. $3\frac{1}{3}$ hours   **C.** $4\frac{1}{4}$ hours

   B. $3\frac{3}{4}$ hours   **D.** $4\frac{3}{4}$ hours

4. Ava made a rectangular drawing. The width of the drawing is $3\frac{1}{2}$ inches. The length is $1\frac{7}{8}$ inches longer than the width. What is the length of the drawing?

   A. $4\frac{4}{5}$ inches

   B. $5\frac{1}{8}$ inches

   C. $5\frac{1}{4}$ inches

   D. $5\frac{3}{8}$ inches

5. Find the sum.
   $$\frac{5}{12} + \frac{3}{5} = \boxed{}$$

   A. $1\frac{1}{30}$

   B. $1\frac{1}{60}$

   C. $\frac{59}{60}$

   D. $\frac{8}{17}$

6. Brooke walked $1\frac{1}{4}$ miles from her home to the park. She walked $\frac{5}{8}$ mile longer on the way home. How far did Brooke walk in all?

   A. $1\frac{1}{2}$ miles   **C.** $2\frac{1}{2}$ miles

   B. $1\frac{7}{8}$ miles   **D.** $3\frac{1}{8}$ miles

7. Which sum is greater than 1?

   A. $\frac{1}{2} + \frac{7}{12}$

   B. $\frac{1}{4} + \frac{2}{5}$

   C. $\frac{3}{8} + \frac{1}{4}$

   D. $\frac{2}{3} + \frac{1}{10}$

8. Camden jogged $3\frac{7}{10}$ miles in the park and then $\frac{3}{4}$ mile back home. How far did Camden jog in all?

   A. $4\frac{9}{20}$ miles

   B. $4\frac{2}{5}$ miles

   C. $4\frac{7}{20}$ miles

   D. $3\frac{11}{14}$ miles

9. Find the sum.

$$4\frac{2}{3} + 1\frac{5}{6} = \boxed{}$$

   A. $5\frac{7}{9}$ **C.** $6\frac{1}{2}$

   B. $6\frac{1}{3}$ **D.** $6\frac{2}{3}$

10. Emilia lives $1\frac{3}{5}$ miles east of school. Valentina lives $1\frac{1}{2}$ miles west of school. How far do Emilia and Valentina live from each other?

   A. $2\frac{4}{7}$ miles

   B. $2\frac{9}{10}$ miles

   C. 3 miles

   D. $3\frac{1}{10}$ miles

11. Of the DVDs sold at the Meloy garage sale, $\frac{1}{3}$ are comedies, $\frac{1}{4}$ are dramas, and $\frac{1}{6}$ are music.

   A. What fraction of the DVDs are comedies or dramas? Show your work.

   B. What fraction of the DVDs are dramas or music? Show your work.

   C. Did the Meloys sell any other type of DVDs? Explain your answer.

   _____

   _____

   _____

12. Use numbers from the box to complete the number sentence.

$$\frac{1}{4} + \frac{3}{8} = \frac{\square}{\square} + \frac{3}{8} = \frac{\square}{8}$$

| 2 |
| 5 |
| 6 |
| 8 |

13. Select True or False for each number sentence.

A. $\frac{2}{4} + \frac{3}{8} = \frac{5}{12}$ ○ True   ○ False

B. $\frac{5}{6} + \frac{4}{12} = \frac{1}{2}$ ○ True   ○ False

C. $\frac{2}{5} + \frac{7}{10} = \frac{11}{10}$ ○ True   ○ False

D. $\frac{4}{9} + \frac{1}{3} = \frac{7}{9}$ ○ True   ○ False

14. Draw a line from each expression to its sum.

A. $1\frac{1}{3} + 2\frac{7}{12}$ •   • $4\frac{9}{10}$

B. $3\frac{3}{10} + 2\frac{3}{5}$ •   • $4\frac{7}{12}$

C. $1\frac{5}{6} + 2\frac{9}{12}$ •   • $3\frac{11}{12}$

D. $2\frac{1}{10} + 2\frac{4}{5}$ •   • $5\frac{9}{10}$

15. Find each sum. Write the expression in the correct box.

| $1\frac{1}{4} + 1\frac{1}{2}$ | $\frac{3}{4} + 1\frac{1}{2}$ | $\frac{7}{8} + 1\frac{7}{8}$ | $\frac{1}{2} + 2\frac{1}{4}$ | $\frac{7}{8} + 1\frac{3}{8}$ | $1\frac{3}{4} + \frac{1}{2}$ |

sum equal to $2\frac{1}{4}$	sum equal to $2\frac{3}{4}$

16. Who has 6 yards of ribbon? Circle all that apply.

A. Michael has $4\frac{1}{3}$ yards of blue ribbon and $1\frac{2}{5}$ yards of red ribbon.

B. Ella has $3\frac{5}{6}$ yards of purple ribbon and $2\frac{2}{12}$ yards of yellow ribbon.

C. Marco has $1\frac{2}{3}$ yards of green ribbon and $4\frac{2}{6}$ yards of gold ribbon.

D. Jill has $2\frac{3}{4}$ yards of orange ribbon and $3\frac{2}{8}$ yards of white ribbon.

17. Use numbers from the box to complete the number sentence.

$$3\frac{3}{12} + 5\frac{3}{8} = 3\frac{\square}{\square} + 5\frac{\square}{24} = 8\frac{\square}{24}$$

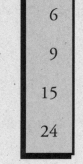

6

9

15

24

Subtract Fractions

Getting the Idea

To subtract fractions that have like denominators, subtract the numerators. The denominator remains the same. Write the difference in simplest form.

Example 1

Subtract.

$\frac{7}{8} - \frac{5}{8} = \boxed{}$

Strategy **Use fraction strips to find the difference.**

Step 1 Shade fraction strips to show $\frac{7}{8}$.

$\frac{1}{8}$	$\frac{1}{8}$	$\frac{1}{8}$	$\frac{1}{8}$	$\frac{1}{8}$	$\frac{1}{8}$	$\frac{1}{8}$	$\frac{1}{8}$

Step 2 Cross out $\frac{5}{8}$ of the shaded parts.

Step 3 Count the remaining shaded parts.

There are 2 shaded parts.

Write 2 as the numerator. The denominator stays the same.

$\frac{7}{8} - \frac{5}{8} = \frac{2}{8}$

Step 4 Write the fraction in simplest form.

$\frac{2}{8} = \frac{2 \div 2}{8 \div 2} = \frac{1}{4}$

Solution $\frac{7}{8} - \frac{5}{8} = \frac{1}{4}$

To subtract fractions with unlike denominators, rename one or both fractions so that they have like denominators.

Example 2

Subtract: $\frac{5}{9} - \frac{1}{6}$

Strategy   **Write equivalent fractions using a common denominator. Then subtract.**

Step 1   Find a common denominator of $\frac{5}{9}$ and $\frac{1}{6}$.

$9 \times 6 = 54$

Step 2   Write equivalent fractions with 54 as the denominator.

$$\frac{5}{9} = \frac{5 \times 6}{9 \times 6} = \frac{30}{54}$$

$$\frac{1}{6} = \frac{1 \times 9}{6 \times 9} = \frac{9}{54}$$

Step 3   Subtract.

$$\frac{30}{54} - \frac{9}{54} = \frac{21}{54}$$

Step 4   Write the difference in simplest form.

$$\frac{21}{54} = \frac{21 \div 3}{54 \div 3} = \frac{7}{18}$$

Solution $\frac{5}{9} - \frac{1}{6} = \frac{7}{18}$

You can use the least common denominator (LCD) to rename fractions. When the LCD is used, the difference will be in simplest form.

Example 3

Subtract: $\frac{5}{6} - \frac{3}{8}$

Strategy   **Use the LCD to write equivalent fractions. Then subtract.**

Step 1   Find the LCD of $\frac{5}{6}$ and $\frac{3}{8}$.

Multiples of 6: 6, 12, 18, 24

Multiples of 8: 8, 16, 24

The LCD is 24.

Step 2   Write equivalent fractions with 24 as the denominator.

$$\frac{5}{6} = \frac{5}{6} \times \frac{4}{4} = \frac{20}{24}$$

$$\frac{3}{8} = \frac{3}{8} \times \frac{3}{3} = \frac{9}{24}$$

Step 3	Subtract.

$$\frac{20}{24} - \frac{9}{24} = \frac{11}{24}$$

Solution $\frac{5}{6} - \frac{3}{8} = \frac{11}{24}$

To subtract mixed numbers, you can subtract the fraction parts and then the whole-number parts.

Example 4

Leo walked a total of $3\frac{1}{4}$ miles before and after school yesterday. He walked $1\frac{7}{8}$ miles before school. How many miles did he walk after school?

Strategy **Use the LCD to write equivalent mixed numbers. Then subtract.**

Step 1	Find the LCD of $\frac{1}{4}$ and $\frac{7}{8}$.
	Since 8 is a multiple of 4, the LCD is 8.

Step 2	Rename $\frac{1}{4}$, so that is has 8 as the denominator.

$$\frac{1}{4} = \frac{1}{4} \times \frac{2}{2} = \frac{2}{8}$$

Step 3	Subtract $3\frac{2}{8} - 1\frac{7}{8}$.
	There are not enough eighths to subtract.
	Regroup 1 whole as $\frac{8}{8}$.

$$3\frac{2}{8} = 2\frac{10}{8}$$

Step 4	Subtract the fractions and then the whole numbers.

$$\frac{10}{8} - \frac{7}{8} = \frac{3}{8}$$
$$2 - 1 = 1$$

Step 5	Add the differences.

$$\frac{3}{8} + 1 = 1\frac{3}{8}$$

Solution **Leo walked $1\frac{3}{8}$ miles after school.**

You can subtract mixed numbers by renaming them as improper fractions.

Example 5

Mr. Ramos bought two packages of chicken. One package weighed $2\frac{5}{8}$ pounds and the other weighed $4\frac{1}{2}$ pounds. How much more does the heavier package weigh?

Strategy   **Rename the mixed numbers as improper fractions. Then subtract.**

Step 1   Find a common denominator for $\frac{5}{8}$ and $\frac{1}{2}$.

Since 2 is a multiple of 8, the LCD is 8.

Step 2   Rename $4\frac{1}{2}$ so that is has 8 as a denominator.

$\frac{1}{2} = \frac{1}{2} \times \frac{4}{4} = \frac{4}{8}$, so $4\frac{1}{2} = 4\frac{4}{8}$

Step 3   Rename both mixed numbers as improper fractions.

$2\frac{5}{8} = \frac{2 \times 8 + 5}{8} = \frac{21}{8}$

$4\frac{4}{8} = \frac{4 \times 8 + 4}{8} = \frac{36}{8}$

Step 4   Subtract. Write the difference as a mixed number.

$\frac{36}{8} - \frac{21}{8} = \frac{15}{8} = 1\frac{7}{8}$

Solution   **The heavier package weighs $1\frac{7}{8}$ pounds more.**

You can subtract fractions with unlike denominators by multiplying the denominators to write a common denominator. For the numerators, you can multiply each numerator by the denominator of the other fraction and subtract the products.

Example 6

Subtract: $\frac{7}{9} - \frac{3}{5}$

Strategy   **Use multiplication to subtract fractions.**

Step 1   Multiply the denominators to find a common denominator.

$9 \times 5 = 45$

Use 45 for the denominator.

Step 2   Multiply the numerator of one fraction by the denominator of the other fraction. These provide the numerators.

$\frac{7}{9} - \frac{3}{5} = \frac{(7 \times 5) - (3 \times 9)}{45}$

Step 3   Subtract.

$$\frac{35}{45} - \frac{27}{45} = \frac{8}{45}$$

Solution $\frac{7}{9} - \frac{3}{5} = \frac{8}{45}$

Coached Example

Jillian poured milk into a glass $\frac{9}{10}$ full. When she finished drinking, the glass was $\frac{1}{4}$ full. How much of the milk in the glass did she drink?

Find the difference.

Find the least common denominator (LCD).

Multiples of 10: _____

Multiples of 4: _____

The least number that is a common multiple of 10 and 4 is _____.

Find equivalent fractions with _____ as the denominator.

$$\frac{9}{10} = \frac{9 \times 2}{10 \times 2} = \frac{\square}{\square}$$

$$\frac{1}{4} = \frac{1 \times \square}{4 \times \square} = \frac{\square}{\square}$$

Subtract.

$$\frac{\square}{20} - \frac{\square}{20} = \frac{\square}{\square}$$

Jillian drank _____ of the milk in the glass.

Lesson Practice • Part 1

Choose the correct answer.

1. What is $\frac{5}{8} - \frac{1}{8}$ in simplest form?

   A. $\frac{1}{2}$

   B. $\frac{3}{4}$

   C. $\frac{7}{8}$

   D. 1

2. What is $\frac{2}{3} - \frac{5}{12}$ in simplest form?

   A. $\frac{1}{12}$

   B. $\frac{1}{6}$

   C. $\frac{1}{4}$

   D. $\frac{1}{3}$

3. Find the difference.

   $$8\frac{9}{10} - 4\frac{3}{5} = \square$$

   A. $4\frac{6}{50}$

   B. $4\frac{3}{10}$

   C. $4\frac{27}{50}$

   D. $4\frac{6}{5}$

4. Jessica is typing a report. She typed $\frac{5}{8}$ of the pages in the report in the morning and $\frac{1}{4}$ of the pages in the afternoon. What fraction more of the pages did she type in the morning?

   A. $\frac{3}{8}$

   B. $\frac{1}{2}$

   C. $\frac{3}{4}$

   D. $\frac{7}{8}$

5. Wally took $\frac{1}{6}$ of the stickers from the pack. Alex took $\frac{1}{2}$ of the stickers. How much more of the pack did Alex take?

   A. $\frac{4}{3}$ C. $\frac{1}{3}$

   B. $\frac{2}{3}$ D. $\frac{1}{6}$

6. Callie spent $\frac{3}{4}$ hour on a science report and $\frac{1}{3}$ hour on a social studies report. What fraction of an hour longer did she spend on the science report?

   A. $\frac{1}{12}$ hour   C. $\frac{1}{2}$ hour

   B. $\frac{5}{12}$ hour   D. $1\frac{1}{12}$ hours

7. Jordan bought $6\frac{4}{5}$ yards of pink ribbon and $3\frac{1}{4}$ yards of purple ribbon. How much more pink ribbon than purple ribbon did she buy?

A. $3\frac{1}{5}$ yards

B. $3\frac{11}{20}$ yards

C. $4\frac{1}{6}$ yards

D. $10\frac{1}{20}$ yards

8. Of the students in Ms. Martinez's class, $\frac{11}{24}$ walk to school. Another $\frac{3}{8}$ of the students ride their bikes to school. What fraction more of the students walk than ride their bikes to school?

A. $\frac{5}{24}$

B. $\frac{1}{6}$

C. $\frac{1}{8}$

D. $\frac{1}{12}$

9. Of the pizzas sold at a pizzeria, $\frac{1}{2}$ were cheese, $\frac{1}{4}$ were sausage, and $\frac{1}{6}$ were pepperoni.

A. What fraction more of the pizzas were cheese than sausage and pepperoni combined?

_____

B. Explain how you found your answer.

_____

_____

_____

Lesson Practice • Part 2

Choose the correct answer.

1. Find the difference.

   $$\frac{7}{12} - \frac{3}{8} = \boxed{}$$

   A. $\frac{1}{6}$

   B. $\frac{5}{24}$

   C. $\frac{1}{4}$

   D. $\frac{7}{24}$

2. Stella has completed $\frac{13}{16}$ of a painting. She had completed $\frac{1}{2}$ of the painting before starting today. What fraction of the painting did Stella complete today?

   A. $\frac{3}{16}$

   B. $\frac{1}{4}$

   C. $\frac{5}{16}$

   D. $\frac{3}{8}$

3. A race is $3\frac{1}{10}$ miles. Lincoln's shoelaces untied after $1\frac{3}{4}$ miles, but he kept running. How many miles did Lincoln run with his shoelaces undone?

   A. $1\frac{7}{20}$ miles   C. $1\frac{9}{20}$ miles

   B. $1\frac{2}{5}$ miles   D. $2\frac{13}{20}$ miles

4. Carson drew a rectangle that has a length of $7\frac{3}{8}$ inches and a width of $4\frac{1}{2}$ inches. How much greater is the length than the width?

   A. $3\frac{1}{4}$ inches

   B. $3\frac{1}{8}$ inches

   C. $2\frac{7}{8}$ inches

   D. $2\frac{3}{4}$ inches

5. Of the CDs in Mr. Bijur's collection, $\frac{7}{10}$ are rock and $\frac{1}{8}$ are classical. What fraction of Mr. Bijur's CDs are something other than rock or classical?

   A. $\frac{3}{20}$

   B. $\frac{7}{40}$

   C. $\frac{1}{5}$

   D. $\frac{9}{40}$

6. Find the difference.

   $$5\frac{1}{3} - 2\frac{1}{10} = \boxed{}$$

   A. $3\frac{7}{30}$ C. $3\frac{1}{7}$

   B. $3\frac{1}{5}$ D. $2\frac{23}{30}$

7. There are $5\frac{3}{4}$ pounds of recycling in a bin collected over 3 days. On Monday, $2\frac{1}{2}$ pounds of recycling went into the bin. Another $1\frac{7}{8}$ pounds went in on Tuesday. How much recycling went in the bin on Wednesday?

A. 1 pound

B. $1\frac{1}{8}$ pounds

C. $1\frac{1}{4}$ pounds

D. $1\frac{3}{8}$ pounds

8. Tani wrote thank-you cards after her birthday party. She wrote $\frac{2}{5}$ of the cards on Thursday, $\frac{1}{4}$ of the cards on Friday, and the rest on Saturday. What fraction of the cards did Tani write on Saturday?

A. $\frac{1}{4}$

B. $\frac{3}{10}$

C. $\frac{7}{20}$

D. $\frac{2}{5}$

9. Autumn rode her bike $7\frac{1}{2}$ miles this week. She biked $2\frac{1}{4}$ miles on Sunday, $1\frac{7}{10}$ miles on Monday, and the rest on Friday.

A. How many more miles did Autumn bike on Sunday than on Monday? Show your work.

B. How many miles did Autumn bike on Friday? Show your work.

10. Use numbers from the box to complete the number sentence.

$$\frac{3}{4} - \frac{3}{8} = \frac{\boxed{}}{\boxed{}} - \frac{3}{8} = \frac{\boxed{}}{8}$$

```
3
4
6
8
```

11. Select True or False for each number sentence.

A. $\frac{2}{4} - \frac{3}{8} = \frac{1}{8}$ ○ True ○ False

B. $\frac{5}{6} - \frac{4}{12} = \frac{1}{3}$ ○ True ○ False

C. $\frac{4}{5} - \frac{7}{15} = \frac{1}{3}$ ○ True ○ False

D. $\frac{4}{9} - \frac{1}{3} = \frac{1}{2}$ ○ True ○ False

12. Draw a line from each expression to its difference.

A. $\frac{2}{3} - \frac{7}{12}$ • • $\frac{1}{10}$

B. $\frac{7}{10} - \frac{3}{5}$ • • $\frac{1}{6}$

C. $\frac{11}{12} - \frac{3}{4}$ • • $\frac{1}{12}$

D. $\frac{3}{5} - \frac{4}{10}$ • • $\frac{1}{5}$

13. Find each difference. Write the expression in the correct box.

| $\frac{3}{4} - \frac{1}{2}$ | $\frac{9}{10} - \frac{2}{5}$ | $\frac{7}{8} - \frac{6}{16}$ | $\frac{11}{12} - \frac{8}{12}$ | $\frac{7}{8} - \frac{3}{8}$ | $\frac{9}{12} - \frac{1}{2}$ |

difference equal to $\frac{1}{4}$	difference equal to $\frac{1}{2}$

14. Who has to jog another $\frac{3}{8}$ mile to reach the goal? Circle all that apply.

    A. Amanda jogs $4\frac{1}{3}$ miles. Her goal is 5 miles.

    B. Badri jogs $5\frac{3}{8}$ miles. His goal is $5\frac{3}{4}$ miles.

    C. Camilla jogs $3\frac{1}{4}$ miles. Her goal is $3\frac{5}{8}$ miles.

    D. Dwight jogs $3\frac{3}{16}$ miles. His goal is $3\frac{3}{4}$ miles.

15. Use numbers from the box to complete the number sentence.

$$3\frac{3}{4} - 1\frac{2}{3} = 3\frac{\square}{\square} - 1\frac{\square}{12} = 2\frac{\square}{12}$$

| 1 |
| 8 |
| 9 |
| 12 |

16. Is each expression equivalent to $\frac{1}{4}$? Select Yes or No.

    A. $\frac{3}{4} - \frac{5}{8}$ ○ Yes   ○ No

    B. $\frac{2}{3} - \frac{5}{12}$ ○ Yes   ○ No

    C. $\frac{5}{6} - \frac{2}{3}$ ○ Yes   ○ No

    D. $\frac{1}{3} - \frac{1}{12}$ ○ Yes   ○ No

Understand Multiplication of Fractions

Getting the Idea

To multiply a fraction by a fraction, multiply the numerators and then multiply the denominators. Write the product in simplest form. For example:

$$\frac{3}{4} \times \frac{2}{5} = \frac{3 \times 2}{4 \times 5} = \frac{6}{20} = \frac{6 \div 2}{20 \div 2} = \frac{3}{10}$$

When both factors in a multiplication sentence are fractions less than 1, the product is less than either of its factors. Because a fraction is a part of a whole and the product is a part of a factor, the product must be less than either factor.

Example 1

The product of $\frac{3}{4} \times \frac{1}{2}$ is less than $\frac{3}{4}$. Without multiplying, is the product greater than or less than $\frac{1}{2}$?

Strategy   **Compare the factors to 1.**

Step 1   Compare the factors $\frac{3}{4}$ and $\frac{1}{2}$ to 1.

$\frac{3}{4} < 1$ and $\frac{1}{2} < 1$

Step 2   Compare the factors to the product.

Both factors are fractions less than 1.
So, the product must be less than either factor.
The product is less than $\frac{3}{4}$.
The product must also be less than $\frac{1}{2}$.

Solution   **The product is less than $\frac{1}{2}$.**

When a whole number is multiplied by a fraction greater than 1, the product is greater than the whole number. When a whole number is multiplied by a fraction less than 1, the product is less than the whole number.

Example 2

The length of Jeff's new garden is $2\frac{1}{2}$ times its old length. The old garden was 8 feet long. What is the length of the new garden?

Strategy **Multiply a whole number by a mixed number.**

Step 1 Compare the factors 8 and $2\frac{1}{2}$ to 1.

$8 > 1$ and $2\frac{1}{2} > 1$

So, the product will be greater than the whole number factor, 8.

The new garden is longer than the old garden.

Step 2 Multiply the fractions.

$8 \times 2\frac{1}{2} = \frac{8}{1} \times \frac{5}{2}$ Write each factor as an improper fraction.

$= \frac{8 \times 5}{1 \times 2}$ Multiply the numerators and the denominators.

$= \frac{40}{2}$ Simplify.

$= 20$ Write the product in simplest form.

Solution **The new garden is 20 feet long.**

When a mixed number is multiplied by a fraction less than 1, the product is less than the mixed number. When a mixed number is multiplied by a fraction greater than 1, the product is greater than the mixed number.

Example 3

A recipe calls for $6\frac{1}{2}$ cups of vegetable stock to make soup. A chef needs to make $\frac{3}{4}$ of the recipe. How much vegetable stock does she need?

Strategy **Multiply a mixed number by a fraction.**

Step 1 Compare the factors $6\frac{1}{2}$ and $\frac{3}{4}$ to 1.

$6\frac{1}{2} > 1$ and $\frac{3}{4} < 1$

The product will be less than the mixed number factor, $6\frac{1}{2}$.

The chef needs less than $6\frac{1}{2}$ cups of stock.

Step 2 Multiply the fractions.

$$6\frac{1}{2} \times \frac{3}{4} = \frac{13}{2} \times \frac{3}{4}$$ Write the mixed number as an improper fraction.

$$= \frac{13 \times 3}{2 \times 4}$$ Multiply the numerators and the denominators.

$$= \frac{39}{8}$$ Simplify.

$$= 4\frac{7}{8}$$ Write the product in simplest form.

Solution She needs $4\frac{7}{8}$ cups of stock.

Coached Example

A spool has $8\frac{3}{4}$ feet of ribbon. Amber needs $1\frac{1}{3}$ times the ribbon that is on the spool. How much ribbon does she need?

To decide if the product is greater or less than $8\frac{3}{4}$ feet, compare the factors _____ and _____ to 1.

Compare: $8\frac{3}{4}$ _____ 1 and $1\frac{1}{3}$ _____ 1.

The product of $8\frac{3}{4} \times 1\frac{1}{3}$ is _____ than $8\frac{3}{4}$.

Convert $8\frac{3}{4}$ to an improper fraction. _____

Convert $1\frac{1}{3}$ to an improper fraction. _____

Multiply $8\frac{3}{4} \times 1\frac{1}{3}$.

In simplest form, $8\frac{3}{4} \times 1\frac{1}{3} =$ _____.

Amber needs _____ feet of ribbon.

Lesson Practice • Part 1

Choose the correct answer.

1. Which of the following has a product less than $\frac{2}{3}$?

   A. $\frac{2}{3} \times \frac{9}{10}$

   B. $\frac{2}{3} \times 1\frac{1}{6}$

   C. $\frac{2}{3} \times 1\frac{1}{2}$

   D. $\frac{2}{3} \times 2$

2. The product of $\frac{7}{10}$ and another factor is less than $\frac{7}{10}$. Which could be the other factor?

   A. $\frac{4}{3}$ C. $\frac{10}{7}$

   B. $\frac{5}{9}$ D. $\frac{7}{4}$

3. George has 6 cups of tomato sauce. He needs $\frac{3}{4}$ of the sauce to make lasagna. Which best describes how much sauce George will use?

   A. George will use more than 6 cups of the sauce.

   B. George will use all 6 cups of the sauce.

   C. George will use less than 6 cups of the sauce.

   D. George will use less than $\frac{3}{4}$ cup of the sauce.

4. Lina ran $3\frac{1}{2}$ miles on Monday. On Wednesday, she ran $1\frac{1}{3}$ times as far as she ran on Monday. Which best describes how far Lina ran on Wednesday?

   A. Lina ran less than $1\frac{1}{3}$ miles.

   B. Lina ran $1\frac{1}{3}$ miles.

   C. Lina ran $3\frac{1}{2}$ miles.

   D. Lina ran more than $3\frac{1}{2}$ miles.

5. A piece of webbing is $2\frac{2}{3}$ yards long. Drew needs $\frac{3}{8}$ of the webbing to make a climbing harness. How much webbing does Drew need to make the harness?

   A. less than $\frac{3}{8}$ yard

   B. 1 yard

   C. $2\frac{7}{24}$ yards

   D. more than $2\frac{2}{3}$ yards

6. Deion practiced piano for $\frac{5}{6}$ hour on Saturday. On Sunday, he practiced $\frac{1}{2}$ as long as on Saturday. Which best describes how long Deion practiced on Sunday?

A. Deion practiced less than $\frac{1}{2}$ hour.

B. Deion practiced more than $\frac{1}{2}$ hour.

C. Deion practiced $\frac{5}{6}$ hour.

D. Deion practiced more than $\frac{5}{6}$ hour.

7. The trail to a waterfall is $4\frac{1}{5}$ miles long. The trail to an overlook is $1\frac{2}{3}$ times as long as the trail to the waterfall. Which best describes the length of the trail to the overlook?

A. The trail is $5\frac{13}{15}$ miles long.

B. The trail is no more than 6 miles long.

C. The trail is 7 miles long.

D. The trail is more than 8 miles long.

8. Raul ate $\frac{7}{8}$ of $\frac{1}{2}$ of a pizza.

A. Did Raul eat more or less than $\frac{7}{8}$ of the pizza? Did he eat more or less than $\frac{1}{2}$ of the pizza? Explain without finding the exact product.

_____

_____

_____

B. How much of the pizza did Raul eat?

_____

_____

Lesson Practice • Part 2

Choose the correct answer.

1. Which has a product greater than $\frac{3}{4}$?

    A. $\frac{3}{4} \times \frac{1}{2}$

    B. $\frac{3}{4} \times 2$

    C. $\frac{3}{4} \times \frac{3}{4}$

    D. $\frac{3}{4} \times 1$

2. Which describes the product when two fractions greater than 0 and less than 1 are multiplied?

    A. It is less than both factors.

    B. It is greater than one factor and less than the other.

    C. It is greater than both factors, but less than 1.

    D. It is greater than both factors and greater than 1.

3. Ruby multiplied a fraction by a number and the product was the same as the fraction. By what number did Ruby multiply the fraction?

    A. 0

    B. $\frac{1}{2}$

    C. 1

    D. 2

4. Which describes the product when a fraction greater than 0 and less than 1 is multiplied by a mixed number?

    A. It is less than both factors.

    B. It is greater than one factor and less than the other.

    C. It is greater than both factors, but less than 1.

    D. It is greater than both factors and greater than 1.

5. Two improper fractions are going to be multiplied. Neither improper fraction is equivalent to a whole number. Which sentence is true?

    A. It is less than both factors.

    B. It is greater than one factor and less than the other.

    C. It is greater than both factors, but less than 1.

    D. It is greater than both factors and greater than 1.

6. Which has a product less than $\frac{1}{2}$?

    A. $\frac{1}{2} \times \frac{1}{2}$ C. $\frac{1}{2} \times 1\frac{2}{3}$

    B. $\frac{1}{2} \times \frac{5}{2}$ D. $\frac{1}{2} \times 1$

7. Which describes the product when two mixed numbers are multiplied?

   A. It is less than both factors.

   B. It is greater than one factor and less than the other.

   C. It is equal to one of the factors.

   D. It is greater than both factors and greater than 1.

8. A whole number greater than 0 will be multiplied by a fraction that has the same numerator and denominator. Which sentence about the product is true?

   A. It is less than both factors.

   B. It is greater than one factor and less than the other.

   C. It is equal to one of the factors.

   D. It is greater than both factors.

9. Maria normally walks for $\frac{3}{4}$ hour each morning. Today she walked $\frac{5}{2}$ times as long as normal.

   A. Did Maria walk for more than $\frac{3}{4}$ hour? Explain without finding the product.

   _____

   _____

   _____

   B. Did Maria walk for more than $\frac{5}{2}$ hours? Explain without finding the product.

   _____

   _____

   _____

10. Circle the number that makes the product have a value less than $\frac{3}{4}$.

$\frac{3}{4} \times$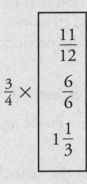

      $\frac{11}{12}$

      $\frac{6}{6}$

      $1\frac{1}{3}$

11. Select True or False for each statement.

A. The product of $2\frac{2}{3} \times \frac{5}{8}$ is less than $2\frac{2}{3}$.   ○ True   ○ False

B. The product of $\frac{1}{3} \times \frac{5}{7}$ is less than $\frac{1}{3}$.   ○ True   ○ False

C. The product of $1\frac{3}{4} \times 1\frac{4}{7}$ is less than $1\frac{3}{4}$.   ○ True   ○ False

D. The product of $\frac{8}{10} \times 4\frac{5}{6}$ is less than $\frac{8}{10}$.   ○ True   ○ False

12. Describe the product of each expression. Write the expression in the correct box.

| $1\frac{2}{3} \times 2\frac{1}{3}$ | $1\frac{2}{3} \times \frac{3}{12}$ | $1\frac{2}{3} \times \frac{11}{7}$ | $1\frac{2}{3} \times \frac{6}{10}$ | $1\frac{2}{3} \times \frac{5}{9}$ | $1\frac{2}{3} \times \frac{1}{2}$ |

Less than $1\frac{2}{3}$	Greater than $1\frac{2}{3}$

13. Which products are greater than $\frac{3}{5}$? Circle all that apply.

   A. $\frac{3}{5} \times 1\frac{6}{7}$

   B. $\frac{3}{5} \times \frac{1}{5}$

   C. $\frac{3}{5} \times 2\frac{4}{5}$

   D. $\frac{3}{5} \times \frac{2}{3}$

   E. $\frac{3}{5} \times \frac{12}{7}$

14. Circle the number that makes the product have a value greater than $1\frac{5}{9}$.

$$1\frac{5}{9} \times \begin{array}{|c|} \hline \frac{7}{9} \\[6pt] \frac{4}{4} \\[6pt] 2\frac{2}{3} \\ \hline \end{array}$$

15. Select True or False for each statement.

   A. Oliver used $\frac{2}{3}$ of a 16-ounce box of spaghetti. He used less than 16 ounces of spaghetti.   ○ True   ○ False

   B. Celia ate $\frac{1}{2}$ of $\frac{1}{4}$ of a blueberry pie. She ate more than $\frac{1}{4}$ of the pie.   ○ True   ○ False

   C. Jorge ran $\frac{3}{8}$ mile on Saturday and $1\frac{1}{2}$ times as far on Sunday. He ran more than $1\frac{1}{2}$ miles on Sunday.   ○ True   ○ False

   D. Patricia studied for $2\frac{1}{3}$ hours on Monday and $\frac{8}{3}$ as long on Tuesday. Patricia studied more than $2\frac{1}{3}$ hours on Tuesday.   ○ True   ○ False

Multiply Fractions

Getting the Idea

When you multiply a fraction by a whole number, first rename the whole number as an improper fraction with a denominator of 1.

Example 1

Isabella drank $\frac{2}{3}$ quart of iced tea each day for 5 days. How many quarts of iced tea did she drink in all?

Strategy   **Convert the whole number to an improper fraction.**

   Step 1   Write an equation for the problem.

            Let n represent the number of quarts she drank in all.

            $5 \times \frac{2}{3} = n$

   Step 2   Rename the whole number as an improper fraction.

            $5 = \frac{5}{1}$

   Step 3   Multiply the numerators and the denominators.

            $\frac{5}{1} \times \frac{2}{3} = \frac{5 \times 2}{1 \times 3} = \frac{10}{3}$

   Step 4   Use models to check.

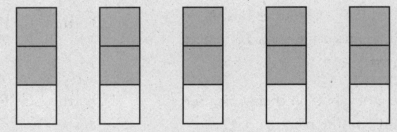

   Step 5   Convert the improper fraction to a mixed number in simplest form.

            $\frac{10}{3} = 3$ R1 or $3\frac{1}{3}$

Solution   **Isabella drank $3\frac{1}{3}$ quarts of iced tea in 5 days**

Remember that when multiplying fractions that are between 0 and 1, the product will be less than either of the fractions.

Example 2

In a flower garden, $\frac{3}{5}$ of the flowers are tulips. Of the tulips, $\frac{1}{2}$ are yellow tulips. What fraction of the flowers are yellow tulips?

Strategy   **Use a model.**

Step 1   Make a model to show $\frac{3}{5}$.

Step 2   Divide and shade the rectangle to show $\frac{1}{2}$.

Step 3   Write a fraction to show the parts that were shaded twice.

        3 parts were shaded twice out of 10 equal parts.

        So, $\frac{3}{10}$ of the parts are shaded twice.

Solution $\frac{3}{10}$ **of the flowers are yellow tulips.**

Example 3

A scientist mixed $\frac{3}{8}$ liter of salt water. He used $\frac{1}{3}$ of the salt water for an experiment. How much salt water did he use?

Strategy   **Multiply the fractions.**

Step 1   Write an equation for the problem.

        Let w represent the amount of salt water the scientist use.

        $\frac{3}{8} \times \frac{1}{3} = w$

Step 2   Multiply the numerators and the denominators.

        $\frac{3}{8} \times \frac{1}{3} = \frac{3 \times 1}{8 \times 3} = \frac{3}{24}$

Step 3   Write the product in simplest form.

        $\frac{3}{24} = \frac{3 \div 3}{24 \div 3} = \frac{1}{8}$

Solution   **The scientist used $\frac{1}{8}$ liter of salt water.**

To find the **area** of a rectangle, multiply the length times the width and express the area in **square units**.

$$A = l \times w$$

Example 4

A rectangle has a length of $\frac{3}{4}$ foot and a width of $\frac{2}{3}$ foot. What is the area of the rectangle?

Strategy   **Use a model.**

Step 1   Draw a model.

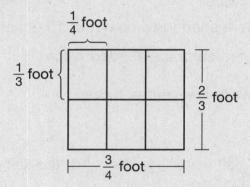

Step 2   Multiply the numerators and denominators.

Substitute the values for l and w into the formula $A = l \times w$.

$$A = \frac{3}{4} \text{ ft} \times \frac{2}{3} \text{ ft} = \frac{3 \times 2}{4 \times 3} = \frac{6}{12} \text{ square foot}$$

Step 3   Write the product in simplest form.

$$\frac{6}{12} = \frac{6 \div 6}{12 \div 6} = \frac{1}{2}$$

Solution   **The area of the rectangle is $\frac{1}{2}$ square foot.**

To multiply mixed numbers, convert the mixed numbers to improper fractions. Multiply the numerators, multiply the denominators, then simplify the product.

Example 5

Asia needs $2\frac{1}{4}$ cups of flour for each batch of cookies she makes. How many cups of flour will she need for $3\frac{1}{2}$ batches of cookies?

Strategy   **Convert the mixed numbers to improper fractions and multiply.**

Step 1   Write an equation for the problem.

Let f represent the total number of cups of flour.

$$2\frac{1}{4} \times 3\frac{1}{2} = f$$

Step 2   Convert the mixed numbers to improper fractions.

$$2\frac{1}{4} = \frac{4}{4} + \frac{4}{4} + \frac{1}{4} = \frac{9}{4}$$

$$3\frac{1}{2} = \frac{2}{2} + \frac{2}{2} + \frac{2}{2} + \frac{1}{2} = \frac{7}{2}$$

Step 3   Multiply the fractions.

$$\frac{9}{4} \times \frac{7}{2} = \frac{9 \times 7}{4 \times 2} = \frac{63}{8}$$

Step 4   Simplify the product.

$$\frac{63}{8} = 7\frac{7}{8}$$

Solution   Asia needs $7\frac{7}{8}$ cups of flour to make $3\frac{1}{2}$ batches of cookies.

You can use the properties of operations to make computation easier.

Multiplicative identity property of 1 The product of any number and 1 is that number.	$a \times 1 = 1 \times a = a$	$\frac{5}{6} \times 1 = 1 \times \frac{5}{6} = \frac{5}{6}$
Commutative property of multiplication The order of factors can be changed. The product does not change.	$a \times b = b \times a$	$\frac{2}{3} \times \frac{1}{5} = \frac{1}{5} \times \frac{2}{3}$ $\frac{2}{15} = \frac{2}{15}$
Associative property of multiplication Factors can be grouped in different ways. The product does not change.	$(a \times b) \times c = a \times (b \times c)$	$\frac{3}{4} \times \left(\frac{1}{3} \times \frac{5}{6}\right) = \left(\frac{3}{4} \times \frac{1}{3}\right) \times \frac{5}{6}$ $\frac{3}{4} \times \left(\frac{1}{3} \times \frac{5}{6}\right) =$ $\frac{3}{4} \times \quad \frac{5}{18} \quad = \frac{15}{72}$ $\frac{15}{72} \div \frac{3}{3} = \frac{5}{24}$

Example 6

Multiply: $\frac{3}{4} \times \frac{5}{8} \times \frac{4}{5}$

Strategy   **Use the associative property of multiplication.**

   Step 1   Use the associative property of multiplication.

$$\frac{3}{4} \times \frac{5}{8} \times \frac{4}{5} = \frac{3}{4} \times \left(\frac{5}{8} \times \frac{4}{5}\right)$$

   Step 2   Multiply inside the parentheses. Write the product in simplest form.

$$\frac{5}{8} \times \frac{4}{5} = \frac{20}{40}$$

$$\frac{20}{40} = \frac{20}{40} \div \frac{20}{20} = \frac{1}{2}$$

   Step 3   Multiply the product times the other factor.

$$\frac{3}{4} \times \frac{1}{2} = \frac{3}{8}$$

Solution $\frac{3}{4} \times \frac{5}{8} \times \frac{4}{5} = \frac{3}{8}$

Coached Example

A rectangle has a length of $\frac{5}{6}$ foot and a width of $\frac{1}{4}$ foot.

What is the area of the rectangle?

The formula for the area of a rectangle is $A = $ _____.

$A = $ _____ $\times$ _____

Multiply the numerators. _____ $\times$ _____ $= $ _____

Multiply the denominators. _____ $\times$ _____ $= $ _____

The product is _____.

The area of the rectangle is _____ **square foot.**

Lesson Practice • Part 1

Choose the correct answer.

1. What multiplication problem does the model show?

A. $\frac{2}{5} \times \frac{3}{5} = \frac{6}{25}$

B. $\frac{2}{3} \times \frac{3}{5} = \frac{6}{15}$

C. $\frac{2}{5} \times \frac{1}{3} = \frac{2}{15}$

D. $\frac{1}{5} \times \frac{2}{3} = \frac{2}{15}$

2. What is $\frac{9}{12} \times \frac{2}{3}$?

A. $\frac{1}{4}$ **C.** $\frac{3}{4}$

B. $\frac{1}{2}$ **D.** $\frac{11}{15}$

3. What is $\frac{4}{9} \times \frac{3}{8}$?

A. $\frac{1}{6}$

B. $\frac{1}{3}$

C. $\frac{2}{3}$

D. $\frac{5}{6}$

4. What is $\frac{1}{2} \times \frac{3}{4}$?

A. $\frac{3}{16}$

B. $\frac{1}{4}$

C. $\frac{1}{3}$

D. $\frac{3}{8}$

5. In a vegetable garden, $\frac{1}{4}$ of the plants are peppers. Of the pepper plants, $\frac{1}{3}$ are yellow peppers. What fraction of the plants are yellow peppers?

A. $\frac{1}{12}$

B. $\frac{1}{7}$

C. $\frac{7}{12}$

D. $\frac{3}{4}$

6. A new road that is $\frac{9}{10}$ mile long is being built. So far, $\frac{5}{8}$ of the road has been built. How long is the section that has been built?

A. $\frac{7}{9}$ mile   **C.** $\frac{1}{2}$ mile

B. $\frac{9}{16}$ mile   **D.** $\frac{11}{40}$ mile

7. A rectangle has a length of $\frac{3}{8}$ foot and a width of $\frac{2}{3}$ foot. What is the area of the rectangle?

A. $\frac{1}{2}$ square feet

B. $\frac{1}{3}$ square feet

C. $\frac{1}{4}$ square feet

D. $\frac{1}{8}$ square feet

8. Which shows the multiplicative identity property of 1?

A. $\frac{4}{5} \times \frac{1}{5} = \frac{1}{5} \times \frac{4}{5}$

B. $\frac{3}{8} \times \left(\frac{1}{2} \times \frac{2}{3}\right) = \left(\frac{3}{8} \times \frac{1}{2}\right) \times \frac{2}{3}$

C. $\frac{1}{4} \times 4 = 1$

D. $\frac{9}{10} \times 1 = \frac{9}{10}$

9. Tamera earned an A on $\frac{5}{8}$ of her spelling tests. Of those spelling tests, she earned a perfect score on $\frac{1}{5}$ of them.

A. On what fraction of Tamera's total spelling tests did she earn a perfect score? Show your work.

B. If Tamera took 32 spelling tests, on how many did she earn a perfect score? Show your work.

Lesson Practice • Part 2

Choose the correct answer.

1. Which shows how to multiply $\frac{2}{5} \times 4$?

   A. $2 \times 5 \div 4$

   B. $2 \times 4 \div 5$

   C. $4 \times 2 \div 5$

   D. $4 \times 5 \div 2$

2. What is the area of this rectangle?

   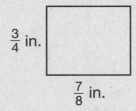

   $\frac{3}{4}$ in.

   $\frac{7}{8}$ in.

   A. $\frac{21}{32}$ square inch

   B. $\frac{5}{6}$ square inch

   C. $1\frac{5}{8}$ square inches

   D. $1\frac{3}{4}$ square inches

3. Each lap around Spring Lake Park is $2\frac{1}{2}$ miles. Brax walked $1\frac{3}{4}$ laps before leaving the park. What distance did Brax walk around Spring Lake Park?

   A. $2\frac{3}{8}$ miles   **C.** $4\frac{1}{4}$ miles

   B. $3\frac{5}{8}$ miles   **D.** $4\frac{3}{8}$ miles

4. Mrs. Campbell bought $1\frac{1}{2}$ pounds of turkey meat and $\frac{3}{8}$ as much cucumber salad. How much cucumber salad did Mrs. Campbell buy?

   A. $\frac{9}{16}$ pound

   B. $1\frac{1}{8}$ pounds

   C. $1\frac{7}{8}$ pounds

   D. $2\frac{1}{16}$ pounds

5. The length of each small square is $\frac{1}{8}$ inch.

   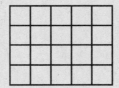

   What is the area of the rectangle?

   A. $\frac{5}{64}$ square inch

   B. $\frac{5}{16}$ square inch

   C. $1\frac{1}{8}$ square inches

   D. $2\frac{1}{2}$ square inches

6. Emmett allotted $2\frac{1}{2}$ hours to study for a science test. He has studied for $\frac{3}{10}$ of that time. How much more time did Emmett allot for studying for the science test?

   A. $\frac{3}{4}$ hour

   B. 1 hour

   C. $1\frac{3}{4}$ hours

   D. $2\frac{1}{5}$ hours

7. Find the product.
   $$\frac{2}{3} \times \frac{4}{5} \times \frac{3}{2} = \square$$

   A. $\frac{2}{3}$

   B. $\frac{4}{5}$

   C. $1\frac{1}{10}$

   D. $1\frac{1}{2}$

8. Kinsley used a $\frac{1}{4}$-cup measuring cup to make iced tea from mix. She filled the measuring cup $8\frac{1}{2}$ times. How much mix did Kinsley use?

   A. $8\frac{1}{8}$ cups   C. $2\frac{1}{8}$ cups

   B. $4\frac{1}{4}$ cups   D. $1\frac{7}{8}$ cups

9. A square has sides of $2\frac{1}{2}$ inches. What is the area of the square?

   A. $4\frac{1}{4}$ square inches

   B. 5 square inches

   C. $6\frac{1}{4}$ square inches

   D. 10 square inches

10. Find the product.
    $$3\frac{7}{8} \times \frac{2}{5} = \square$$

    A. $1\frac{11}{20}$ C. $3\frac{19}{40}$

    B. $1\frac{17}{20}$ D. $3\frac{7}{20}$

11. The Red Trail is $3\frac{1}{4}$ miles long. The Blue Trail is $\frac{7}{8}$ times as long as the Red Trail.

   A. A group finished hiking $\frac{3}{5}$ of the Red Trail when it started to rain. What is the distance that they hiked before it started to rain? Show your work.

   B. The group planned on hiking the Blue Trail after hiking the Red Trail. How far did the group plan on hiking? Show your work.

12. Use numbers from the box to complete an expression that has a product of $\frac{8}{15}$.

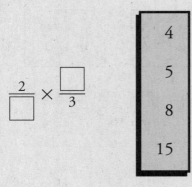

13. Select True or False for each equation.

A. $\frac{1}{4} \times \frac{3}{5} = \frac{3}{20}$ ○ True ○ False

B. $\frac{7}{10} \times \frac{5}{8} = \frac{7}{80}$ ○ True ○ False

C. $\frac{3}{4} \times \frac{7}{12} = \frac{21}{16}$ ○ True ○ False

D. $\frac{3}{8} \times \frac{4}{6} = \frac{1}{4}$ ○ True ○ False

14. Draw a line from each expression to its product.

A. $\frac{3}{8} \times \frac{4}{12}$ •   • $\frac{1}{9}$

B. $\frac{5}{9} \times \frac{1}{5}$ •   • $\frac{1}{8}$

C. $\frac{3}{10} \times \frac{5}{8}$ •   • $\frac{2}{15}$

D. $\frac{4}{9} \times \frac{3}{10}$ •   • $\frac{3}{16}$

15. Find each product. Write the expression in the correct box.

| $\frac{3}{4} \times \frac{1}{2}$ | $\frac{3}{6} \times \frac{9}{12}$ | $\frac{1}{2} \times \frac{1}{2}$ | $\frac{5}{10} \times \frac{6}{12}$ | $\frac{4}{8} \times \frac{3}{6}$ | $\frac{5}{10} \times \frac{9}{12}$ |

product equal to $\frac{1}{4}$	product equal to $\frac{3}{8}$

16. Which number sentences show the associative property of multiplication? Circle all that apply.

A. $\frac{3}{10} \times \frac{4}{9} = \frac{4}{9} \times \frac{3}{10}$

B. $\frac{5}{9} \times \left(\frac{1}{2} \times \frac{3}{4}\right) = \left(\frac{5}{9} \times \frac{1}{2}\right) \times \frac{3}{4}$

C. $\frac{5}{6} \times 1 = \frac{5}{6}$

D. $\left(\frac{3}{7} \times \frac{2}{3}\right) \times \frac{1}{8} = \frac{3}{7} \times \left(\frac{2}{3} \times \frac{1}{8}\right)$

E. $\frac{1}{3} \times 3 = 1$

17. In a vase, $\frac{2}{9}$ of the flowers are roses. Of the roses, $\frac{3}{8}$ are pink roses. Does the expression represent the fraction of the flowers that are pink roses? Select Yes or No.

A. $\frac{2}{9} + \frac{3}{8}$ ○ Yes   ○ No

B. $\frac{1}{12}$ ○ Yes   ○ No

C. $\frac{2}{9} \times \frac{3}{8}$ ○ Yes   ○ No

D. $\frac{43}{72}$ ○ Yes   ○ No

Fractions as Division

Getting the Idea

A fraction is related to division. The fraction $\frac{2}{3}$ is the same as 2 divided by 3.

Remember that division and multiplication are inverse operations. Since $2 \div 3 = \frac{2}{3}$, then $\frac{2}{3} \times 3 = 2$.

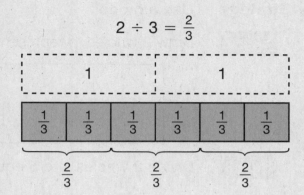

Example 1

Show $\frac{3}{4}$ as division, and show that $\frac{3}{4} \times 4 = 3$.

Strategy   **Use fraction strips.**

Step 1   Show the fraction as division.

$$\frac{3}{4} = 3 \div 4$$

Step 2   Use fraction strips to model 3 divided by 4.

Step 3   Show that $\frac{3}{4} \times 4 = 3$.

The model above shows $3 \div 4$. It also shows that $\frac{3}{4} \times 4 = 3$, as you can see below.

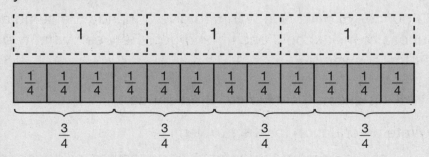

Solution $3 \div 4 = \frac{3}{4}$ and $\frac{3}{4} \times 4 = 3$

Example 2

Dan had 2 feet of ribbon. He cut the ribbon into 5 equal pieces. How long is each piece of ribbon?

Strategy   **Use a model.**

Step 1   Draw 2 wholes to represent 2 feet of ribbon. Each whole represents 1 foot.

Step 2   Divide 2 wholes into 5 equal pieces.

$$2 = \frac{10}{5}$$

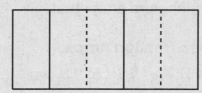

Step 3   What fraction of the whole is each part?

Each part is $\frac{2}{5}$.

Solution   **Each piece of ribbon is $\frac{2}{5}$ foot.**

In Example 2, use multiplication to check that $2 \div 5 = \frac{2}{5}$.

$$\frac{2}{5} \times 5 = \frac{2}{5} \times \frac{5}{1} = \frac{2 \times 5}{5 \times 1} = \frac{10}{5} = 2$$

Example 3

Mohini has 60 ounces of milk. She wants to give 8 friends the same amount of milk. How many ounces of milk should each friend get? Between what two whole numbers does the answer lie?

Strategy   **Write a division sentence, then divide.**

Step 1   Write an equation for the problem.

Let o represent the number of ounces of milk each friend will get.

$$60 \div 8 = o$$

Step 2   Divide.

$60 \div 8 = 7 \text{ R}4$

Step 3   Write the quotient as a mixed number. Then simplify.

$7 \text{ R}4 \longrightarrow 7\frac{4}{8}$ $7\frac{4}{8} = 7\frac{1}{2}$

Step 4   What two whole numbers does the answer lie between?

$7\frac{1}{2}$ is between 7 and 8.

Solution   **Each friend should get $7\frac{1}{2}$ ounces of milk. The answer is between the whole numbers 7 and 8.**

Coached Example

If 4 friends want to share 45 ounces of jelly beans equally by weight, how many ounces should each friend get? Between what two whole numbers does your answer lie?

Write a division sentence for the problem.

Let *o* represent the number of ounces of jelly beans each friend will get.

_____ ÷ _____ = _____

Divide. Show your work.

$4\overline{)45}$

Write the quotient as a mixed number. _____

Is the mixed number in simplest form? _____

Each friend should get _____ ounces of jelly beans. The answer lies between the whole numbers _____ and _____.

Lesson Practice • Part 1

Choose the correct answer.

1. Which fraction is the same as this division?

$$1 \div 5$$

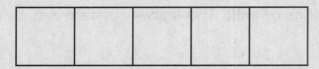

A. $\frac{1}{5}$ **C.** $\frac{1}{4}$

B. $\frac{5}{1}$ **D.** $\frac{4}{5}$

2. Which fraction is the same as this division?

$$3 \div 8$$

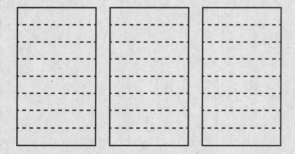

A. $\frac{8}{3}$ **C.** $\frac{3}{5}$

B. $\frac{3}{8}$ **D.** $\frac{5}{8}$

3. Which division is the same as the fraction $\frac{2}{7}$?

A. $7 \div 2$ **C.** $2 \div 5$

B. $2 \div 7$ **D.** $5 \div 7$

4. Which division is the same as the fraction $\frac{1}{3}$?

A. $3 \div 1$

B. $1 \div 2$

C. $2 \div 3$

D. $1 \div 3$

5. Which multiplication sentence can you use to check this division sentence?

$$5 \div 6 = \frac{5}{6}$$

A. $\frac{5}{6} \times 5$ **C.** $\frac{5}{6} \times 1$

B. $\frac{1}{6} \times 5$ **D.** $\frac{5}{6} \times 6$

6. Which multiplication sentence can you use to check this division sentence?

$$3 \div 7 = \frac{3}{7}$$

A. $\frac{4}{7} \times 3$

B. $\frac{3}{7} \times 7$

C. $\frac{4}{7} \times 7$

D. $\frac{3}{7} \times 3$

7. For a 5-mile race, there will be 8 water stops. All the stops will be the same distance apart. How far apart are the water stops?

   A. $\frac{8}{5}$ miles

   B. $\frac{5}{8}$ mile

   C. $\frac{3}{8}$ mile

   D. $\frac{5}{3}$ mile

8. Shannon bought 2 pies. She cut the pies into 3 equal amounts. How much pie is in each amount?

   A. $\frac{2}{3}$ pie

   B. $\frac{1}{3}$ pie

   C. $\frac{1}{2}$ pie

   D. 1 pie

9. The baker made 4 carrot cakes to sell in the next 8 hours.

   A. If the baker wants to sell the same amount of cake each hour, how much cake does he have to sell each hour?

   _____

   B. Make a model to show how much cake the baker will sell each hour.

Lesson Practice • Part 2

Choose the correct answer.

1. Ed printed 31 photos that he will put on pages in an album. Each page holds 4 photos. How many pages can Ed fill?

   A. $7\frac{1}{4}$

   B. $7\frac{1}{2}$

   C. $7\frac{3}{4}$

   D. $8\frac{1}{2}$

2. The Barry family is trying to sell their house. Their realtor has brought them 12 potential buyers in 15 weeks. How many potential buyers have been brought per week?

   A. $\frac{3}{4}$

   B. $\frac{4}{5}$

   C. $1\frac{1}{3}$

   D. $1\frac{1}{4}$

3. Sam is writing a book. He has written 72 pages in 5 weeks. How many pages has Sam written per week?

   A. $14\frac{2}{5}$ C. $15\frac{2}{5}$

   B. $14\frac{3}{5}$ D. $15\frac{3}{5}$

4. How can you tell if a quotient is less than 1?

   A. the divisor is greater than the dividend

   B. the divisor is less than the dividend

   C. the divisor is equal to the dividend

   D. the dividend is greater than the divisor

5. Springfield Avenue is 3 miles long. There are 8 sets of stop signs along Springfield Avenue. The stop signs are the same distance apart. How far apart are the stop signs?

   A. $2\frac{2}{3}$ miles

   B. $2\frac{1}{3}$ mile

   C. $\frac{3}{8}$ mile

   D. $\frac{1}{3}$ mile

6. A bag of mulch weighs 40 pounds. Mr. Downs wants to use more than 4 pounds and less than 5 pounds for each tree. He will use the same amount for each tree. How many trees will Mr. Downs's mulch plan cover?

A. 6   **C.** 8

B. 7   **D.** 9

7. Mrs. Block will give her 6 grandchildren $50 to share equally. Which describes the amount of money that each grandchild will receive?

A. more than $6 and less than $7

B. more than $7 and less than $8

C. more than $8 and less than $9

D. more than $9 and less than $10

8. Which has the same value as $\frac{3}{5}$?

A. $3 \div 5$ **C.** $5 \div 3$

B. $3 \div 2$ **D.** $5 \div 2$

9. There are 64 fluid ounces of lemonade in a pitcher. Molly is going to pour an equal amount of lemonade into 5 glasses. How much lemonade will be in each glass?

A. $13\frac{1}{5}$ fluid ounces

B. $12\frac{4}{5}$ fluid ounces

C. $11\frac{1}{5}$ fluid ounces

D. $10\frac{4}{5}$ fluid ounces

10. How can you tell if a quotient is greater than 1?

A. the divisor is greater than the dividend

B. the divisor is less than the dividend

C. the divisor is equal to the dividend

D. the dividend is less than the divisor

11. A board is 5 feet or 60 inches long. Natalia is going to cut the board into 8 equal pieces.

A. What will be the length, in feet, of each piece of the board? Show your work.

B. What will be the length, in inches, of each piece of the board? Show your work.

12. Select True or False for each division sentence.

A. $1 \div 8 = \frac{7}{8}$ ◯ True ◯ False

B. $1 \div 6 = \frac{1}{6}$ ◯ True ◯ False

C. $2 \div 3 = \frac{3}{2}$ ◯ True ◯ False

D. $3 \div 4 = \frac{3}{4}$ ◯ True ◯ False

E. $8 \div 9 = \frac{1}{9}$ ◯ True ◯ False

13. Draw a line from each fraction to the matching division problem.

A. $\frac{2}{3}$ •   • $4 \div 5$

B. $\frac{4}{5}$ •   • $3 \div 5$

C. $\frac{3}{5}$ •   • $1 \div 3$

D. $\frac{1}{3}$ •   • $2 \div 3$

14. Draw a line from each division sentence to the multiplication sentence you can use to check it.

A. $2 \div 5 = \frac{2}{5}$ •   • $\frac{3}{5} \times 5$

B. $5 \div 8 = \frac{5}{8}$ •   • $\frac{2}{5} \times 5$

C. $2 \div 8 = \frac{2}{8}$ •   • $\frac{5}{8} \times 8$

D. $3 \div 5 = \frac{3}{5}$ •   • $\frac{2}{8} \times 8$

15. For a 3-mile work zone, there will be 7 warning signs. All the signs will be about the same distance apart. Which show how far apart the signs will be? Circle all that apply.

A. $\frac{3}{7}$ mile

B. 7 miles ÷ 3

C. $\frac{7}{3}$ mile

D. 3 miles ÷ 7

16. Look at each multiplication problem. Can it be used to check the division sentence below? Select Yes or No.

$$4 \div 9 = \frac{4}{9}$$

A. $\frac{5}{9} \times 4$ ○ Yes   ○ No

B. $\frac{4}{9} \times 9$ ○ Yes   ○ No

C. $\frac{4}{9} \times 4$ ○ Yes   ○ No

D. $9 \times \frac{4}{9}$ ○ Yes   ○ No

E. $4 \times \frac{4}{9}$ ○ Yes   ○ No

17. Use numbers from the box to complete the division sentence.

$$3 \div \boxed{} = \frac{\boxed{}}{11}$$

| 3 |
| 8 |
| 11 |
| 14 |

Divide Fractions

Getting the Idea

Fraction strips can help you divide a whole number by a fraction.

Example 1

Samara has 3 yards of ribbon. She wants to cut the ribbon into pieces that are each $\frac{1}{4}$ yard long. How many pieces of ribbon will Samara have?

Strategy   **Use fraction strips.**

Step 1   Write an equation for the problem.

Let p represent the number of $\frac{1}{4}$ yard long pieces.

$3 \div \frac{1}{4} = p$

Step 2   Use three whole fraction strips to model 3 yards.

| 1 | 1 | 1 |

Step 3   Use $\frac{1}{4}$ fraction strips below the wholes to model $\frac{1}{4}$ yard.

| 1 | 1 | 1 |

| $\frac{1}{4}$ | $\frac{1}{4}$ | $\frac{1}{4}$ | $\frac{1}{4}$ | $\frac{1}{4}$ | $\frac{1}{4}$ | $\frac{1}{4}$ | $\frac{1}{4}$ | $\frac{1}{4}$ | $\frac{1}{4}$ | $\frac{1}{4}$ | $\frac{1}{4}$ |

Step 4   Count the number of $\frac{1}{4}$ fraction strips.

There are 12.

$3 \div \frac{1}{4} = 12$

Solution   **Samara will have 12 pieces of $\frac{1}{4}$ yard long ribbon.**

Dividing a whole number by a fraction is the same as multiplying by the **reciprocal** of the divisor. To find the reciprocal, switch the numerator and the denominator of the divisor. In Example 1, the reciprocal of $\frac{1}{4}$ is $\frac{4}{1}$, or 4, so $3 \div \frac{1}{4} = 3 \times 4 = 12$.

In a **unit fraction**, which is a fraction with a numerator of 1, the reciprocal will always be a whole number. When you divide a whole number by a unit fraction, the quotient will always be a greater whole number than the dividend.

Example 2

Caleb bought 2 pounds of trail mix in a large bag. He wants to put $\frac{1}{8}$ pound of trail mix into small bags. How many small bags of trail mix will Caleb have?

Strategy   **Write the reciprocal of the divisor and multiply.**

Step 1   Write an equation for the problem.

Let b represent the number of small bags of trail mix.

$2 \div \frac{1}{8} = b$

Step 2   Write the reciprocal of $\frac{1}{8}$.

Switch the numerator and denominator of $\frac{1}{8}$.

$\frac{8}{1}$ or 8

Step 3   Multiply 2 by the reciprocal.

$2 \times 8 = 16$

$2 \div \frac{1}{8} = 16$

Solution   **Caleb will have 16 small bags of trail mix.**

You can use multiplication to check division. In Example 2, multiply the quotient by the divisor.

$16 \times \frac{1}{8} = \frac{16}{1} \times \frac{1}{8} = \frac{16}{8} = 2$

Since $16 \times \frac{1}{8} = 2$, the quotient is correct.

When you divide a unit fraction by a whole number, the quotient will always be a unit fraction less than the dividend. For example, $\frac{1}{2} \div 5 = \frac{1}{10}$ because when $\frac{1}{2}$ is divided into 5 equal parts, the size of each part is $\frac{1}{10}$.

Example 3

What is $\frac{1}{6} \div 2$?

Strategy **Write the reciprocal of the divisor and multiply.**

Step 1 Write the reciprocal of 2.

The reciprocal of 2 is $\frac{1}{2}$.

Step 2 Multiply $\frac{1}{6}$ by the reciprocal.

$$\frac{1}{6} \times \frac{1}{2} = \frac{1}{12}$$

Solution $\frac{1}{6} \div 2 = \frac{1}{12}$

Example 4

What is the missing number?

$$\boxed{} \div \frac{1}{3} = 15$$

Strategy **Use the inverse operation of division.**

Step 1 Multiplication and division are inverse operations.

Since $\boxed{} \div \frac{1}{3} = 15$, $15 \times \frac{1}{3} = \boxed{}$.

Step 2 Multiply.

$$15 \times \frac{1}{3} = \frac{15}{1} \times \frac{1}{3} = \frac{15}{3} = 5$$

So $\boxed{} = 5$.

Step 3 Check your answer.

$$\boxed{} \div \frac{1}{3} = 15$$

$$5 \div \frac{1}{3} = 5 \times \frac{3}{1} = \frac{5}{1} \times \frac{3}{1} = \frac{15}{1} = 15$$

Solution **The missing number is 5.**

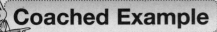

Coached Example

Lucy baked a loaf of banana bread. She took half of the loaf to school. She wants to share the banana bread equally among 6 friends. What fraction of the loaf of banana bread will each friend get?

Write an equation for the problem. _____

When dividing a unit fraction by a whole number, the quotient is always a unit fraction _____ than the dividend.

Divide $\frac{1}{2}$ by 6 to find the size of each slice of banana bread.

To divide fractions, multiply the dividend by the _____ of the divisor.

The reciprocal of 6 is _____.

Multiply.

$\frac{1}{2} \times$ _____ = _____

Each friend will get _____ of the banana bread.

Lesson Practice • Part 1

Choose the correct answer.

1. What division sentence does the model show?

1

1

$\frac{1}{3}$	$\frac{1}{3}$	$\frac{1}{3}$

$\frac{1}{3}$	$\frac{1}{3}$	$\frac{1}{3}$

   A. $6 \div 3 = 2$

   B. $2 \div \frac{1}{3} = 6$

   C. $\frac{1}{3} \div 2 = 6$

   D. $\frac{1}{3} \div 6 = 2$

2. Which explains why $\frac{1}{3} \div 4 = \frac{1}{12}$?

   A. When $\frac{1}{3}$ is divided into 12 equal parts, the size of each part is $\frac{1}{4}$.

   B. When 4 is divided into $\frac{1}{3}$ equal parts, the size of each part is $\frac{1}{12}$.

   C. When $\frac{1}{3}$ is divided into 4 equal parts, the size of each part is $\frac{1}{12}$.

   D. When $\frac{1}{12}$ is divided into 4 equal parts, the size of each part is $\frac{1}{3}$.

3. $\frac{1}{5} \div 4 = \boxed{}$

   A. $\frac{1}{20}$ C. 9

   B. $\frac{1}{9}$ D. 20

4. $9 \div \frac{1}{3} = \boxed{}$

   A. $\frac{1}{27}$ C. 3

   B. $\frac{1}{3}$ D. 27

5. When you divide a unit fraction by a whole number, which statement is true?

   A. The quotient will be greater than the whole number.

   B. The quotient will be greater than the unit fraction.

   C. The quotient will be less than the unit fraction.

   D. The quotient will be equal to the unit fraction.

6. The length of a running trail in a park is 12 miles. There are water fountains every $\frac{1}{4}$ mile. How many water fountains are along the running trail?

   A. 3   C. 16

   B. 8   D. 48

7. Jamal ordered 4 pizzas. How many slices of pizza did Jamal order if each slice is $\frac{1}{8}$ of a pizza?

   A. 2

   B. 8

   C. 16

   D. 32

8. Denise divided $\frac{1}{2}$ pound of butter into 4 equal parts. How much butter was in each part?

   A. $\frac{1}{8}$ pound

   B. $\frac{1}{2}$ pound

   C. 2 pounds

   D. 8 pounds

9. Anna is making a gallon of iced tea, which requires 6 cups of iced tea mix. She only has a $\frac{1}{4}$-cup measuring cup.

   A. How many $\frac{1}{4}$-cup scoops of iced tea mix does Anna need?

   _____

   B. Use words and/or numbers to explain your answer to Part A.

   _____

   _____

   _____

Lesson Practice • Part 2

Choose the correct answer.

1. Find the quotient.

   $\frac{1}{3} \div 4 = \boxed{}$

   A. $\frac{1}{12}$

   B. $\frac{3}{4}$

   C. $1\frac{1}{3}$

   D. 12

2. When a whole number is divided by a unit fraction, which statement is true?

   A. The quotient can be found by dividing the whole number by the numerator.

   B. The quotient can be found by dividing the whole number by the denominator.

   C. The quotient can be found by multiplying the whole number times the denominator.

   D. The quotient can be found by multiplying the whole number times the numerator.

3. There are 3 sets of traffic lights along Adams Street, which is $\frac{1}{2}$ mile long. The sets of traffic lights are the same distance apart. What is the distance between the sets of traffic lights?

   A. $\frac{1}{6}$ mile

   B. $\frac{1}{5}$ mile

   C. $\frac{2}{3}$ mile

   D. $1\frac{1}{2}$ miles

4. Find the quotient.

   $6 \div \frac{1}{3} = \boxed{}$

   A. $\frac{1}{18}$

   B. $\frac{1}{2}$

   C. 2

   D. 18

5. The length of a county highway is 5 miles. There are mile marker signs every $\frac{1}{10}$ mile. How many mile marker signs are there?

   A. 2   **C.** 15

   B. 5   **D.** 50

6. Four friends are going to equally share $\frac{1}{2}$ gallon of frozen yogurt. How many gallons of frozen yogurt will each friend receive?

A. $\frac{1}{8}$ gallon

B. $\frac{1}{6}$ gallon

C. 2 gallons

D. 8 gallons

7. Which number makes this sentence true?

$$4 \div \boxed{} = 20$$

A. $\frac{1}{16}$

B. $\frac{1}{5}$

C. 5

D. 16

8. A teaspoon has the capacity of $\frac{1}{3}$ tablespoon. If Adam puts 3 tablespoons of sweetener in his iced tea, how many teaspoons of sweetener did he use?

A. 1 teaspoon

B. 2 teaspoons

C. 6 teaspoons

D. 9 teaspoons

9. Each magazine in a pile weighs $\frac{1}{4}$ pound. The pile weighs 8 pounds. How many magazines are in the pile?

A. 2   **C.** 12

B. 4   **D.** 32

10. Which means the same as $\frac{1}{4} \div 2$?

A. $\dfrac{1}{4 + 2}$

B. $\dfrac{1}{4 \times 2}$

C. $\dfrac{1}{4 - 2}$

D. $\dfrac{1}{4 \div 2}$

11. A nickel is worth $\frac{1}{20}$ of a dollar. Each dime is worth $\frac{1}{10}$ of a dollar.

A. How many nickels are worth $2? Show your work.

B. How many dimes are worth $3? Show your work.

12. Use numbers from the box to complete the division sentence shown by the model.

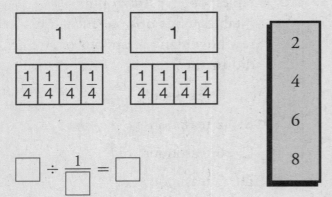

$$\boxed{} \div \dfrac{1}{\boxed{}} = \boxed{}$$

13. A hallway is 30 yards long. There is a light every $\frac{1}{2}$ yard. Which show the number of lights in the hallway? Circle all that apply.

A. 15

B. $\dfrac{1}{30} \div \dfrac{1}{2}$

C. $30 \div \dfrac{1}{2}$

D. 60

14. Three puppies were given equal portions of food. They shared a total of $\frac{1}{5}$ pound of food. How much food, in pounds, did each puppy get? Use numbers from the box to complete the division sentence.

$$\dfrac{\boxed{}}{\boxed{}} \div \boxed{} = \dfrac{1}{\boxed{}}$$

1
3
5
15

15. Draw a line from each explanation to the division sentence it explains.

A. When $\frac{1}{4}$ is divided into 5 equal parts, the size of each part is $\frac{1}{20}$.   •

  • $\frac{1}{5} \div 4 = \frac{1}{20}$

B. When $\frac{1}{5}$ is divided into 4 equal parts, the size of each part is $\frac{1}{20}$.   •

  • $\frac{1}{4} \div 8 = \frac{1}{32}$

C. When $\frac{1}{4}$ is divided into 8 equal parts, the size of each part is $\frac{1}{32}$.   •

  • $\frac{1}{8} \div 4 = \frac{1}{32}$

D. When $\frac{1}{8}$ is divided into 4 equal parts, the size of each part is $\frac{1}{32}$.   •

  • $\frac{1}{4} \div 5 = \frac{1}{20}$

16. Rosa ordered 5 pizzas. How many slices did she get? Select True or False for each statement.

A. She got 20 slices if each slice were $\frac{1}{5}$ of a pizza.   ○ True   ○ False

B. She got 40 slices if each slice were $\frac{1}{8}$ of a pizza.   ○ True   ○ False

C. She got 30 slices if each slice were $\frac{1}{6}$ of a pizza.   ○ True   ○ False

D. She got 50 slices if each slice were $\frac{1}{12}$ of a pizza.   ○ True   ○ False

17. Draw a line from each division problem to its quotient.

A. $4 \div \frac{1}{6}$ •   • 12

B. $5 \div \frac{1}{8}$ •   • 18

C. $6 \div \frac{1}{3}$ •   • 24

D. $6 \div \frac{1}{2}$ •   • 40

Domain 3: Cumulative Assessment for Lessons 17–24

1. Which fraction is equivalent to $\frac{10}{12}$?

   A. $\frac{5}{6}$

   B. $\frac{5}{7}$

   C. $\frac{3}{4}$

   D. $\frac{10}{22}$

2. Find the sum.

   $$\frac{3}{10} + \frac{1}{2} = \square$$

   A. $\frac{3}{20}$

   B. $\frac{1}{3}$

   C. $\frac{4}{12}$

   D. $\frac{4}{5}$

3. Heather lives $\frac{7}{10}$ mile from the school and $\frac{2}{5}$ mile from the library. How much closer does Heather live to the library than to the school?

   A. $\frac{2}{10}$ mile

   B. $\frac{3}{10}$ mile

   C. $\frac{9}{15}$ mile

   D. 1 mile

4. A rectangle has a length of $\frac{2}{3}$ foot and a width of $\frac{3}{10}$ foot. What is the area of the rectangle?

   A. $\frac{1}{5}$ square foot

   B. $\frac{1}{6}$ square foot

   C. $\frac{11}{30}$ square foot

   D. $\frac{29}{30}$ square foot

5. The product of $\frac{1}{2}$ and another factor is less than $\frac{1}{2}$. Which could be the other factor?

   A. $\frac{4}{3}$

   B. $\frac{4}{2}$

   C. $\frac{5}{2}$

   D. $\frac{3}{4}$

6. Marty lives $\frac{2}{3}$ mile from school. Linda lives $\frac{3}{4}$ as far from school as Marty does. How far does Linda live from school?

   A. $\frac{1}{2}$ mile   C. $\frac{5}{7}$ mile

   B. $\frac{7}{12}$ mile   D. 1 mile

7. Find the quotient.

    $\frac{1}{3} \div 5 = \boxed{}$

    A. $1\frac{2}{3}$

    B. $1\frac{2}{4}$

    C. $\frac{2}{8}$

    D. $\frac{1}{15}$

8. How much milk will each friend get if 3 friends share $\frac{1}{4}$ gallon equally?

    A. $\frac{1}{12}$ gallon

    B. $\frac{1}{6}$ gallon

    C. $\frac{1}{3}$ gallon

    D. $\frac{3}{4}$ gallon

9. What is $2\frac{7}{10} + \frac{4}{5}$?

    _____

10. If 3 dogs are going to share 32 ounces of canned dog food equally by weight, how many ounces should each dog get?

    A. Write an equation for the problem.

    _____

    B. Solve the problem. Show your work.

Domain 4

Measurement and Data

Domain 4: Diagnostic Assessment for Lessons 25–29

Domain 4: Cumulative Assessment for Lessons 25–29

Domain 4: Diagnostic Assessment for Lessons 25–29

1. What is the volume of this cube?

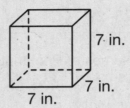

   A. 21 inches

   B. 49 cubic inches

   C. 343 square inches

   D. 343 cubic inches

2. Calvin is 5 feet 2 inches tall. What is Calvin's height in inches?

   A. 50 inches

   B. 52 inches

   C. 62 inches

   D. 64 inches

3. Julia poured 250 milliliters (mL) of juice into each of 11 glasses. How many liters (L) of juice did she use?

   A.   2.75 L

   B.   27.5 L

   C.   275 L

   D. 2,750 L

4. What is the volume of this rectangular prism?

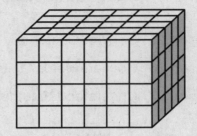

   A. 120 cubic units

   B. 100 cubic units

   C.   25 cubic units

   D.   15 cubic units

5. This figure is made up of 1-inch cubes.

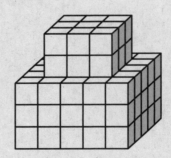

   What is the volume of the figure in cubic inches?

   A. 21 cubic inches

   B. 34 cubic inches

   C. 75 cubic inches

   D. 93 cubic inches

6. Carla packed 1-centimeter cubes into the base of this box. The box is 4 centimeters high.

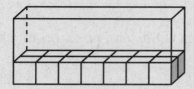

What is the volume of the box?

A. 14 cubic centimeters

B. 28 cubic centimeters

C. 42 cubic centimeters

D. 56 cubic centimeters

7. The line plot shows the number of pounds of hard candy in bags on a store shelf.

Hard Candy in Bags (in pounds)

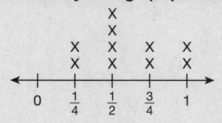

How many pounds of hard candy are on the shelf?

A. 0.25 pound

B. 2 pounds

C. 6 pounds

D. 10 pounds

8. What is the volume of this swimming pool?

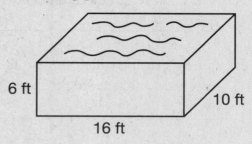

A. 32 cubic feet

B. 160 cubic feet

C. 900 cubic feet

D. 960 cubic feet

9. In the long jump, Lou leapt 754 centimeters. How many meters did Lou leap?

_____

10. Jenny put 10 cups of chicken stock into a pot to make soup.

    A. How many quarts of chicken stock did Jenny put into the pot?

        _____

    B. Jenny's recipe called for 2 quarts of chicken stock. Did Jenny use too much or too little chicken stock? Explain.

        _____

        _____

        _____

Convert Customary Units

Getting the Idea

When you want to know how long or tall something is, you measure its **length**. Units of length in the customary system include **inches**, **feet**, **yards**, and **miles**.

When measuring the length of an object, more units are needed when smaller units are used. For example, a piece of paper that is 12 inches long also has a length of 1 foot. More inches than feet are used to measure the length of the paper. This is because a foot is a longer unit than an inch.

You can convert units if you know their equivalent measures. For example, since there are 24 hours in a day, 48 hours is equivalent to 2 days. The table shows the conversions for length in the customary system.

Customary Units of Length

1 foot (ft) = 12 inches (in.)
1 yard (yd) = 3 feet
1 mile (mi) = 1,760 yards

To convert a smaller unit to a larger unit, divide.

Example 1

Ms. Richards's car is 198 inches long. How many feet is that?

Strategy   **Divide to convert a smaller unit to a larger unit.**

Step 1   Write the relationship between feet and inches.

1 foot = 12 inches

Step 2   Divide the number of inches by 12 to find the number of feet.

198 ÷ 12 = 16 R6

Step 3   Interpret the remainder.

The remainder means there are 6 inches left over.

Solution   Ms. Richards's car is 16 feet 6 inches long.

If the quotient of 198 ÷ 12 is written with the remainder as a fraction, the quotient is $16\frac{1}{2}$. So the length of the car can also be written as $16\frac{1}{2}$ feet, because 6 inches is $\frac{1}{2}$ foot.

When you want to know how heavy something is, you measure its **weight**. Units of weight in the customary system include **ounces**, **pounds**, and **tons**.

The table shows the conversions for weight in the customary system.

Customary Units of Weight

1 pound (lb) = 16 ounces (oz)
1 ton (T) = 2,000 pounds

To convert a larger unit to a smaller unit, multiply.

Example 2

Henry weighed 7 pounds 9 ounces when he was born. How many ounces is that?

Strategy   **Multiply to convert a larger unit to a smaller unit. Then add.**

Step 1   Write the relationship between ounces and pounds.

1 pound = 16 ounces

Step 2   Multiply the number of pounds by 16.

$7 \times 16 = 112$ ounces

Step 3   Add the extra ounces to the product

$112 + 9 = 121$ ounces

Solution   **Henry weighed 121 ounces.**

Capacity measures the amount of dry or liquid volume a container can hold. Units of capacity in the customary system include **fluid ounces**, **cups**, **pints**, **quarts**, and **gallons**.

The table shows the conversions for capacity in the customary system. Fluid ounces are not the same as ounces, although they are often called ounces.

Customary Units of Capacity

1 cup (c) = 8 fluid ounces (fl oz)
1 pint (pt) = 2 cups
1 quart (qt) = 2 pints
1 gallon (gal) = 4 quarts

Example 3

Regina made 10 quarts of fruit punch. How many gallons of fruit punch did she make?

Strategy   **Divide to convert a smaller unit to a larger unit.**

Step 1   Write the relationship between gallons and quarts.

1 gallon = 4 quarts

Step 2   Divide the number of quarts by 4.

10 ÷ 4 = 2 R2

The remainder represents $\frac{2}{4}$ of a gallon.

Step 3   Write the remainder in simplest form.

$\frac{2}{4} = \frac{1}{2}$

Solution   **Regina made $2\frac{1}{2}$ gallons of fruit punch.**

Example 4

At lunch, a group of students drank 5 quarts of milk in all. Each student in the group drank 1 cup of milk. How many students were in the group?

Strategy   **Multiply to convert a larger unit to a smaller unit.**

Step 1   Write the relationship between quarts and pints.

1 quart = 2 pints

Multiply the number of quarts by 2.

5 × 2 = 10 pints

5 quarts = 10 pints

Step 2   Write the relationship between pints and cups.

1 pint = 2 cups

Multiply the number of pints by 2.

10 × 2 = 20 cups

10 pints = 20 cups

Solution   **There were 20 students in the group.**

Coached Example

Luanne needs to fill a pot with 1 gallon of water. She only has a 1-pint measuring cup. How many times must Luanne fill the 1-pint measuring cup to have 1 gallon of water?

Use the relationships between the different units to find how many times Luanne must fill the 1-pint measuring cup.

How many pints are in 1 quart? _____

How many quarts are in 1 gallon? _____

Multiply to find how many pints are equal to 1 gallon.

_____ × _____ = _____

Luanne must fill the 1-pint measuring cup _____ times to have 1 gallon of water.

Lesson Practice • Part 1

Choose the correct answer.

1. Each Thanksgiving in Barry's hometown, there is a 5-mile road race. How many feet are there in 5 miles?

   A. 4,400 feet

   B. 8,800 feet

   C. 17,600 feet

   D. 26,400 feet

2. Which does **not** show the same capacity as the others?

   A. 96 fluid ounces

   B. 18 cups

   C. 6 pints

   D. 3 quarts

3. Leroy's favorite basketball player is 6 feet 8 inches tall. How tall is Leroy's favorite basketball player in inches?

   A. 68 inches

   B. 76 inches

   C. 80 inches

   D. 84 inches

4. Mike's cat weighs 12 pounds 9 ounces. How many ounces is that?

   A. 129 ounces

   B. 153 ounces

   C. 183 ounces

   D. 201 ounces

5. Which of these lengths is the greatest?

   A. 3 yards

   B. 6 feet 10 inches

   C. 8 feet

   D. 100 inches

6. An elevator has a weight limit of 1 ton. There are 3 people inside the elevator. Each person weighs 150 pounds. How many more pounds can the elevator safely hold?

   A. 450 pounds

   B. 850 pounds

   C. 1,550 pounds

   D. 1,850 pounds

7. Mrs. Rios wants to make curtains for her windows. She needs 25 feet of material. Which is another way of stating how much material she needs?

    A. 2 yards 1 foot

    B. 8 yards 1 foot

    C. 75 yards

    D. 300 yards

8. The distance from Josie's home to Kathy's home is 900 yards. The distance from Josie's home to Sitha's home is 1 mile. How many more yards away is Sitha's home from Josie's home than is Kathy's?

    A. 860 yards

    B. 1,680 yards

    C. 2,660 yards

    D. 4,380 yards

9. For a party, Lori made a fruit punch from 1 gallon of orange juice, 2 quarts of grape juice, 5 pints of pineapple juice, and 12 cups of cranberry juice.

    A. Order the juices from least to greatest amount used in the fruit punch.

    _____

    _____

    B. How many quarts of juice did Lori make in all? Show your work.

    _____

Lesson Practice • Part 2

Choose the correct answer.

1. The rim of a basketball hoop is 10 feet high. When Chase stretches his hand, it is 88 inches high. How many feet does Chase have to jump to be able to touch the rim?

   A. $3\frac{1}{4}$ feet   **C.** 1 foot

   B. $2\frac{3}{4}$ feet   **D.** $\frac{1}{2}$ foot

2. The world record in the long jump is 29 feet $4\frac{1}{2}$ inches. How many inches short of 10 yards is the record long jump?

   A. $3\frac{1}{2}$ inches

   B. $7\frac{1}{2}$ inches

   C. $11\frac{1}{2}$ inches

   D. $79\frac{1}{2}$ inches

3. A pitcher contains 3 quarts of iced tea. John is going to pour the iced tea into glasses that each hold $1\frac{1}{2}$ cups. How many glasses will John fill?

   A. 2

   B. 4

   C. 8

   D. 16

4. Each lap around a track is $\frac{1}{4}$ mile. Hadley jogged 3 laps around the track. How many yards did Hadley jog?

   A. 880 yards

   B. 1,320 yards

   C. 1,760 yards

   D. 3,960 yards

5. Each book inside a box weighs 20 ounces. There are 24 books in the box. How many pounds do the books weigh altogether?

   A. 60 pounds

   B. 40 pounds

   C. 30 pounds

   D. 24 pounds

6. Four friends are going to equally share $\frac{1}{2}$ gallon of fruit punch. Which describes the amount of fruit punch each friend will receive?

   A. 1 cup   **C.** 1 pint

   B. $1\frac{1}{2}$ cups   **D.** $1\frac{1}{2}$ pints

7. A freight elevator has a weight limit of 4 tons. Each crate in the elevator weighs 250 pounds. If there are 25 crates in the elevator, which sentence is true?

   A. The elevator can still hold 1,750 pounds.

   B. The crates are 2,250 pounds over the weight limit.

   C. The crates are 1,250 pounds over the weight limit.

   D. The elevator can still hold 2,750 pounds.

8. Hudson has to fill a pot with 1 quart of water. All he has is a $\frac{1}{4}$-cup measuring cup. How many times does he have to fill the $\frac{1}{4}$-cup measuring cup to have a quart?

   A. 4   **C.** 12

   B. 8   **D.** 16

9. Arianna has two piles of newspapers to take to recycling. The first pile weighs 10 pounds 7 ounces. The second pile weighs 148 ounces. What is the total weight of the newspapers?

   A. 19 pounds 11 ounces

   B. 22 pounds 11 ounces

   C. 25 pounds 3 ounces

   D. 29 pounds 3 ounces

10. Each day, Kylie walks $2\frac{1}{2}$ miles around her neighborhood. How many feet are equivalent to $2\frac{1}{2}$ miles?

   A. 3,520 feet

   B. 4,400 feet

   C. 10,560 feet

   D. 13,200 feet

11. The women's world record for the shot put is 74 feet 3 inches.

   A. How many inches are equivalent to 74 feet 3 inches? Show your work.

   B. How many yards are equivalent to 74 feet 3 inches? Write your answer as a mixed number. Show your work.

12. Draw a line from each length to its equivalent measure in feet.

A. 2 yards •   • 4 feet

B. 48 inches •   • $4\frac{1}{2}$ feet

C. $1\frac{1}{2}$ yards •   • $5\frac{1}{2}$ feet

D. 66 inches •   • 6 feet

13. How many cups are there in each capacity? Write the capacity in the correct box.

96 fluid ounces	3 pints	$1\frac{1}{2}$ quarts

3 quarts	48 fluid ounces	6 pints

Equivalent to 6 cups	Equivalent to 12 cups

14. Select True or False for each measurement conversion.

    A. 26 inches = 3 feet   ○ True ○ False

    B. 5 yards = 15 feet   ○ True ○ False

    C. 2 miles = 10,280 feet   ○ True ○ False

    D. 3 miles = 5,280 yards   ○ True ○ False

15. A bucket can hold 6 quarts of water. Which amounts will just fill the bucket? Circle all that apply.

    A. 12 pints

    B. 22 cups

    C. 160 fluid ounces

    D. $1\frac{1}{2}$ gallons

16. Use numbers from the box to make the measurement conversion true.

122 ounces = _____ pounds _____ ounces

5
7
10
12

17. Look at each capacity. Is it equivalent to 24 pints? Select Yes or No.

    A. 384 fluid ounces   ○ Yes ○ No

    B. 3 gallons   ○ Yes ○ No

    C. 36 cups   ○ Yes ○ No

    D. 12 quarts   ○ Yes ○ No

Convert Metric Units

Getting the Idea

Units of length in the metric system include **millimeters**, **centimeters**, **meters**, and **kilometers**.

When measuring the length of an object, more units are needed when smaller units are used. For example, a desk that has a length of 1 meter also has a length of 100 centimeters. It takes more centimeters than meters to measure the length of the desk because a centimeter is a shorter unit than a meter.

You can convert units if you know their equivalent measures. The table shows the conversions for length in the metric system.

Metric Units of Length

1 centimeter (cm) = 10 millimeters (mm)
1 meter (m) = 100 centimeters
1 kilometer (km) = 1,000 meters

Example 1

Sanjay lives 3 kilometers from school. How many meters does he live from school?

Strategy   **Multiply to convert a larger unit to a smaller unit.**

Step 1   Write the relationship between kilometers and meters.

   1 kilometer = 1,000 meters

Step 2   Multiply the number of kilometers by 1,000.

   3 × 1,000 = 3,000 meters

Solution   **Sanjay lives 3,000 meters away from school.**

Example 2

Benny cut a piece of string that is 2 meters long. Rina cut a piece of string that is 80 centimeters long. How many centimeters longer is Benny's piece of string than Rina's?

Strategy   **Convert the units to centimeters, and then subtract.**

Step 1   Convert 2 meters to centimeters.

        100 centimeters = 1 meter

        There are 200 centimeters in 2 meters since $100 \times 2 = 200$.

Step 2   Subtract 80 centimeters from 200 centimeters.

        $200 - 80 = 120$

Solution   **Benny's string is 120 centimeters longer than Rina's.**

Mass is the measure of how much matter an object has. Unlike weight, which can change according to gravity, mass never changes. Mass can be measured in **milligrams**, **grams**, **kilograms**, and **metric tons** in the metric system. As with weight, you can use a balance or a scale to measure mass. The table shows the conversions for mass in the metric system.

Metric Units of Mass

1 gram (g) = 1,000 milligrams (mg)
1 kilogram (kg) = 1,000 grams
1 metric ton (t) = 1,000 kilograms

Example 3

A book has a mass of 690 grams. What is the mass of the book in kilograms?

Strategy   **Divide to convert a smaller unit to a larger unit.**

Step 1   Write the relationship between kilograms and grams.

        1 kilogram = 1,000 grams

Step 2   Divide the number of grams by 1,000.

        Dividing by 1,000 is the same as moving the decimal point 3 places to the left.

        $690 \div 1000 = 0.690 = 0.69$ kilogram

Solution   **The book has a mass of 0.69 kilogram.**

Example 4

Ling bought a 450-gram box of strawberries, a 2.2-kilogram watermelon, and 0.75 kilogram of apples. What is the total mass, in grams, of the fruit that Ling bought?

Strategy   **Convert the units to grams. Then add.**

Step 1   Find the mass of the strawberries in grams.

The strawberries have a mass of 450 grams.

Step 2   Find the mass of the watermelon in grams.

1 kilogram = 1,000 grams

Multiply the number of kilograms of the watermelon by 1,000.

2.2 × 1,000 = 2,200 grams

The watermelon has a mass of 2,200 grams.

Step 3   Find the mass of the apples in grams.

Multiply the number of kilograms of apples by 1,000.

0.75 × 1,000 = 750 grams

The apples have a mass of 750 grams.

Step 4   Find the total mass of the fruit.

Add the masses.

450 + 2,200 + 750 = 3,400

Solution   **The total mass of the fruit is 3,400 grams.**

Metric units of capacity include **milliliters** and **liters**. The table shows the conversions for capacity in the metric system.

Metric Units of Capacity

1 liter (L) = 1,000 milliliters (mL)

Example 5

Quinn's punch bowl has a capacity of 575 milliliters. How many liters is that?

Strategy   **Multiply to convert a larger unit to a smaller unit.**

  Step 1   Write the relationship between liters and milliliters.

  1 liter = 1,000 milliliters

  Step 2   Divide the number of milliliters by 1,000.

  575 ÷ 1,000 = 0.575

Solution   **Quinn's punch bowl has a capacity of 0.575 liter.**

Coached Example

Alex wants to drink 2 liters of water today. So far, he has drunk five 250-milliliter glasses of water. How many more milliliters of water does Alex need to drink today to reach his goal?

Use the relationship between liters and milliliters.

1 liter = _____ milliliters, so 2 liters = _____ milliliters

Alex wants to drink _____ milliliters of water today.

The amount of water Alex drank so far can be found by multiplying _____ × _____.

How many milliliters of water did Alex drink so far? _____

Subtract: _____ mL − _____ mL = _____ mL

Alex needs to drink _____ milliliters more of water today to reach his goal.

Lesson Practice • Part 1

Choose the correct answer.

1. How many liters are equivalent to 3,200 milliliters?

   A. 0.032 liter

   B. 0.32 liter

   C. 3.2 liters

   D. 32 liters

2. Pedro lives 6,750 meters from his school. How many kilometers does he live from his school?

   A. 0.675 kilometer

   B. 6.75 kilometers

   C. 67.5 kilometers

   D. 675 kilometers

3. Which measure is **not** equivalent to the others?

   A. 0.0008 kilometer

   B. 0.8 meter

   C. 80 centimeters

   D. 0.008 millimeter

4. A brick has a mass of 1,200 grams. What is the mass of the brick in kilograms?

   A. 0.012 kilogram

   B. 0.12 kilogram

   C. 1.2 kilograms

   D. 12 kilograms

5. Which measure is the greatest?

   A. 0.029 kilometer

   B. 290 centimeters

   C. 2.9 meters

   D. 290,000 millimeters

6. Sam's dog Petunia has a mass of 10.5 kilograms. One of Petunia's newborn puppies has a mass of 125 grams. How much more mass does Petunia have than the newborn puppy?

   A. 9.25 kilograms

   B. 10.375 kilograms

   C. 10.625 kilograms

   D. 114.5 kilograms

7. Irene works in a bakery. She uses 250 milliliters of milk to make a loaf of bread. How many liters of milk will she need to make 15 loaves of bread?

   A.　　3.75 liters

   B.　　37.5 liters

   C.　　375 liters

   D.　3,750 liters

8. On his first try, a pole-vaulter cleared 3.7 meters. On his second try, the pole-vaulter cleared 45 centimeters more than on his first try. What height, in meters, did the pole-vaulter clear on his second try?

   A.　3.25 meters

   B.　3.745 meters

   C.　4.15 meters

   D.　8.2 meters

9. Jack ran 1.5 kilometers on a treadmill, then walked 475 meters before running another 2.3 kilometers.

   A. How many kilometers did Jack do on the treadmill in all?

   B. Explain how you found your answer to Part A.

   _____

   _____

   _____

Lesson Practice • Part 2

Choose the correct answer.

1. In training, Kayden does reps where he bench presses 65 kilograms. How many reps does he have to do to bench press a total of 1 metric ton?

   A. 15

   B. 16

   C. 30

   D. 31

2. A garden bed has a length of 6.75 meters and a width of 85 centimeters. What is the perimeter of the garden?

   A. 6.835 meters

   B. 7.6 meters

   C. 13.67 meters

   D. 15.2 meters

3. There were 4 liters of water in a pitcher. Eight glasses were filled with 325 milliliters of water. How much water remains in the pitcher?

   A. 0.4 liter

   B. 0.6 liter

   C. 1.4 liters

   D. 2.6 liters

4. Broadway is 2.6 kilometers long. There are 13 sets of stop signs on Broadway, each the same distance apart. How many meters apart are the stop signs?

   A. 20 meters

   B. 50 meters

   C. 200 meters

   D. 500 meters

5. Each book inside a box has a mass of 475 grams. There are 16 books in the box. What is the mass of the books inside the box?

   A. 7.15 kilograms

   B. 7.6 kilograms

   C. 71.5 kilograms

   D. 76 kilograms

6. A sports cooler holds 20 liters of water. There are 22 players and 3 coaches involved with a youth soccer team. If they all equally share the water, how much will each person drink?

   A. 80 milliliters

   B. 125 milliliters

   C. 800 milliliters

   D. 1,250 milliliters

7. The ceiling in Clara's basement is 2.75 meters high. When Clara jumps she is 18 centimeters short of being able to touch the ceiling. How high can Clara reach when she jumps?

A. 2.57 meters

B. 2.732 meters

C. 2.768 meters

D. 2.93 meters

8. Nolan tries to drink 2 liters of water each day. After he finished his lunch, Nolan had finished 0.6 of his daily goal. How much water does Nolan have left to drink today?

A. 1,200 milliliters

B.   800 milliliters

C.   120 milliliters

D.   80 milliliters

9. Reagan has 3 books in her backpack. Two of the books each have a mass of 0.45 kilogram. The mass of the third book is 200 grams greater than the combined mass of the other two books. What is the mass of the third book in Reagan's backpack?

A. 0.25 kilogram

B. 0.65 kilogram

C. 0.7 kilogram

D. 1.1 kilograms

10. A race is 5 kilometers long. There are 16 water stops evenly spread throughout the course. How far apart are the water stops?

A.   31.25 meters

B.   37.5 meters

C. 312.5 meters

D. 375 meters

11. Each day, Alyssa jogs for 25 minutes on a treadmill. She jogs 135 meters each minute.

A. How many kilometers will Alyssa jog in 25 minutes? Show your work.

B. At the speed at which Alyssa is jogging, how many centimeters does she jog each second? Show your work.

12. Draw a line from each length to its equivalent measure in meters.

A. 0.05 kilometer •   • 0.05 meter

B. 55 millimeters •   • 0.055 meter

C. 5 centimeters •   • 5.5 meters

D. 550 centimeters •   • 50 meters

13. A paper bag can hold at most 16,000 grams before breaking. Write each mass in the correct box.

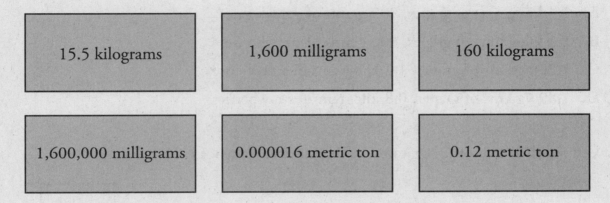

| 15.5 kilograms | 1,600 milligrams | 160 kilograms |

| 1,600,000 milligrams | 0.000016 metric ton | 0.12 metric ton |

Bag Does Not Break	Bag Breaks

14. Select True or False for each measurement conversion.

    A. 400 milliliters = 4 liters   ○ True ○ False

    B. 2.7 liters = 0.0027 milliliter ○ True ○ False

    C. 0.25 liter = 250 milliliters   ○ True ○ False

    D. 1,600 milliliters = 1.6 liters ○ True ○ False

15. Which ingredients are enough to make 2,500 grams of fruit salad? Circle all that apply.

    A. 1.4 kilograms of grapes, 900 grams of strawberries

    B. 2.1 kilograms of grapes, 600 grams of strawberries

    C. 1,200 grams of grapes, 1.2 kilograms of strawberries

    D. 1,800 grams of grapes, 0.8 kilogram of strawberries

16. Use numbers from the box to make the number sentence true.

2,750 grams = _____ kilograms − _____ grams

| 2.9 |
| 3.1 |
| 250 |
| 350 |

17. Look at each distance. Is it equivalent to 2.5 meters? Select Yes or No.

    A. 25 millimeters   ○ Yes ○ No

    B. 250 centimeters   ○ Yes ○ No

    C. 0.25 kilometer   ○ Yes ○ No

    D. 2,500 millimeters ○ Yes ○ No

Understand Volume

Getting the Idea

Recall that capacity is a measure of how much a container can hold. Capacity is measured in units such as cups and milliliters. The **volume** of a three-dimensional figure is the number of **cubic units** that fit inside it. A cubic unit is a **cube** with each **edge** measuring 1 unit. For the cube below, let u represent 1 unit. The volume of this cube can then be expressed as u^3. The notation u^3 means $u \times u \times u$.

u

Common units of volume are the cubic inch (in.^{3}) and the cubic centimeter (cm^3). When measuring the volume of an object, more units are needed when smaller cubic units are used.

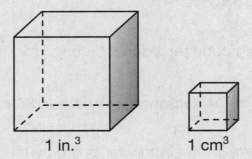

1 in.^{3} 1 cm^3

To find the volume of a rectangular prism or a cube, you can count the number of cubic units that would fit inside the figure.

Example 1

What is the volume of the rectangular prism in cubic units?

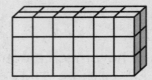

Strategy   **Find the area of each layer. Then multiply by the number of layers.**

Step 1   Find the number of cubes in the bottom layer.

There are 2 rows and 6 columns of cubes.

Step 2   Find the area of the bottom layer.

$2 \times 6 = 12$

The area of each layer is 12 square units.

Step 3   Multiply the area of one layer by the number of layers.

There are 3 layers.

$3 \times 12 = 36$

Since each cube represents 1 cubic unit, the volume is 36 cubic units.

Solution   **The volume of the rectangular prism is 36 cubic units.**

You can also find the volume of a rectangular prism by multiplying the number of cubic units needed to cover the base by the number of layers of cubes needed to fill the height of the prism.

The number of cubes needed to cover the base tells you the area of the base. This is the same as multiplying the edge lengths to find the area of the base. Then multiply the area of the base by the height of the rectangular prism to find the volume of the prism. Remember, area is the number of square units needed to cover a two-dimensional figure.

Example 2

The rectangular prism below has a height of 10 centimeters.

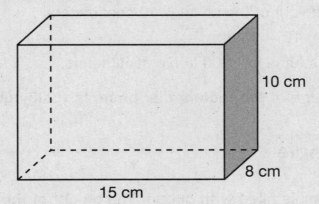

10 cm

8 cm

15 cm

What is the volume of the rectangular prism in cubic centimeters?

Strategy   **Use cubes to find the area of the base. Then multiply the area of the base by the height of the prism.**

Step 1   Find the area of the bottom layer.

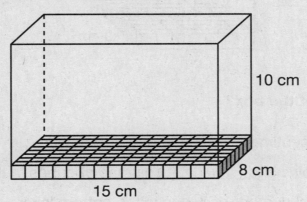

10 cm

8 cm

15 cm

There are 8 rows and 15 columns in the bottom layer.

Multiply: 8 × 15 = 120

The area of the base of the prism is 120 square centimeters.

Step 2   Multiply the area of the base by the height of the prism.

The area of the base is 120 square centimeters.

The height of the prism is 10 centimeters.

120 × 10 = 1,200

The volume is 1,200 cubic centimeters.

Solution   **The volume of the rectangular prism is 1,200 cubic centimeters.**

Coached Example

The first layer of a box is filled with cubes. The height of the prism is 6 centimeters.

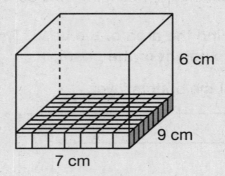

What is the volume of the box?

Find the number of 1-centimeter cubes in the bottom layer.

There are _____ rows and _____ columns of cubes in the bottom layer.

Multiply to find the total number of cubes in the bottom layer.

_____ × _____ = _____

The area of the base of the prism is _____ square centimeters.

Multiply the area of the base by the height of the prism.

The height of the prism is _____ centimeters.

_____ × 6 = _____

The volume of the cube is _____ cubic centimeters.

Lesson Practice • Part 1

Choose the correct answer.

1. What is the volume of this rectangular prism?

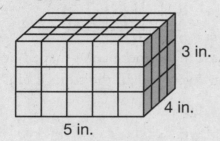

3 in.

4 in.

5 in.

   A. 12 cubic inches

   B. 20 cubic inches

   C. 47 cubic inches

   D. 60 cubic inches

2. What is the volume of this rectangular prism?

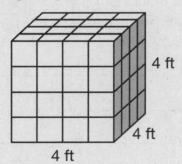

4 ft

4 ft

4 ft

   A. 64 cubic feet

   B. 45 cubic feet

   C. 16 cubic feet

   D. 12 cubic feet

3. What is the volume of this rectangular prism?

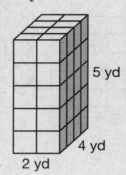

5 yd

4 yd

2 yd

   A. 40 yd^3 **C.** 11 yd^3

   B. 20 yd^3 **D.** 10 yd^3

4. Which rectangular prism does **not** have a volume of 48 cubic units?

   A.

   B.

   C.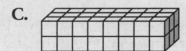

   D.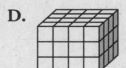

5. What is the volume of this rectangular prism?

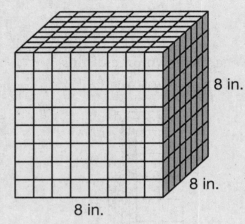

8 in.

8 in.

8 in.

A. 8 cu in.

B. 24 cu in.

C. 64 cu in.

D. 512 cu in.

6. Avery is stacking cube-shaped boxes in a rectangular-shaped storage bin.

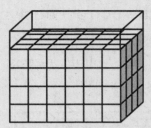

How many more cube-shaped boxes can Avery put in the storage bin?

A. 96

B. 30

C. 24

D. 20

7. Keiko is putting these blocks into a large box.

A. If Keiko makes layers of blocks, how many of the blocks can Keiko put into a box that is 6 inches long, 4 inches wide, and 6 inches high? Explain how you found your answer.

1 in.

1 in.

1 in.

_____

_____

_____

B. Multiply length × width to find the area of the base of the box. Then find the volume by multiplying the area of the base by the height. Compare the volume to your answer in part A. What do you notice?

_____

_____

_____

Lesson Practice • Part 2

Choose the correct answer.

Use the rectangular prisms for questions 1 and 2.

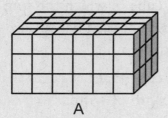

A

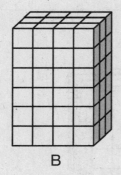

B

1. Which sentence is true?

   A. Prism A has the greater volume because it has a greater length and width than prism B.

   B. Prism B has the greater volume because it has a greater height than prism A.

   C. The prisms have the same volume because the sums of the dimensions are the same.

   D. The prisms have the same volume because the dimensions are the same, but ordered differently.

2. What is the volume of prism A?

   A. 13 cubic units

   B. 24 cubic units

   C. 72 cubic units

   D. 96 cubic units

3. What is the volume of this rectangular prism?

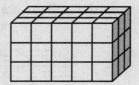

   A. 60 cubic units

   B. 45 cubic units

   C. 30 cubic units

   D. 15 cubic units

4. If the top layer were taken off, what would be the volume of this rectangular prism?

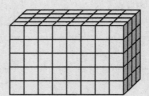

   A. 120 cubic units

   B. 128 cubic units

   C. 150 cubic units

   D. 160 cubic units

5. A rectangular prism has a volume of 30 cubic inches. Which describes the rectangular prism?

   A. It is made of 30 one-inch cubes that have no gaps or overlaps.

   B. It is made of 30 one-inch cubes that have gaps but no overlaps.

   C. It is made of 1 thirty-inch cube that has no gaps or overlaps.

   D. It is made of 1 thirty-inch cube that has gaps but no overlaps.

6. Which describes a unit cube?

   A. a cube with a length, width, and height that has a sum of 1

   B. a cube in which each flat surface has a perimeter of 1 unit

   C. a cube in which the sum of the areas of each flat surface is 1 square unit

   D. a cube that has edges that have a length of 1 unit

---

7. Two rectangular prisms are shown.

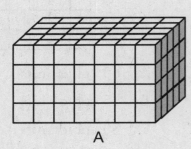 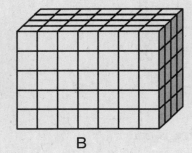

         A   B

   A. What is the volume of prism A? Show your work.

   _____

   B. Explain how you can tell the volume of prism B without multiplying or counting cubes.

   _____

   _____

   C. Give the dimensions of two rectangular prisms that have the same volume as prism A.

   Prism C: _____

   Prism D: _____

---

8. Draw a line from each rectangular prism to its volume.

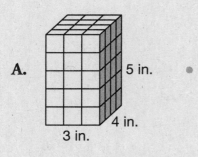

A. 5 in. 4 in. 3 in.   •   • 24 cubic inches

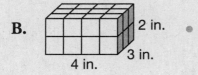

B. 2 in. 3 in. 4 in.   •   • 27 cubic inches

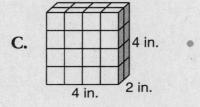

C. 4 in. 2 in. 4 in.   •   • 32 cubic inches

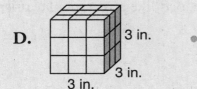

D. 3 in. 3 in. 3 in.   •   • 60 cubic inches

9. Which statements describe this rectangular prism? Circle all that apply.

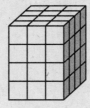

A. The total volume of the prism is 48 cubic units.

B. Adding another layer on top of the prism would add 9 cubic units.

C. The volume of the bottom 2 layers is 30 cubic units.

D. Adding another layer to the right of the prism would add 16 cubic units.

10. Which rectangular prisms have a volume of 36 cubic units? Circle all that apply.

A.

B.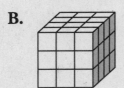

C.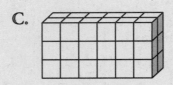

D.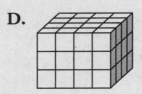

11. Cora is packing cube-shaped blocks into a storage bin shaped like a rectangular prism. Use numbers from the box to complete the statements.

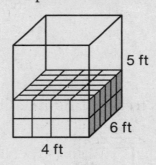

5 ft

6 ft

4 ft

The storage bin can hold a total of _____ blocks.

Cora can pack _____ more blocks into the bin.

| 24 |
| 48 |
| 72 |
| 120 |

Volumes of Rectangular Prisms

Getting the Idea

To find the volume of a **rectangular prism** you can use the formula $V = lwh$, where l is the length, w is the width, and h is the height.

Example 1

What is the volume of the fish tank?

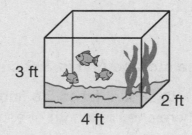

3 ft

2 ft

4 ft

Strategy   Use the formula $V = lwh$ for the volume of a rectangular prism.

Step 1   Substitute the values into the formula $V = lwh$.

$V = 4 \times 2 \times 3$

Step 2   Multiply using the associative property.

$V = 4 \text{ ft} \times 2 \text{ ft} \times 3 \text{ ft}$

$= 8 \text{ ft}^2 \times 3 \text{ ft}$

$= 24 \text{ ft}^3$

Solution   The volume of the fish tank is 24 cubic feet.

Another formula that you can use to find the volume of a rectangular prism is $V = Bh$, where B is the area of the base and h is the height of the prism. No matter which of the two formulas you use, the result will be the same.

Example 2

A storage unit in the shape of a rectangular prism has a length of 12 feet, a width of 8 feet, and a height of 8 feet. What is the volume of the storage unit?

Strategy   **Use the formula $V = Bh$ for the volume of a rectangular prism.**

Step 1   Find the area of the base.

$$B = 12 \times 8$$
$$= 96 \text{ square feet}$$

Step 2   Multiply the area of the base times the height.

$$V = 96 \text{ ft}^2 \times 8 \text{ ft}$$
$$= 768 \text{ ft}^3$$

Solution   **The volume of the storage unit is 768 cubic feet.**

A cube is a rectangular prism with square faces. To find the volume of a cube, you can use the formula $V = e^3$, where e is the length of each edge of the cube.

Example 3

What is the volume of this cube?

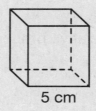

5 cm

Strategy   **Use the formula for the volume of a cube.**

Step 1   Substitute the value into the formula

$$V = e^3$$
$$V = 5 \text{ cm} \times 5 \text{ cm} \times 5 \text{ cm}$$

Step 2   Multiply using the associative property.

$$V = 25 \text{ cm}^2 \times 5 \text{ cm}$$
$$V = 125 \text{ cm}^3$$

Solution   **The volume of the cube is 125 cubic centimeters.**

Example 4

What is the volume of this solid figure?

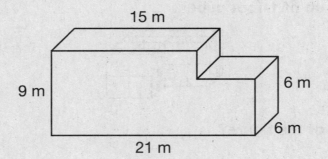

Strategy   Separate the figure into rectangular prisms and find the volume of each part.

Step 1   Separate the figure into two rectangular prisms.

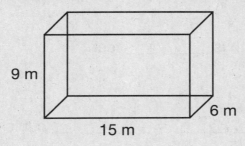 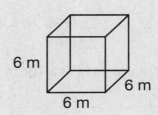

Step 2   Find the volume or the larger prism.

$$V = 15 \text{ m} \times 6 \text{ m} \times 9 \text{ m}$$
$$= 90 \text{ m}^2 \times 9 \text{ m}$$
$$= 810 \text{ m}^3$$

Step 3   Find the volume of the smaller prism.

$$V = 6 \text{ m} \times 6 \text{ m} \times 6 \text{ m}$$
$$= 36 \text{ m}^2 \times 6 \text{ m}$$
$$= 216 \text{ m}^3$$

Step 4   Add the volumes.

$$810 \text{ m}^3 + 216 \text{ m}^3 = 1{,}026 \text{ m}^3$$

Solution   **The volume of the figure is 1,026 cubic meters.**

Coached Example

This figure is made up of 1-foot cubes.

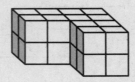

What is the volume of the figure?

Separate the figure into 2 rectangular prisms, one on the left and one on the right.

Use the formula for finding the volume of a rectangular prism.

$V =$ _____ $\times$ _____ $\times$ _____

Start with the prism on the left.

The length is _____ feet. The width is _____ feet.
The height is _____ feet.

Substitute the values into the formula.

$V =$ _____ $\times$ _____ $\times$ _____ $=$ _____ cubic feet

The volume of the prism on the left is _____.

Next find the volume of the prism on the right.

The length is _____ feet. The width is _____ feet.
The height is _____ feet.

Substitute the values into the formula.

$V =$ _____ $\times$ _____ $\times$ _____ $=$ _____ cubic feet

The volume of the prism on the right is _____ cubic feet.

Add to find the total volume.

_____ cubic feet + _____ cubic feet = _____ cubic feet

The volume of the figure is _____**.**

Lesson Practice • Part 1

Choose the correct answer.

1. What is the volume of this rectangular prism?

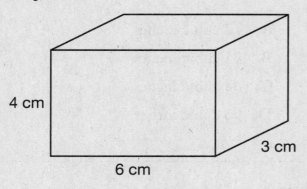

4 cm

3 cm

6 cm

 A. 36 cubic centimeters

 B. 42 cubic centimeters

 C. 54 cubic centimeters

 D. 72 cubic centimeters

2. The trunk in Gary's garage is shaped like a rectangular prism. It has a length of 3 feet, a width of 2 feet, and a height of 3 feet. What is the volume of the trunk?

 A. 18 cubic feet

 B. 15 cubic feet

 C. 12 cubic feet

 D. 8 cubic feet

3. This figure is made up of 1-inch cubes.

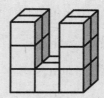

 What is the volume of the figure?

 A. 10 cubic units

 B. 14 cubic units

 C. 18 cubic units

 D. 20 cubic units

4. A box has a volume 240 cubic inches. The width is 6 inches and the height of the box is 5 inches. What is the length of the box?

 A. 8 inches

 B. 40 inches

 C. 48 inches

 D. 210 inches

5. This figure is made up of 1-inch cubes.

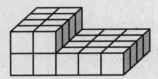

What is the volume of the figure?

A. 12 cubic inches

B. 16 cubic inches

C. 28 cubic inches

D. 35 cubic inches

6. What is the volume of this cube?

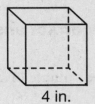

4 in.

A. 12 cubic inches

B. 32 cubic inches

C. 64 cubic inches

D. 96 cubic inches

7. A rectangular prism and a cube are shown below.

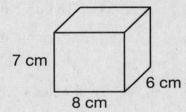

7 cm
8 cm
6 cm

7 cm

A. What is the volume of the rectangular prism? Show your work.

B. What is the volume of the cube? Show your work.

Lesson Practice • Part 2

Choose the correct answer.

1. Paul has two boxes. One is a cylinder and has a volume of 280 cubic inches. The other is a rectangular prism and has a length of 9 inches, a width of 5 inches, and a height of 6 inches. Which sentence is true?

   A. The cylinder has a greater volume by 10 cubic inches.

   B. The cylinder has a greater volume by 20 cubic inches.

   C. The rectangular prism has a greater volume by 10 cubic inches.

   D. The rectangular prism has a greater volume by 20 cubic inches.

2. How many 1-inch cubes can fit inside this rectangular prism?

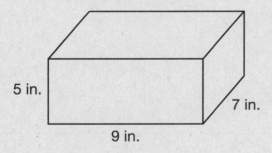

   5 in.   7 in.   9 in.

   A. 80   C. 108

   B. 105   D. 315

3. What is the volume of the solid figure?

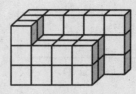

   A. 45 cubic units

   B. 36 cubic units

   C. 33 cubic units

   D. 24 cubic units

4. A desk drawer is a rectangular prism. It has a volume of 3,528 cubic inches. The base has an area of 252 square inches. Which equation shows how to find the height, in inches, h, of the desk drawer?

   A. $h \div 252 \div 3{,}528$

   B. $3{,}528 \div 252 = h$

   C. $3{,}528 \times 252 = h$

   D. $h \times 3{,}528 = 252$

5. How many 2-inch cubes can fit inside this rectangular prism?

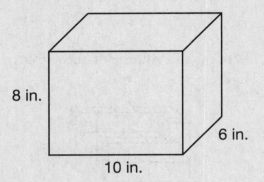

8 in.

6 in.

10 in.

A. 60   **C.** 120

B. 80   **D.** 240

6. A rectangular prism has the same length and width. Its volume is 144 cubic inches and its height is 4 inches. What is the length of the rectangular prism?

A. 36 inches

B. 12 inches

C. 9 inches

D. 6 inches

7. A composite solid figure is shown.

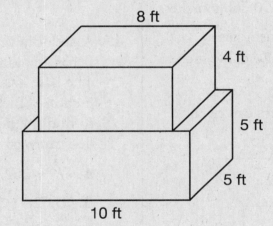

8 ft

4 ft

5 ft

5 ft

10 ft

A. Explain how you can find the volume of the entire figure.

_____

_____

_____

B. What is the volume of the figure? Show your work.

8. Each rectangular prism is made up of 1-foot cubes. Draw a line from each set of dimensions to its volume.

    A. Length: 5 feet

    Width: 3 feet

    Height: 3 feet   24 cubic feet

    B. Length: 4 feet

    Width: 2 feet

    Height: 4 feet   30 cubic feet

    C. Length: 6 feet

    Width: 2 feet

    Height: 2 feet   32 cubic feet

    D. Length: 5 feet

    Width: 2 feet

    Height: 3 feet   45 cubic feet

9. This figure is made up of 1-inch cubes. Which statements describe the figure? Circle all that apply.

    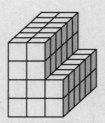

    A. The total volume of the figure is 48 cubic inches.

    B. The volume of the rectangular prism on the right is 12 cubic inches.

    C. The volume of the rectangular prism on the left is 48 cubic inches.

    D. The bottom layer of the figure is made up of 9 cubes.

10. Which rectangular prisms have a volume of 60 cubic inches? Circle all that apply.

A.

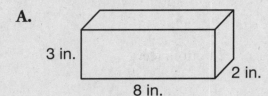

3 in.
8 in.
2 in.

B.

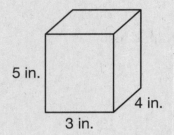

5 in.
3 in.
4 in.

C.

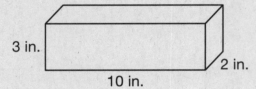

3 in.
10 in.
2 in.

D.

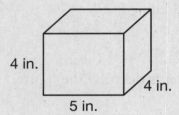

4 in.
5 in.
4 in.

11. This figure is made up of 1-inch cubes. Use numbers from the box to complete the statements.

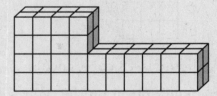

The volume of the rectangular prism on the right is _____ cubic inches.

The total volume of the figure is _____ cubic inches.

| 24 |
| 32 |
| 56 |
| 80 |

Line Plots

Getting the Idea

A **line plot** uses a number line and Xs or dots to organize **data**. The number of Xs above each number indicates how many times that value occurs in a data set.

Example 1

The line plot shows beakers of water in a lab.

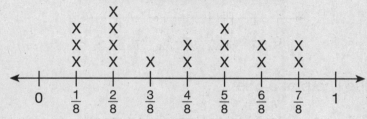

Water in Beakers (in pints)

How many beakers contain less than $\frac{1}{2}$ pint of water?

Strategy   Find the total number of beakers that contain less than $\frac{1}{2}$ pint of water.

Step 1   Look at the line plot to find all the fractions that are less than $\frac{1}{2}$.

$\frac{1}{2} = \frac{4}{8}$

So 0, $\frac{1}{8}$, $\frac{2}{8}$, and $\frac{3}{8}$ are less than $\frac{4}{8}$.

Step 2   Identify the number of Xs above $\frac{1}{8}$, $\frac{2}{8}$, and $\frac{3}{8}$ pints.

There are no Xs above 0.

There are 3 Xs above $\frac{1}{8}$.

There are 4 Xs above $\frac{2}{8}$.

There is 1 X above $\frac{3}{8}$.

Step 3   Add to find the total number of beakers.

$0 + 3 + 4 + 1 = 8$

Solution   **8 beakers contain less than $\frac{1}{2}$ pint of water.**

Data can be collected using a line plot.

Example 2

The weights, in pounds, of different amounts of bagged trail mix that were sold at a health food store is shown below.

$1\frac{1}{4}$, $\frac{1}{2}$, $1\frac{1}{2}$, $\frac{1}{4}$, $\frac{1}{2}$, $1\frac{1}{2}$, $1\frac{3}{4}$, 1, $1\frac{1}{2}$, $\frac{3}{4}$, $1\frac{1}{4}$, $1\frac{1}{2}$

Make a line plot to represent the data.

Strategy   **Make an X for each value.**

Step 1   Draw a number line from 0 to 2 by fourths.

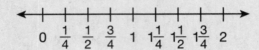

Step 2   Give the line plot a title.

Trail Mix in Bags (in pounds)

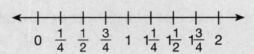

Step 3   Write an X for each value.

Trail Mix in Bags (in pounds)

```
                              X
                              X
            X          X      X
        X   X   X   X  X   X  X
    ←───┼───┼───┼───┼──┼───┼──┼───┼──→
        0   1   1   3   1  1  1  1  2
            ─   ─   ─      ─  ─  ─
            4   2   4      4  2  4
                           1  1  1
```

Solution   **The line plot is shown in Step 3.**

Example 3

Using the line plot in Example 2, find the total weight of the bags of trail mix that were sold.

Trail Mix in Bags (in pounds)

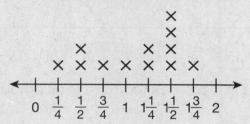

Strategy	**Add to find the total number of pounds.**
Step 1	Write an equation to represent the total number of pounds, p.

$$\frac{1}{4} + \left(2 \times \frac{1}{2}\right) + \frac{3}{4} + 1 + \left(2 \times 1\frac{1}{4}\right) + \left(4 \times 1\frac{1}{2}\right) + 1\frac{3}{4} = p$$

Step 2	Rename the mixed numbers as improper fractions.

$$\frac{1}{4} + \left(\frac{2}{1} \times \frac{1}{2}\right) + \frac{3}{4} + 1 + \left(\frac{2}{1} \times \frac{5}{4}\right) + \left(\frac{4}{1} \times \frac{3}{2}\right) + \frac{7}{4} = p$$

Step 3	Work inside the parentheses.

$$\frac{1}{4} + \frac{2}{2} + \frac{3}{4} + 1 + \frac{10}{4} + \frac{12}{2} + \frac{7}{4} = p$$

Step 4	Rename the addends using the common denominator, 4.

$$\frac{1}{4} + \frac{4}{4} + \frac{3}{4} + \frac{4}{4} + \frac{10}{4} + \frac{24}{4} + \frac{7}{4} = p$$

Step 5	Add the numerators.

$$\frac{1}{4} + \frac{4}{4} + \frac{3}{4} + \frac{4}{4} + \frac{10}{4} + \frac{24}{4} + \frac{7}{4} = \frac{53}{4}$$

Step 6	Write the sum as a mixed number.

$$\frac{53}{4} = 13\frac{1}{4}$$

Solution	**The total weight of the bags of trail mix was $13\frac{1}{4}$ pounds.**

Example 4

The line plot shows beakers of liquid.

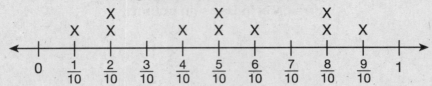

Liquid in Beakers (in liters)

How much liquid would be in each beaker if the total amount in all the beakers was redistributed equally?

Strategy   **Find the total amount of liquid. Then divide by the number of beakers.**

Step 1   Find the total number of liters.

$$\frac{1}{10} + \left(2 \times \frac{2}{10}\right) + \frac{4}{10} + \left(2 \times \frac{5}{10}\right) + \frac{6}{10} + \left(2 \times \frac{8}{10}\right) + \frac{9}{10}$$

$$\frac{1}{10} + \frac{4}{10} + \frac{4}{10} + \frac{10}{10} + \frac{6}{10} + \frac{16}{10} + \frac{9}{10} = \frac{50}{10}$$

There are $\frac{50}{10}$ liters of liquid in all the beakers.

Step 2   Divide to redistribute the liquid equally.

There are 10 beakers, so divide by 10.

$$\frac{50}{10} \div 10 = \frac{50}{10} \times \frac{1}{10} = \frac{50}{100}$$

Step 3   Simplify.

$$\frac{50}{100} = \frac{50 \div 50}{100 \div 50} = \frac{1}{2}$$

Solution   There would be $\frac{1}{2}$ liter in each beaker if the liquid was redistributed equally.

Coached Example

The line plot shows the weight of each piece of fruit that Logan bought today.

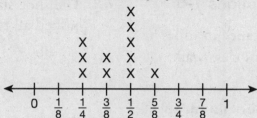

Pieces of Fruit (in pounds)

What is the total weight of the fruit that Logan bought?

Find the total weight of the pieces of fruit that weigh $\frac{1}{4}$ pound.

_____ $\times \frac{1}{4} =$ _____

Find the total weight of the pieces of fruit that weigh $\frac{3}{8}$ pound.

_____ $\times \frac{3}{8} =$ _____

Find the total weight of the pieces of fruit that weigh $\frac{1}{2}$ pound.

_____ $\times \frac{1}{2} =$ _____

Find the total weight of the pieces of fruit that weigh $\frac{5}{8}$ pound.

_____ $\times \frac{5}{8} =$ _____

Rename the products, so they all have a denominator of _____.

Add.

_____ + _____ + _____ + _____ = _____

Write the sum as a mixed number in simplest form.

_____ = _____

The total weight of the fruit that Logan bought is _____ pounds.

Lesson Practice • Part 1

Choose the correct answer.

Use the line plot for questions 1–3.

The line plot shows the distance in miles that students in Mr. Becker's class walk to school.

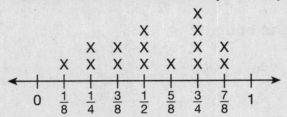

Distance Walked to School (in miles)

1. How many students walk to school?

   A. 8   **C.** 12

   B. 10   **D.** 15

2. How many students walk more than $\frac{1}{2}$ mile to school?

   A. 7   **C.** 9

   B. 8   **D.** 10

3. What is the greatest distance that any student walks to school?

   A. $\frac{1}{2}$ mile

   B. $\frac{5}{8}$ mile

   C. $\frac{3}{4}$ mile

   D. $\frac{7}{8}$ mile

4. The shoe sizes of players on the basketball team are shown below.

   $6\frac{1}{2}, 5\frac{1}{2}, 7, 6, 6\frac{1}{2}, 5\frac{1}{2},$

   $7, 8, 5\frac{1}{2}, 7\frac{1}{2}, 6\frac{1}{2}, 8$

   Which line plot represents the data?

   A.   **Shoe Sizes**

   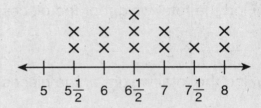

   B.   **Shoe Sizes**

   C.   **Shoe Sizes**

   D.   **Shoe Sizes**

   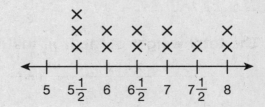

Use the line plot for questions 5 and 6.

The line plot shows the amounts of juice in glasses after a breakfast meeting.

Juice in Glasses (in cups)

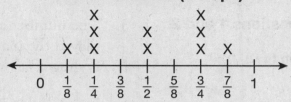

5. What is the total number of cups of juice?

   A. 3 cups

   B. 4 cups

   C. 5 cups

   D. 6 cups

6. How much juice would be in each glass if the total amount in all the glasses was redistributed equally?

   A. $\frac{1}{10}$ cup   **C.** $\frac{1}{8}$ cup

   B. $\frac{1}{2}$ cup   **D.** 1 cup

---

7. Suri planted some seedlings. After one week she measured the heights of the seedlings. The heights, in inches, of the seedlings are shown below.

$\frac{1}{4}, \frac{5}{8}, \frac{3}{4}, \frac{3}{8}, \frac{5}{8}, \frac{7}{8}, \frac{1}{2}, \frac{5}{8}, \frac{3}{8}, \frac{1}{2}, \frac{7}{8}, \frac{5}{8}, \frac{1}{2}$

   A. Complete the line plot.

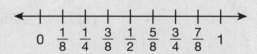

   B. What is the difference in heights, in inches, between the tallest and the shortest seedlings? Show your work.

Lesson Practice • Part 2

Choose the correct answer.

Use the line plot for questions 1 and 2.

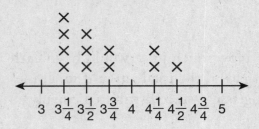

High Jumps (in feet)

1. What is the difference between the greatest and the least high jump?

   A. $\frac{3}{4}$ foot

   B. 1 foot

   C. $1\frac{1}{4}$ feet

   D. $1\frac{1}{2}$ feet

2. How many more students high jumped less than 4 feet than greater than 4 feet?

   A. 2

   B. 4

   C. 6

   D. 8

3. The number of hours that Odette played the piano each day for 12 days is shown below.

   $\frac{3}{4}$, $1\frac{1}{4}$, $1\frac{1}{2}$, 1, $\frac{1}{2}$, 2, $1\frac{3}{4}$, $\frac{1}{2}$, $\frac{3}{4}$, $1\frac{1}{2}$, $1\frac{1}{4}$, $\frac{3}{4}$

   Which line plot represents the data?

   A.   **Piano Playing (in hours)**

   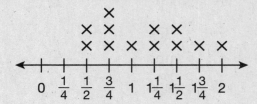

   B.   **Piano Playing (in hours)**

   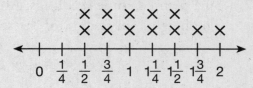

   C.   **Piano Playing (in hours)**

   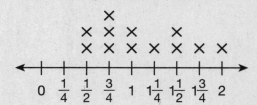

   D.   **Piano Playing (in hours)**

   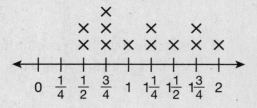

Use the line plot for questions 4 and 5.

The line plot shows the amount of recycling in bins.

Pounds of Recycling

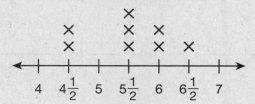

4. What is the total weight of recycling in the bins?

    A. 35 pounds

    B. 44 pounds

    C. 45 pounds

    D. 47 pounds

5. How many pounds would be in each bin if all of the recycling was redistributed equally?

    A. 5 pounds

    B. $5\frac{1}{2}$ pounds

    C. 6 pounds

    D. $6\frac{1}{2}$ pounds

6. The number of miles that Leanne jogged each day for 2 weeks is shown.

    $2\frac{1}{4}$, $2\frac{1}{2}$, 3, $2\frac{1}{4}$, $1\frac{1}{2}$, $1\frac{3}{4}$, $2\frac{1}{2}$, $1\frac{3}{4}$, $2\frac{1}{2}$, $2\frac{1}{2}$, 2, $1\frac{1}{2}$, $1\frac{1}{4}$, $1\frac{1}{2}$

    A. Complete the line plot. Remember to give it a title.

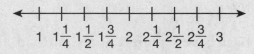

    B. What was the total number of miles Leanne jogged during the 2 weeks? Show your work.

7. The line plot shows the distance in miles that the members of a soccer team jogged during practice. Select True or False for each statement.

Distance Jogged (in miles)

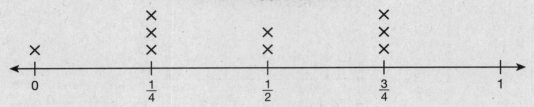

A. There were 8 team members at practice. ○ True ○ False

B. Five members jogged $\frac{1}{2}$ mile or farther. ○ True ○ False

C. More members jogged $\frac{1}{2}$ mile than jogged $\frac{1}{4}$ mile. ○ True ○ False

D. The members jogged a total of 4 miles. ○ True ○ False

8. The line plot shows the weight of cat food that was placed in bags at an animal shelter. Circle all that apply.

Cat Food in Bags (in pounds)

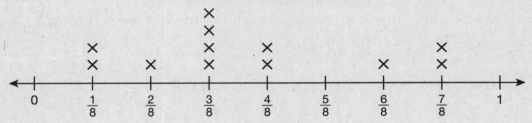

A. Four bags have $\frac{3}{8}$ pound of food.

B. Six pounds of food were bagged in all.

C. Twelve bags were used.

D. More than half the bags have $\frac{3}{8}$ pound or less of food.

9. The line plot shows the lengths of fish caught in a pond. Use numbers from the box to complete the statements.

Lengths of Fish (in feet)

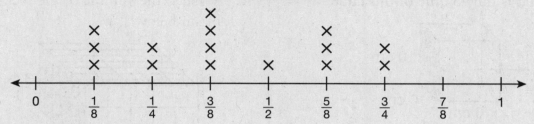

The longest fish was _____ foot.

The total length of fish caught was _____ feet.

The greatest number of fish had a length of _____ foot.

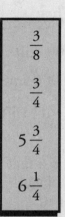

10. The line plot shows the amounts of vinegar in beakers used in a lab. Draw a line from each description to its value.

Vinegar in Beakers (in liters)

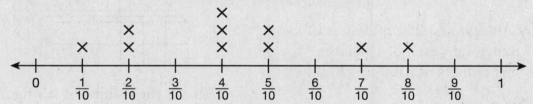

A. the amount of vinegar that was used most often   •

B. the total amount of vinegar in the three beakers with the least vinegar in them   •

C. the total number of beakers   •

D. the number of beakers that have more than $\frac{3}{5}$ liter of vinegar   •

• $\frac{4}{10}$

• $\frac{1}{2}$

• 2

• 10

Domain 4: Cumulative Assessment for Lessons 25–29

1. What is the volume of this cube?

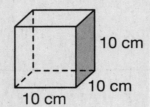

10 cm

10 cm

10 cm

   A. 30 centimeters

   B. 100 cubic centimeters

   C. 1,000 square centimeters

   D. 1,000 cubic centimeters

2. Ryan is 6 feet 1 inch tall. What is Ryan's height in inches?

   A. 61 inches

   B. 67 inches

   C. 73 inches

   D. 77 inches

3. Mary Ann poured 250 milliliters of fruit punch into each of 13 glasses. How many liters of fruit punch did she pour?

   A. 3.25 liters

   B. 32.5 liters

   C. 325 liters

   D. 3,250 liters

4. What is the volume of the rectangular prism below?

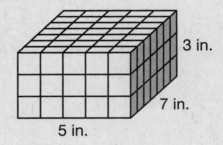

3 in.

7 in.

5 in.

   A. 15 cubic inches

   B. 70 cubic inches

   C. 105 cubic inches

   D. 175 cubic inches

5. The figure below is made up of 1-inch cubes.

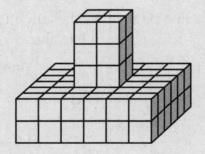

What is the volume of the figure?

   A. 21 cubic inches

   B. 40 cubic inches

   C. 72 cubic inches

   D. 84 cubic inches

6. Nina packed 1-inch cubes into this box. The box is 6 inches high.

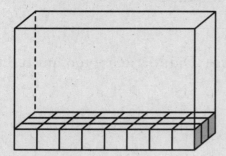

What is the volume of the box?

A. 144 cubic inches

B. 140 cubic inches

C. 144 square inches

D. 24 square inches

7. The line plot shows the bags of dried fruit a teacher bought for a class trip.

Dried Fruit in Bags (in pounds)

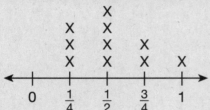

How many pounds of dried fruit did she buy?

A. $4\frac{1}{4}$ pounds

B. $5\frac{1}{4}$ pounds

C. $5\frac{1}{2}$ pounds

D. 10 pounds

8. What is the volume of this fish tank?

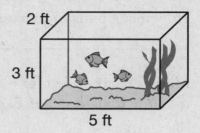

A. 6 cubic feet

B. 10 cubic feet

C. 30 cubic feet

D. 40 cubic feet

9. In the high jump, Quon leapt 183 centimeters. How many meters did Quon leap?

_____

10. Mario put 1.5 quarts of tomato sauce into a pot.

A. How many pints of tomatoes did Mario put into the pot?

_____

B. Mario's recipe called for 8 cups of tomato sauce. Did Mario use too much or too little tomato sauce? Explain.

Domain 5 | Geometry

Domain 5: Diagnostic Assessment for Lessons 30–34

Domain 5: Cumulative Assessment for Lessons 30–34

Domain 5: Diagnostic Assessment for Lessons 30–34

Use the coordinate plane for questions 1–3.

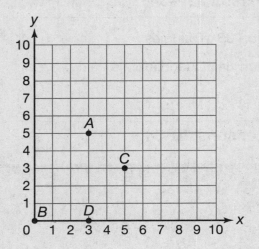

Use this coordinate plane for questions 4 and 5.

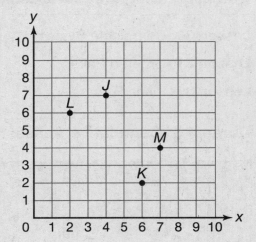

1. Which point represents the origin?

   A. point *A*   **C.** point *C*

   B. point *B*   **D.** point *D*

2. Which two points have the same *x*-coordinate?

   A. points *A* and *B*

   B. points *A* and *C*

   C. points *B* and *D*

   D. points *A* and *D*

3. Which point is 3 units right and 5 units up from the origin?

   A. point *A*   **C.** point *C*

   B. point *B*   **D.** point *D*

4. Which point is located at (7, 4)?

   A. point *J*

   B. point *K*

   C. point *L*

   D. point *M*

5. What are the coordinates of point *K*?

   A. (4, 7)

   B. (6, 2)

   C. (2, 6)

   D. (7, 4)

6. Which figure has 5 sides and 5 angles?

   A. heptagon

   B. hexagon

   C. pentagon

   D. octagon

7. How can you classify this triangle?

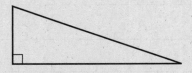

   A. scalene, acute

   B. scalene, right

   C. isosceles, right

   D. isosceles, obtuse

8. Which of the following is a parallelogram and has 4 sides of equal length?

   A. rhombus

   B. trapezoid

   C. hexagon

   D. octagon

9. Graph point A at (2, 7) on the coordinate plane below.

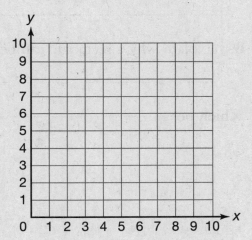

10. Look at figure *ABCD*.

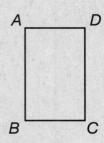

A. Identify all the ways to classify figure *ABCD*.

_____

_____

_____

B. Explain why a rectangle can be classified as a parallelogram.

_____

_____

_____

Coordinate System

Getting the Idea

An **ordered pair** is a pair of numbers used to locate a point on a **coordinate plane**. The left-right or horizontal number line on the coordinate plane is the **x-axis**. The up-down or vertical number line is the **y-axis**. The x-axis and y-axis are perpendicular to each other. The point where the axes meet is called the **origin** and is named by the ordered pair (0, 0).

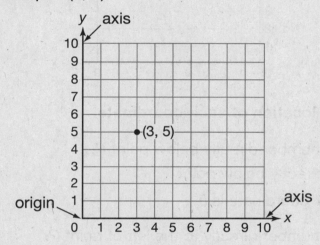

The first number in an ordered pair is the **x-coordinate**. The x-coordinate tells the distance from the origin along the x-axis.

The second number in an ordered pair is the **y-coordinate**. The y-coordinate tells the distance from the origin along the y-axis.

For example, the ordered pair (3, 5) is shown on the coordinate plane above. The x-coordinate is 3 and the y-coordinate is 5.

Example 1

What is the location of point *P*?

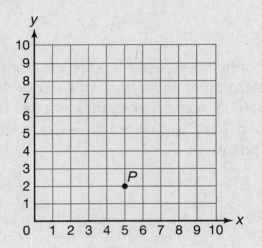

Strategy **Find the location of each coordinate.**

Step 1 Find the number directly below point *P*.

5 is directly below point *P*.

The *x*-coordinate is 5.

Step 2 Find the number directly to the left of point *P*.

2 is directly to the left of point *P*.

The *y*-coordinate is 2.

Step 3 Write the ordered pair.

(5, 2)

Solution **Point *P* is located at (5, 2).**

Example 2

Three points are graphed on the coordinate plane below.

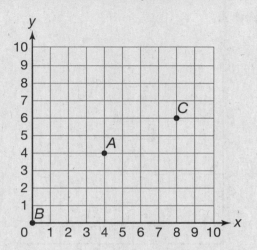

Which letter is not represented by an ordered pair that has the same *x*- and *y*-coordinates?

Strategy   **Write the ordered pair for each point.**

Step 1   Write the ordered pair for point *A*.

Point *A* is 4 units to the right of 0.

Point *A* is 4 units above 0.

Point *A* is located at (4, 4).

Step 2   Write the ordered pair for point *B*.

Point *B* is at the origin, which is (0, 0).

Step 3   Write the ordered pair for point *C*.

Point *C* is 8 units to the right of 0.

Point *C* is 6 units above 0.

Point *C* is located at (8, 6).

Solution   **Point *C* does not have the same *x*- and *y*-coordinates.**

Coached Example

Name the location of point A.

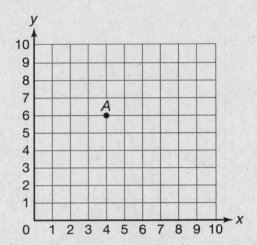

Place your finger on point A.

The number directly below point A is _____.

This is the number of units to the _____ of the origin.

The number directly to the left of point A is _____.

This is the number of units _____ the origin.

The ordered pair _____ gives the location of point A.

Lesson Practice • Part 1

Choose the correct answer.

Use the coordinate plane for questions 1–3.

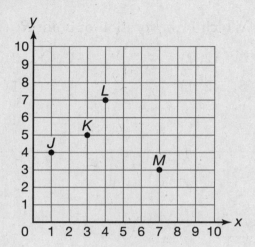

Use the coordinate plane for questions 4–6.

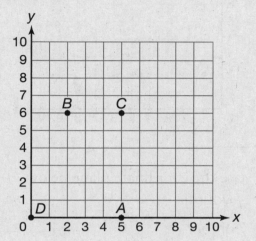

1. Which point is located at (3, 5)?

   A. point *J*

   B. point *K*

   C. point *L*

   D. point *M*

2. Which ordered pair gives the location of point *M*?

   A. (3, 7)   C. (7, 3)

   B. (4, 8)   D. (8, 4)

3. Which ordered pair gives the location of point *J*?

   A. (1, 4)   C. (4, 1)

   B. (2, 5)   D. (5, 2)

4. Which point is at the origin?

   A. point *A*

   B. point *B*

   C. point *C*

   D. point *D*

5. Which point is located at (2, 6)?

   A. point *A*   C. point *C*

   B. point *B*   D. point *D*

6. Which two points have the same *x*-coordinate?

   A. *A* and *B*   C. *B* and *C*

   B. *A* and *C*   D. *A* and *D*

Use the coordinate plane for questions 7 and 8.

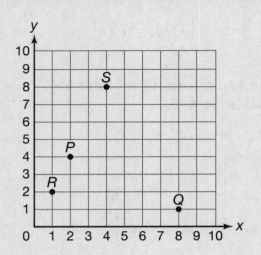

7. Which point is located at (4, 8)?

   A. point *P*   **C.** point *R*

   B. point *Q*   **D.** point *S*

8. Which is the location of point *R*?

   A. (2, 2)   **C.** (1, 2)

   B. (2, 1)   **D.** (1, 1)

9. Use the coordinate plane below.

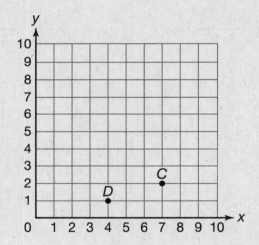

   A. What ordered pair names point *C*? Explain your answer.

   _____

   B. What ordered pair names point *D*? Explain your answer.

   _____

Lesson Practice • Part 2

Choose the correct answer.

Use the coordinate plane for questions 1–3.

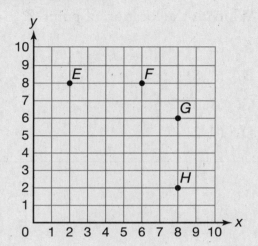

1. Which two points have the same *x*-coordinate?

   A. *E* and *F*   **C.** *E* and *H*

   B. *F* and *G*   **D.** *G* and *H*

2. Which two points have the same *y*-coordinate?

   A. *E* and *F*   **C.** *E* and *H*

   B. *F* and *G*   **D.** *G* and *H*

3. Which point is located at (8, 6)?

   A. point *E*   **C.** point *G*

   B. point *F*   **D.** point *H*

Use the coordinate plane for questions 4–6.

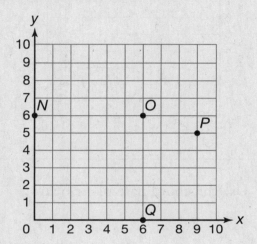

4. Which point is located on the *x*-axis?

   A. point *N*   **C.** point *P*

   B. point *O*   **D.** point *Q*

5. Which point has the same *y*-coordinate as its *x*-coordinate?

   A. point *N*   **C.** point *P*

   B. point *O*   **D.** point *Q*

6. Which is the location of point *P*?

   A. (4, 8)   **C.** (4, 9)

   B. (9, 4)   **D.** (9, 5)

Use the coordinate plane for questions 7 and 8.

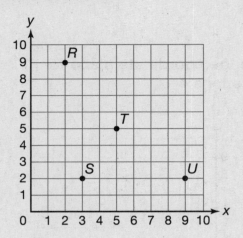

7. Which two points have the same *y*-coordinate?

   A. *R* and *S*   C. *S* and *U*

   B. *S* and *T*   D. *R* and *T*

8. Which is the location of point *R*?

   A. (2, 9)

   B. (3, 8)

   C. (8, 3)

   D. (9, 2)

9. Use the coordinate plane below.

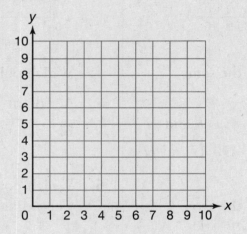

   A. Plot point *A* at (7, 3) on the coordinate plane.

   B. Plot point *B* at (8, 0) on the coordinate plane.

10. Which statements are correct? Circle all that apply.

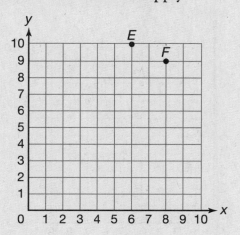

A. Point *F* is 9 units above the origin.

B. The *x*-coordinate of point *E* is 6.

C. Point *F* is 9 units to the right of the origin.

D. The *y*-coordinate of point *E* is 9.

11. Use numbers from the box to complete the statements.

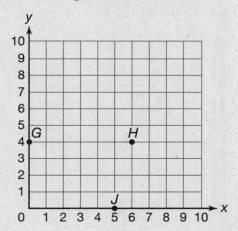

The *y*-coordinate of point *G* is _____.

The *x*-coordinate of point *H* is _____.

Point *J* is _____ units to the right of the origin.

| 0 |
| 4 |
| 5 |
| 6 |

12. Select True or False for each statement.

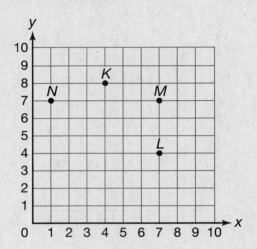

A. Point *K* is located at (8, 4).   ○ True   ○ False

B. Point *L* is located at (7, 3).   ○ True   ○ False

C. Points *M* and *N* have the same *y*-coordinate.   ○ True   ○ False

D. Point *N* is located at (7, 1).   ○ True   ○ False

13. Draw a line from each ordered pair to the correct point.

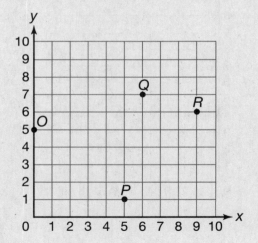

A. (5, 1)   ●   ● point *O*

B. (6, 7)   ●   ● point *P*

C. (9, 6)   ●   ● point *Q*

D. (0, 5)   ●   ● point *R*

Ordered Pairs

Getting the Idea

The first number in an ordered pair is the *x*-coordinate. The second number is the *y*-coordinate. The point where the two axes meet is the origin (0, 0).

To locate a point on the part of the coordinate plane that is shown in Example 1, you follow these steps:

- Start at the origin.
- For the *x*-coordinate, move to the right.
- For the *y*-coordinate, move up.

You can plot a point on a coordinate plane using an ordered pair.

Example 1

Plot a point at (5, 8) on the coordinate plane.

Strategy   **Use each number in the ordered pair to find the exact location on the coordinate plane.**

Step 1   Start at the origin.

Step 2   Look at the *x*-coordinate and the *y*-coordinate.

  The *x*-coordinate is 5, so move 5 units to the right of the origin.

  The *y*-coordinate is 8, so move 8 units up.

Step 3   Label the point (5, 8).

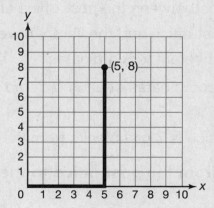

Solution   **The coordinate plane with a point plotted at (5, 8) is shown in Step 3.**

To find the distance between two points, count the number of units to the left or right (west and east) and the number of units up or down (north or south).

Example 2

Emile made the map below.

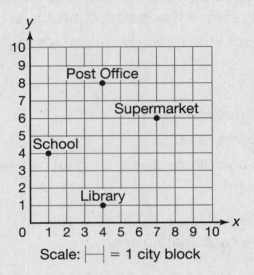

Scale: ⊢⊣ = 1 city block

What is the distance from the post office to the library?
You can only go right and left and up and down.

Strategy	**Name the ordered pairs. Then use subtraction.**
Step 1	Find the location of the post office and the library.
	The post office is located at (4, 8).
	The library is located at (4, 1).
Step 2	Find the distance between the post office and the library.
	Both the post office and the library have the same *x*-coordinate.
	They have different *y*-coordinates.
Step 3	Subtract the *y*-coordinates of each ordered pair.
	$8 - 1 = 7$
	The post office is 7 city blocks from the library.

Solution **The distance from the post office to the library is 7 city blocks.**

In Example 2, you could also have solved the problem by counting the units between the post office and the library. There are 7 units between the post office and the library.

You can use the lengths of line segments to find the perimeter and area.

Example 3

What is the area of rectangle *ABCD*?

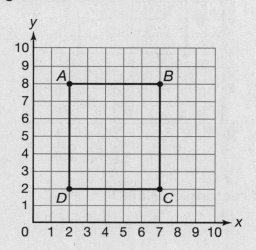

Strategy   **Find the length of each side.**

Step 1   Find the length of line segment *AB*.

Points *A* and *B* have the same *y*-coordinates.

Subtract the *x*-coordinates: 7 − 2 = 5

The length of line segment *AB* is 5 units.

Step 2   Find the length of line segment *BC*.

Points *B* and *C* have the same *x*-coordinates.

Subtract the *y*-coordinates: 8 − 2 = 6

The length of line segment *BC* is 6 units.

Step 3   Use the formula for the area of a rectangle.

$A = lw$

$A = 5 \times 6$

$A = 30$ square units

Solution   **The area of rectangle *ABCD* is 30 square units.**

Coached Example

Rectangle *JKLM* is shown on the coordinate plane below.

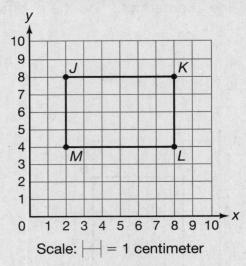

Scale: ├─┤ = 1 centimeter

What is the perimeter of rectangle *JKLM*?

Look at line segment *JK*.

Points *J* and *K* have the same _____-coordinates.

To find the length of line segment *JK*, subtract the _____-coordinates.

_____ − _____ = _____

Look at line segment *KL*.

Points *K* and *L* have the same _____-coordinates.

To find the length of line segment *KL*, subtract the _____-coordinates.

_____ − _____ = _____

Use the formula for the perimeter of a rectangle: $P = 2l + 2w$

$P = 2 \times$ _____ $+ 2 \times$ _____

$P =$ _____ $+$ _____

$P =$ _____ units

The perimeter of rectangle *JKLM* is _____ units.

Lesson Practice • Part 1

Choose the correct answer.

Use this coordinate plane for questions 1 and 2.

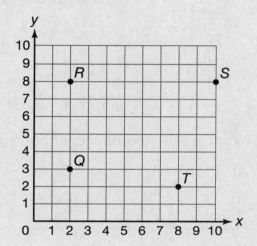

Use this coordinate plane for questions 3 and 4.

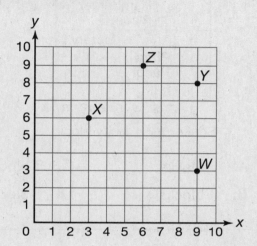

1. What are the coordinates of point *S*?

   A. (2, 8)

   B. (10, 8)

   C. (8, 10)

   D. (8, 2)

3. Which point is located at (9, 8)?

   A. point *W*

   B. point *X*

   C. point *Y*

   D. point *Z*

2. What are the coordinates of point *Q*?

   A. (2, 3)

   B. (2, 8)

   C. (3, 2)

   D. (8, 2)

4. What are the coordinates of point *X*?

   A. (6, 3)

   B. (4, 7)

   C. (3, 5)

   D. (3, 6)

5. What is the distance between the pizza parlor and the library?

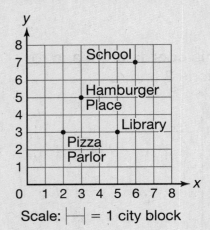

Scale: ⊢—⊣ = 1 city block

A. 5 blocks   **C.** 2 blocks

B. 3 blocks   **D.** 1 block

6. Look at the coordinate plane below.

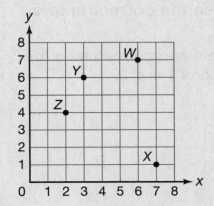

What are the coordinates of point *W*?

A. (3, 6)   **C.** (6, 7)

B. (7, 6)   **D.** (7, 1)

7. Look at the coordinate plane below.

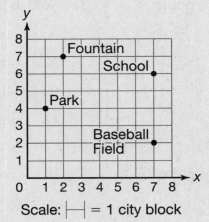

Scale: ⊢—⊣ = 1 city block

A. What is located at (2, 7)? Explain your answer.

_____

_____

B. What is the distance between the school and baseball field? Explain your answer.

_____

_____

_____

Lesson Practice • Part 2

Choose the correct answer.

Use the coordinate plane for questions 1–4.

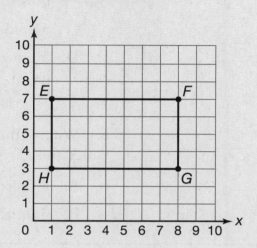

1. Which is the length of line segment *EF* ?

   A. 6 units

   B. 7 units

   C. 8 units

   D. 9 units

2. Which is the length of line segment *FG*?

   A. 4 units

   B. 5 units

   C. 6 units

   D. 7 units

3. Which is the perimeter of rectangle *EFGH*?

   A. 11 units

   B. 12 units

   C. 22 units

   D. 24 units

4. Which is the area of rectangle *EFGH*?

   A. 24 square units

   B. 28 square units

   C. 30 square units

   D. 35 square units

Use the coordinate plane for questions 5 and 6.

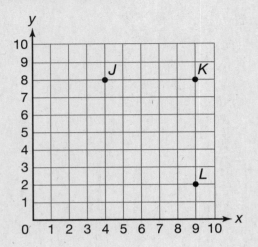

5. Which describes how to get from point *J* to point *L*

   A. 5 units to the left and 6 units up

   B. 5 units to the left and 6 units down

   C. 5 units to the right and 6 units up

   D. 5 units to the right and 6 units down

6. What is the distance between points *K* and *L*?

   A. 4 units   **C.** 6 units

   B. 5 units   **D.** 7 units

7. Look at the coordinate plane below.

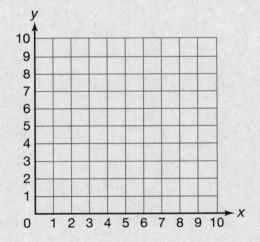

   A. Plot the following points *A* at (1, 9), *B* at (7, 9), *C* at (7, 3), and *D* at (1, 3). Then connect the points.

   B. What is the perimeter, in units, of rectangle *ABCD*?

   _____

   C. What is the area, in square units, of rectangle *ABCD*?

   _____

8. Draw a line from each point to its coordinates.

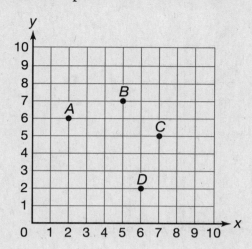

A. point *A* •

B. point *B* •

C. point *C* •

D. point *D* •

• (2, 6)

• (6, 2)

• (5, 7)

• (7, 5)

9. Draw a line from the coordinates to the building located there.

Scale: |—| = 1 city block

A. (8, 4) •

B. (0, 7) •

C. (7, 0) •

D. (4, 8) •

• Hospital

• Police Station

• Laundromat

• Gas Station

10. Select True or False for each statement.

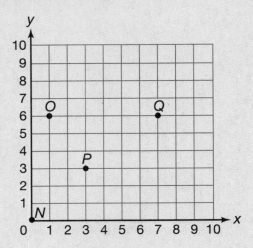

A. The coordinates of point *N* are (0, 0). ◯ True ◯ False

B. The coordinates of point *O* are (6, 1). ◯ True ◯ False

C. The coordinates of point *P* are (3, 3). ◯ True ◯ False

D. The coordinates of point *Q* are (7, 6). ◯ True ◯ False

11. Which are the correct distances between points on the map? You can only go right and left or up and down. Circle all that apply.

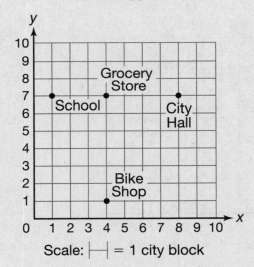

Scale: ⊢⊣ = 1 city block

A. The distance from the grocery store to the school is 4 city blocks.

B. The distance from the bike shop to the grocery store is 5 city blocks.

C. The distance from City Hall to the grocery store is 4 city blocks.

D. The distance from the school to City Hall is 7 city blocks.

Plane Figures

Getting the Idea

A **two-dimensional figure** is a **plane figure**. A **polygon** is a closed plane figure with straight sides. A side is a **line segment**. A polygon is classified by its number of **sides**, **angles**, or **vertices**.

A **regular polygon** has all equal sides and all equal angles. Some regular polygons are shown below.

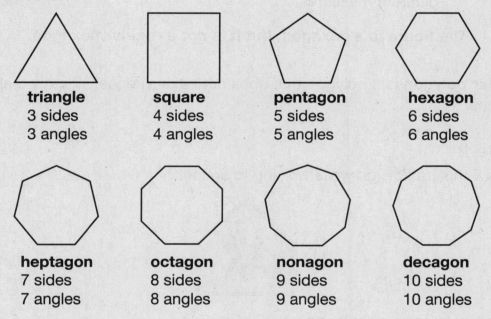

triangle	**square**	**pentagon**	**hexagon**
3 sides	4 sides	5 sides	6 sides
3 angles	4 angles	5 angles	6 angles

heptagon	**octagon**	**nonagon**	**decagon**
7 sides	8 sides	9 sides	10 sides
7 angles	8 angles	9 angles	10 angles

A **circle** is a plane figure with all points an equal distance from a point called the **center**. A circle is not a polygon because it does not have straight sides.

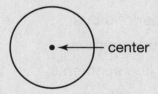

center

Example 1

How can you classify this polygon? Is the figure a regular polygon?

Strategy   **Count the number of sides.**

> **Step 1**   A side is a line segment.
>
> There are 6 line segments.

> **Step 2**   A regular polygon has all equal sides and equal angles.
>
> The sides are different lengths and the angles have different measures.

Solution   **The figure is a hexagon, but it is not a regular hexagon.**

An **irregular polygon** is a polygon that does not have all equal sides and all equal angles.

Example 2

Jerome saw this traffic sign while walking to school.

Is the sign a regular or irregular polygon?

Strategy   **Identify the two-dimensional figure.**

> **Step 1**   Count the number of sides.
>
> A side is a line segment.
>
> There are 5 line segments.
>
> The sign is a pentagon.

> **Step 2**   A regular polygon has all equal sides and equal angles.
>
> The sides are not all the same length and the angles do not all have the same measure.
>
> The sign is an irregular polygon.

Solution   **The traffic sign is an irregular pentagon.**

Example 3

Sort the figures below.

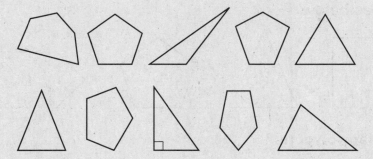

Strategy   **Determine how the figures are alike and different.**

Step 1   Determine how the figures are alike.

All of the figures are polygons.

Some figures have 3 sides.

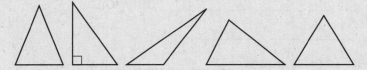

Some figures have 5 sides.

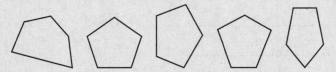

Some figures are regular polygons.

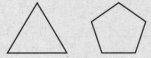

Step 2   Determine how the figures are different.

Some figures have unequal side lengths.
They are irregular polygons.

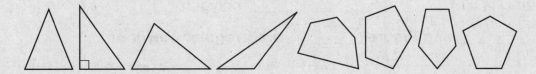

Solution   **The figures are shown sorted in the steps above.**

Coached Example

Look at the figures below.

A

B

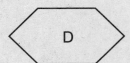
C

D

Which are irregular polygons?

Sort the figures.

Figure A is a _____.

    Do all of its sides appear equal? _____

    Do all of its angles appear equal? _____

    Figure A is a(n) _____ polygon.

Figure B is a _____.

    Do all of its sides appear equal? _____

    Do all of its angles appear equal? _____

    Figure B is a(n) _____ polygon.

Figure C is a _____.

    Do all of its sides appear equal? _____

    Do all of its angles appear equal? _____

    Figure C is a(n) _____ polygon.

Figure D is a _____.

    Do all of its sides appear equal? _____

    Do all of its angles appear equal? _____

    Figure D is a(n) _____ polygon.

Figure _____ and Figure _____ are irregular polygons.

Lesson Practice • Part 1

Choose the correct answer.

1. Which has 7 sides and 7 angles?

   A. heptagon

   B. hexagon

   C. pentagon

   D. octagon

2. Which is a regular polygon?

   A.

   B.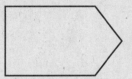

   C.

   D.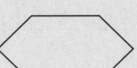

3. Which is **not** a polygon?

   A.

   B.

   C.

   D.

4. How many sides does a decagon have?

   A. 6

   B. 8

   C. 10

   D. 12

5. Which best classifies this figure?

   A. triangle

   B. rectangle

   C. heptagon

   D. octagon

6. Which best classifies this figure?

   A. decagon

   B. nonagon

   C. hexagon

   D. pentagon

7. Look at the figure below.

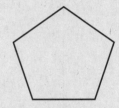

   A. Classify the figure.

_____

   B. Does the figure appear to be a regular or an irregular polygon? Explain your answer.

_____

_____

Lesson Practice • Part 2

Choose the correct answer.

1. How many more sides does a hexagon have than a triangle?

   A. 2

   B. 3

   C. 4

   D. 5

2. Which is the classification for this figure?

   A. regular hexagon

   B. regular heptagon

   C. irregular hexagon

   D. irregular heptagon

3. Why is a circle not a polygon?

   A. It is made from a curve.

   B. It is not two-dimensional.

   C. It is not closed.

   D. It is made from line segments.

4. Which is the classification of this figure?

   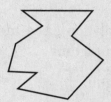

   A. regular nonagon

   B. regular decagon

   C. irregular nonagon

   D. irregular decagon

5. Which sentence about the relationship between the number of sides and the number of angles that a figure has is true?

   A. The number of sides and the number of angles are always equal.

   B. A polygon can have more sides than angles.

   C. A polygon can have more angles than sides.

   D. The number of sides and the number of angles are always different.

6. Each side length of a regular triangle is a whole number of inches. Which could be the perimeter of the triangle?

A. 6 inches   **C.** 10 inches

B. 8 inches   **D.** 14 inches

7. Which polygon has 4 more angles than a pentagon?

A. hexagon   **C.** octagon

B. heptagon   **D.** nonagon

8. Which describes a regular polygon?

A. It has all side lengths equal, but can have different angle measures.

B. It has all angle measures equal, but can have different side lengths.

C. It has all side lengths and angle measures equal.

D. The side lengths and the angle measures are not all the same.

9. The sum of the angle measures of any quadrilateral is 360°. The perimeter of a regular quadrilateral is 24 inches.

A. What is the measure of each angle of a regular quadrilateral?

_____

B. Does the angle measure change as the size of a regular quadrilateral increases? Explain your reasoning.

_____

_____

10. Use numbers from the box to complete the statements.

| 5 |
| 6 |
| 7 |
| 8 |

A hexagon has _____ sides.

An octagon has _____ angles.

A pentagon has _____ sides.

11. Select True or False for each statement.

    A. A decagon has 5 sides and 5 angles.   ○ True   ○ False

    B. A regular polygon has all equal sides and angles.   ○ True   ○ False

    C. A circle is a polygon.   ○ True   ○ False

    D. All sides of a polygon must be straight.   ○ True   ○ False

12. Draw a line from each polygon to its name.

    A.   •   • nonagon

    B.   •   • triangle

    C.   •   • heptagon

    D.   •   • pentagon

13. Classify each polygon as regular or irregular. Draw the polygon in the correct box.

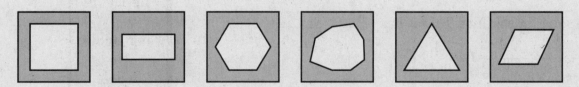

Regular	Irregular

14. Select True or False for each statement.

    A. A polygon is a closed figure.   ◯ True   ◯ False

    B. An irregular polygon can have one curved side.   ◯ True   ◯ False

    C. A square is a regular polygon.   ◯ True   ◯ False

    D. All angles in a regular polygon must be equal.   ◯ True   ◯ False

15. Which statements correctly describe the figures? Circle all that apply.

    A. The figure on the right is irregular.

    B. Both figures have 6 sides.

    C. The figure on the right is not a polygon.

    D. Both figures are heptagons.

16. Use the names of figures from the box to complete the statements.

A regular polygon that has 4 sides is a _____.

A polygon that has 9 sides is a _____.

A _____ has 10 sides.

decagon
nonagon
pentagon
square

Triangles

Getting the Idea

You can classify and sort triangles into different groups.

You can classify a triangle by the number of equal sides. The length of the longest side of a triangle is less than the sum of the lengths of the two shorter sides.

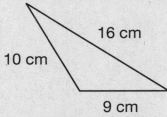

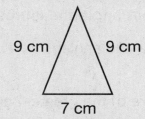

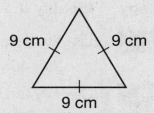

scalene triangle
No sides are equal.

isosceles triangle
At least 2 sides are equal.

equilateral triangle
All sides are equal.

The sum of the angle measures for any triangle is 180 **degrees (°)**. You can classify a triangle by the measure of its greatest angle.

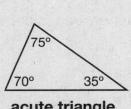

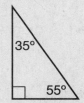

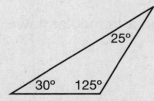

acute triangle
3 **acute** angles

right triangle
One angle is a **right angle**.

obtuse triangle
One angle is an **obtuse angle**.

Example 1

Classify this triangle by the number of equal sides.

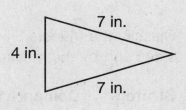

Strategy   **Identify the lengths of the sides.**

There are two equal sides.

An isosceles triangle has at least two equal sides.

Solution   **The triangle is an isosceles triangle.**

Example 2

Classify this triangle by the measures of its angles.

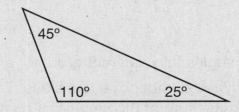

Strategy   **Identify the greatest angle measure.**

Step 1   List the measures of the angles.

25°, 45°, 110°

Step 2   Classify the measure of the greatest angle.

The greatest angle measure is 110°.

The greatest angle is an obtuse angle.

Solution   **The triangle is an obtuse triangle.**

Example 3

Ellie designed a triangular flower garden. A diagram of her garden is shown below.

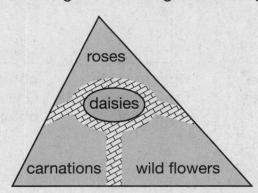

Classify the triangle Ellie used to design her flower garden by the number of equal sides and by the measure of its angles.

Strategy   **Compare the angles to a right angle, then compare the side lengths.**

Step 1   Decide if any of the angles are right angles.

None of the angles are right angles.

Step 2   Compare each angle measure to a right, or 90°, angle.

Each of the angles measures less than 90°.

Step 3   Classify each of the angles.

Each angle is an acute angle.

Step 4   Compare the side lengths.

Each side is a different length.

The triangle is scalene.

Solution   **Ellie used an acute, scalene triangle to design her flower garden.**

Coached Example

Classify the triangle by its number of equal sides and by the measures of its angles.

Classify the triangle by its sides.

Measure the lengths of the sides to the nearest centimeter.

The lengths of the sides are _____ cm, _____ cm, and _____ cm.

A(n) _____ triangle has _____ equal sides.

Classify the triangle by the measure of its greatest angle.

The triangle has a(n) _____ angle, so the triangle is a
_____ triangle.

The triangle is a(n) _____, _____ triangle.

Lesson Practice • Part 1

Choose the correct answer.

1. Which best classifies this triangle?

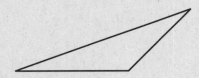

   A. acute

   B. obtuse

   C. right

   D. equilateral

2. How can you classify this triangle?

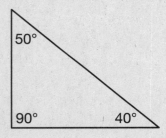

   A. isosceles, right

   B. isosceles, obtuse

   C. scalene, acute

   D. scalene, right

3. What is the least number of acute angles a triangle can have?

   A. 0   C. 2

   B. 1   D. 3

4. Colin must go from his home to school, then to the baseball field, and then back home. The path he will travel today is shown below.

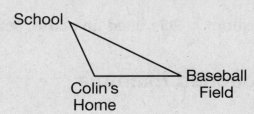

   Which best classifies the triangle formed by Colin's path?

   A. scalene, obtuse

   B. scalene, right

   C. isosceles, acute

   D. isosceles, right

5. Which triangle is a regular polygon?

   A. isosceles, right triangle

   B. scalene, obtuse triangle

   C. isosceles, acute triangle

   D. equilateral triangle

6. Which type of triangle has one obtuse and two acute angles?

   A. right

   B. acute

   C. obtuse

   D. equilateral

7. How can you classify this triangle?

  A. scalene, acute

  B. scalene, right

  C. isosceles, acute

  D. isosceles, obtuse

8. What is the maximum number of right angles a triangle can have?

  A. 0

  B. 1

  C. 2

  D. 3

9. Look at the triangle shown below.

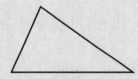

  A. Classify the triangle as scalene, isosceles, or equilateral. Explain your answer.

    _____

    _____

  B. Classify the triangle as acute, right, or obtuse. Explain your answer.

    _____

    _____

Lesson Practice • Part 2

Choose the correct answer.

1. A square is divided into two equal parts by a diagonal.

   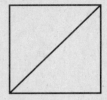

   Which two triangles are formed by the diagonal?

   A. isosceles, acute

   B. isosceles, right

   C. scalene, acute

   D. scalene, right

2. What is the maximum number of obtuse angles a triangle can have?

   A. 0

   B. 1

   C. 2

   D. 3

3. Which describes the angle measures of a scalene, obtuse triangle?

   A. 35°, 40°, 105°

   B. 40°, 40°, 100°

   C. 40°, 50°, 90°

   D. 55°, 60°, 65°

4. What is the measure of each angle of an equilateral triangle?

   A. 60°

   B. 90°

   C. 120°

   D. 180°

5. A rectangle is divided into two equal parts by a diagonal.

   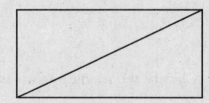

   Which two triangles are formed by the diagonal?

   A. isosceles, acute

   B. isosceles, right

   C. scalene, acute

   D. scalene, right

6. Which set of angle measures does **not** form a triangle?

   A. 28°, 63°, 89°

   B. 34°, 72°, 74°

   C. 42°, 57°, 91°

   D. 47°, 61°, 72°

7. Which set of lengths does **not** form a triangle?

   A. 6 in., 8 in., 10 in.

   B. 7 in., 9 in., 15 in.

   C. 8 in., 8 in., 8 in.

   D. 9 in., 10 in., 19 in.

8. Two of the angle measures of a triangle are 53° and 46°. Which is the classification of the triangle?

   A. isosceles, acute

   B. isosceles, obtuse

   C. scalene, acute

   D. scalene, obtuse

9. A triangle has 3 equal sides and 3 equal angle measures.

   A. Classify the triangle as acute, right, or obtuse.

   _____

   B. Is the triangle equilateral? Explain your reasoning.

   _____

   _____

   C. Is the triangle isosceles? Explain your reasoning.

   _____

   _____

10. Use numbers from the box to complete the statements.

   An obtuse triangle has _____ sides.

   It has _____ obtuse and _____ acute angles.

0
1
2
3

11. Select True or False for each statement.

    A. A polygon that has 3 sides and a 90° angle is   ○ True   ○ False
        a right triangle.

    B. An equilateral triangle has 3 equal sides.   ○ True   ○ False

    C. An acute triangle can have only 2 acute angles.   ○ True   ○ False

    D. An isosceles triangle has 2 equal sides.   ○ True   ○ False

12. Draw a line from each triangle to its description.

    A.   ●   ●   scalene, right

    B.   ●   ●   scalene, obtuse

    C.   ●   ●   isosceles, acute

    D.   ●   ●   scalene, acute

13. Which best describe the triangle? Circle all that apply.

    A. acute

    B. scalene

    C. right

    D. isosceles

    E. obtuse

    F. equilateral

14. Use terms from the box to complete the statements.

A triangle that has a 90° angle is a(n) _____ triangle.

Based on the number of equal sides, it cannot
be a(n) _____ triangle.

| acute |
| equilateral |
| isosceles |
| right |

15. Hana travels from her home to the park. Her mom sends her a text message asking
that she pick up some items at the store before coming home. The path she travels is
shown below. Which describes the triangle formed by Hana's path? Select Yes or No.

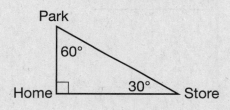

A. acute   ◯ Yes   ◯ No

B. isosceles   ◯ Yes   ◯ No

C. right   ◯ Yes   ◯ No

D. scalene   ◯ Yes   ◯ No

E. obtuse   ◯ Yes   ◯ No

Quadrilaterals

Getting the Idea

A **quadrilateral** is a plane figure with 4 sides and 4 angles. There are many different kinds of quadrilaterals, some of which are shown in the chart below. You can classify and sort quadrilaterals into different groups.

Quadrilateral	Figure	Properties
parallelogram		A parallelogram is a quadrilateral in which both pairs of opposite sides are **parallel**. Opposite sides of a parallelogram have the same length, and opposite angles have the same measure.
rhombus		A rhombus is a parallelogram with four sides that have the same length.
rectangle		A rectangle is a parallelogram with four right angles.
square		A square is a rectangle with four sides that have the same length.
trapezoid		A trapezoid is a quadrilateral with exactly one pair of parallel sides.
kite		A kite is a quadrilateral with two different pairs of connected sides that have the same length.

Some quadrilaterals can be classified in different ways.

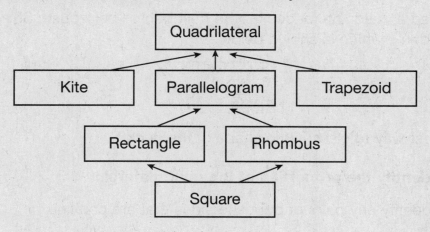

Example 1

Identify all the ways to classify this quadrilateral.

Strategy   **Use the properties to classify the quadrilateral.**

Step 1   Identify any pairs of opposite sides that are parallel.

Both pairs of opposite sides are parallel, so it is a parallelogram.

Step 2   Identify any sides that have the same length.

All of the sides have the same length, so it is a rhombus or a square.

Step 3   Identify any right angles.

All of the angles are right angles, so it is a rectangle or a square.

Solution   **The quadrilateral can be classified as a parallelogram, a rhombus, a rectangle, and a square.**

Example 2

Renee designed a quadrilateral deck to be built behind her house. She drew a sketch of the deck, which is shown below.

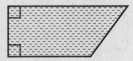

What is the best way to classify the shape of the deck?

Strategy   **Identify the properties of the quadrilateral.**

Step 1   Identify any pairs of opposite sides that are parallel.

Exactly one pair of opposite sides is parallel.

Step 2   Identify any sides that have the same length.

None of the sides have the same length.

Step 3   Identify any right angles.

There are two right angles.

Step 4   Analyze the properties.

There are two right angles, but four right angles are needed for a quadrilateral to be a square or rectangle. Since there is exactly one pair of opposite sides that are parallel, the quadrilateral is a trapezoid.

Solution   **The best way to classify the shape of the deck is as a trapezoid.**

Coached Example

What are two ways you can classify quadrilateral *JKLM*?

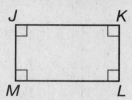

Determine if quadrilateral *JKLM* is a trapezoid or a parallelogram.

A trapezoid has exactly one pair of _____ sides.

A parallelogram has both pairs of opposite sides _____.

$\overline{JK}$ is parallel to _____.

$\overline{JM}$ is parallel to _____.

Is quadrilateral *JKLM* a trapezoid or a parallelogram? _____

Determine if quadrilateral *JKLM* is a rectangle, rhombus, and/or square.

Which quadrilaterals have 4 right angles? _____

Does quadrilateral *JKLM* have 4 right angles? _____

Which quadrilaterals have 4 equal sides? _____

Does quadrilateral *JKLM* have 4 equal sides? _____

The quadrilateral that has 4 right angles, but does not have 4 equal sides, is a

_____.

Quadrilateral *JKLM* can be classified as a _____ **and as a**

_____.

Lesson Practice • Part 1

Choose the correct answer.

Use the following figures for questions 1 and 2.

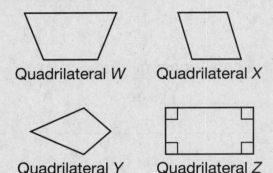

Quadrilateral W   Quadrilateral X

Quadrilateral Y   Quadrilateral Z

1. Which quadrilateral is a kite?

   A. quadrilateral W

   B. quadrilateral X

   C. quadrilateral Y

   D. quadrilateral Z

2. Which quadrilateral has only one pair of parallel sides?

   A. quadrilateral W

   B. quadrilateral X

   C. quadrilateral Y

   D. quadrilateral Z

3. Which sentence is true?

   A. All rhombi are squares.

   B. All rectangles are squares.

   C. All rectangles are rhombi.

   D. All squares are rectangles.

4. Which of the following is a rectangle and has 4 sides of equal length?

   A. square

   B. trapezoid

   C. parallelogram

   D. rhombus

5. Which quadrilateral can have exactly 2 right angles?

   A. square

   B. rectangle

   C. trapezoid

   D. rhombus

6. Which of the following is **not** a parallelogram?

   A. rhombus

   B. kite

   C. rectangle

   D. square

7. Which is the best way to classify the quadrilateral?

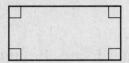

   A. square

   B. rectangle

   C. parallelogram

   D. rhombus

8. Which is the best way to classify the quadrilateral?

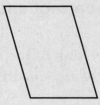

   A. kite

   B. trapezoid

   C. rhombus

   D. parallelogram

9. Look at figure *CDEF*.

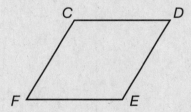

   A. Identify all the ways to classify figure *CDEF*.

_____

_____

_____

   B. Explain why a square can be classified as a rhombus.

_____

_____

_____

Lesson Practice • Part 2

Choose the correct answer.

1. What is the sum of the measures of the angles of any quadrilateral?

   A. 180°

   B. 270°

   C. 360°

   D. 540°

2. What is the maximum number of obtuse angles a quadrilateral can have?

   A. 1

   B. 2

   C. 3

   D. 4

3. Sarah drew a parallelogram that is **not** a rectangle. What is the greatest number of right angles Sarah's parallelogram can have?

   A. 0   C. 2

   B. 1   D. 4

4. Which sentence is true?

   A. All parallelograms are rhombi.

   B. All parallelograms are squares.

   C. All trapezoids are parallelograms.

   D. All rhombi are parallelograms.

5. Which quadrilateral is **not** a parallelogram?

   A. rectangle

   B. rhombus

   C. square

   D. trapezoid

6. What is the least number of acute angles a quadrilateral can have?

   A. 0   C. 2

   B. 1   D. 4

7. Which quadrilateral always has the same angle measures no matter what its shape?

   A. parallelogram

   B. rectangle

   C. rhombus

   D. trapezoid

8. One angle measure of a parallelogram is 64°. Which could be one of the other angle measures of the parallelogram?

   A. 26°   C. 148°

   B. 116°   D. 296°

9. Which sentence is true?

  A. A square can be a trapezoid.

  B. A parallelogram can be a kite.

  C. A rectangle can be a rhombus.

  D. A kite can be a rectangle.

10. Which is the most specific classification for a quadrilateral with exactly 1 right angle?

  A. parallelogram

  B. quadrilateral

  C. rhombus

  D. trapezoid

11. Look at quadrilateral *ABCD*.

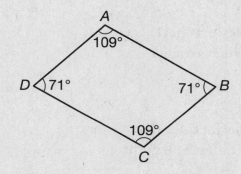

  A. Is the quadrilateral a parallelogram? Explain your reasoning.

  _____

  _____

  B. Is the quadrilateral a rectangle? Explain your reasoning.

  _____

  _____

  C. Is the quadrilateral a rhombus? Explain your reasoning.

  _____

  _____

12. Select True or False for each statement.

    A. All trapezoids are parallelograms.   ○ True   ○ False

    B. All squares are rhombi.   ○ True   ○ False

    C. All kites are quadrilaterals.   ○ True   ○ False

    D. All rectangles are trapezoids.   ○ True   ○ False

13. Draw a line from each description of a polygon to the best name for the figure.

    A. 4 equal sides, opposite sides   •   • kite
are parallel, no right angles

    B. 4 sides, 2 pairs of sides that have   •   • quadrilateral
the same length, no sides parallel

    C. 4 sides   •   • rhombus

    D. 4 sides, a pair of opposite sides that   •   • trapezoid
are parallel but have different lengths

14. Classify each figure. Write the name in the correct box.

square	rectangle	trapezoid	kite	rhombus

Parallelogram	Not a Parallelogram

15. Which best describe the figure? Circle all that apply.

A. rhombus

B. quadrilateral

C. trapezoid

D. square

E. parallelogram

16. Use terms from the box to complete the statement.

kite

rectangle

rhombus

trapezoid

A square is both a _____ and a _____,
but it can never be a _____ or a _____.

17. Does the term describe the figure? Select Yes or No.

A. kite   ○ Yes   ○ No

B. parallelogram ○ Yes   ○ No

C. rhombus   ○ Yes   ○ No

D. quadrilateral ○ Yes   ○ No

E. trapezoid   ○ Yes   ○ No

Domain 5: Cumulative Assessment for Lessons 30–34

Use the coordinate plane for questions 1–3.

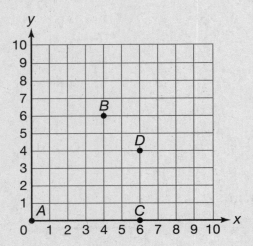

Use this coordinate plane for questions 4 and 5.

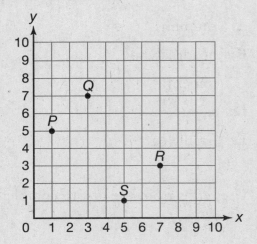

1. Which point represents the origin?

   A. point A **C.** point C

   B. point B **D.** point D

2. Which two points have the same x-coordinate?

   A. A and B

   B. B and C

   C. A and D

   D. C and D

3. Which point is 4 units right and 6 units up from the origin?

   A. point A **C.** point C

   B. point B **D.** point D

4. Which point is located at (5, 1)?

   A. point P **C.** point R

   B. point Q **D.** point S

5. What are the coordinates of point Q?

   A. (1, 5)   **C.** (3, 7)

   B. (5, 1)   **D.** (7, 3)

6. Which figure has 8 sides and 8 angles?

   A. heptagon

   B. hexagon

   C. pentagon

   D. octagon

7. How can you classify this triangle?

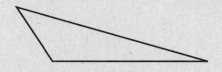

- **A.** scalene, acute
- **B.** scalene, obtuse
- **C.** isosceles, right
- **D.** isosceles, obtuse

8. Which of the following is a parallelogram that must have 4 equal angles?

- **A.** rhombus
- **B.** trapezoid
- **C.** kite
- **D.** rectangle

9. Graph point *B* at (6, 3) on the coordinate plane below.

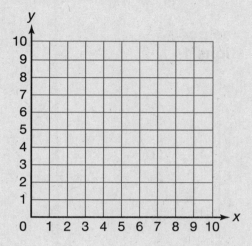

10. Look at the figure below.

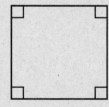

A. Identify all the ways to classify the figure.

_____

B. Explain why a square can be classified as a rectangle.

_____

_____

_____

Glossary

acute angle an angle that measures less than 90° (Lesson 33)

acute triangle a triangle with three acute angles (Lesson 33)

addends numbers that are added (Lesson 6)

additive identity property of 0 the rule that states that any number plus 0 is equal to that number (Lessons 13, 19)

angle a figure made of two rays or two line segments that have the same endpoint (Lesson 32)

area the region inside a closed figure measured in square units (Lesson 22)

associative property of addition the rule that states that the grouping of the addends does not change the sum (Lessons 13, 19)

associative property of multiplication the rule that states that the grouping of the factors does not change the product (Lessons 15, 22)

base-ten numeral a way of writing a number that shows only its digits (Lesson 9)

benchmark a common number that can be compared to another number (Lesson 19)

capacity the amount that a container can hold (Lesson 25)

center the point that is the same distance from all points on a circle (Lesson 32)

centimeter (cm) a metric unit of length; 100 cm = 1 m (Lesson 26)

circle a closed two-dimensional figure having all points the same distance from a given point (Lesson 32)

common denominator a common multiple of two or more denominators (Lesson 19)

commutative property of addition the rule that states that the order of the addends does not change the sum (Lessons 13, 19)

commutative property of multiplication the rule that states that the order of the factors does not change the product (Lessons 15, 22)

coordinate plane a grid formed by a horizontal line called the x-axis and a vertical line called the y-axis (Lessons 5, 30)

cube a three-dimensional figure with six square faces (Lesson 27)

cubic unit a cube with edges of 1 unit (Lesson 27)

cup (c) a customary unit of capacity; 1 cup = 8 fluid ounces (Lesson 25)

data information (Lesson 29)

decagon a polygon with ten sides and ten angles (Lesson 32)

decimal a number with a decimal point (Lesson 9)

decimal point (.) a symbol separating the ones from the tenths in a decimal (Lesson 9)

degree (°) a unit for measuring angles (Lesson 33)

denominator the bottom number of a fraction that tells how many equal parts there are (Lesson 17)

distributive property the rule that states that multiplying a sum by a number gives the same result as multiplying each addend in the sum by that number and then adding the products (Lesson 6)

dividend a number to be divided (Lesson 7)

divisor the number by which the dividend is divided (Lesson 7)

edge a line segment where two faces of a solid figure meet (Lesson 27)

equation a number sentence with an equal sign (Lesson 6)

equilateral triangle a triangle with three equal sides and angles (Lesson 33)

equivalent fractions two or more fractions that name the same part of a whole (Lesson 17)

estimate an answer that is close to the exact amount (Lesson 13)

expanded form a way of writing a number as a sum of the values of its digits (Lesson 9)

exponent a number that tells how many times a given number is used as a factor (Lesson 12)

expression a combination of numbers and operation signs (Lesson 1)

factor a number that can be multiplied by another number to get a product (Lesson 6)

fluid ounce (fl oz) a customary unit of capacity; 8 fl oz = 1 cup (Lesson 25)

foot (ft) (plural: feet) a customary unit of length; 1 foot = 12 inches (Lesson 25)

fraction a number that names a part of a whole or a group (Lesson 17)

gallon (gal) a customary unit of capacity; 1 gallon = 4 quarts (Lesson 25)

gram (g) a metric unit of mass; 1,000 g = 1 kg (Lesson 26)

greatest common factor (GCF) the greatest factor that is common to two or more numbers (Lesson 17)

heptagon a polygon with seven sides and seven angles (Lesson 32)

hexagon a polygon with six sides and six angles (Lesson 32)

improper fraction a fraction with a numerator that is greater than or equal to the denominator (Lesson 18)

inch (in.) a customary unit of length; 12 inches = 1 foot (Lesson 25)

inverse operations operations that undo each other, like addition and subtraction, or multiplication and division (Lesson 7)

irregular polygon a polygon that does not have all equal sides and all equal angles (Lesson 32)

is equal to (=) a symbol that shows that two quantities have the same value (Lesson 10)

is greater than (>) a symbol that shows that the first quantity is greater than the second quantity (Lesson 10)

is less than (<) a symbol that shows that the first quantity is less than the second quantity (Lesson 10)

isosceles triangle a triangle with two equal sides and angles (Lesson 33)

kilogram (kg) a metric unit of mass; 1 kg = 1,000 g (Lesson 26)

kilometer (km) a metric unit of length; 1 km = 1,000 m (Lesson 26)

kite a quadrilateral with two different pairs of connected sides that have the same length (Lesson 34)

least common denominator (LCD) the least common multiple of two or more denominators (Lesson 19)

length the measurement of how long or tall something is (Lesson 25)

like denominators fractions with the same denominators (Lesson 19)

line plot a graph used to organize data by placing Xs on a number line (Lesson 29)

line segment a part of a line (Lesson 32)

liter (L) a metric unit of capacity; 1 L = 1,000 mL (Lesson 26)

mass how much matter an object has (Lesson 26)

meter (m) a metric unit of length; 1 m = 100 cm (Lesson 26)

metric ton (t) a metric unit of mass; 1 metric ton = 1,000 kilograms (Lesson 26)

mile (mi) a customary unit of length; 1 mile = 5,280 feet (Lesson 25)

milligram (mg) a metric unit of mass; 1 mg = 1,000 g (Lesson 26)

milliliter (mL) a metric unit of capacity; 1,000 mL = 1 L (Lesson 26)

millimeter (mm) a metric unit of length; 10 mm = 1 cm (Lesson 26)

mixed number a number that has a whole-number part and a fraction part (Lessons 8, 18)

multiplicative identity property of 1 the rule that states that any number times 1 is equal to that number (Lessons 15, 22)

nonagon a polygon with nine sides and nine angles (Lesson 32)

number name a way of writing numbers using words (Lesson 9)

numerator the top number of a fraction that tells how many of the parts are being considered (Lesson 17)

obtuse angle an angle that measures greater than 90° and less than 180° (Lesson 33)

obtuse triangle a triangle with one obtuse angle (Lesson 33)

octagon a polygon with eight sides and eight angles (Lesson 32)

order of operations rules used to determine the order of evaluating an expression (Lesson 2)

ordered pair two numbers that give a location on a coordinate grid (Lessons 5, 30)

origin the point where the axes meet on a coordinate grid, named by the ordered pair (0, 0) (Lesson 30)

ounce (oz) a customary unit of weight; 1 pound = 16 ounces (Lesson 25)

parallel describes lines or line segments that stay the same distance apart and never cross (Lesson 34)

parallelogram a quadrilateral in which both pairs of opposite sides are parallel (Lesson 34)

pattern a series of numbers or figures that follows a rule (Lesson 4)

pentagon a polygon with five sides and five angles (Lesson 32)

pint (pt) a customary unit of capacity; 1 pint = 2 cups (Lesson 25)

plane figure a two-dimensional figure (Lesson 32)

polygon a closed two-dimensional figure made of line segments that do not cross each other (Lesson 32)

pound (lb) a customary unit of weight; 1 pound = 16 ounces (Lesson 25)

power of ten a number that can be written as 10 raised to some exponent (Lesson 12)

product the result of multiplying two or more numbers (Lesson 6)

quadrilateral a polygon with four sides and four angles (Lesson 34)

quart (qt) a customary unit of capacity; 1 quart = 2 pints (Lesson 25)

quotient the result of division (Lesson 7)

reciprocal number pairs that have a product of 1 (Lesson 24)

rectangle a parallelogram with four right angles (Lesson 34)

rectangular prism a three-dimensional figure with six rectangular faces (Lesson 28)

regroup to rename a number for use in addition or subtraction (Lesson 13)

regular polygon a polygon that has all sides equal in length and all angles equal in measure (Lesson 32)

remainder the number that is left over after division is complete (Lesson 7)

rhombus a parallelogram in which four sides have the same length (Lesson 34)

right angle an angle that measures exactly 90° (Lesson 33)

right triangle a triangle with one right angle (Lesson 33)

round to estimate the value of a number based on a given place (Lesson 11)

rule describes how the terms are related in a pattern (Lesson 4)

scalene triangle a triangle with no sides equal (Lesson 33)

side a line segment of a polygon (Lesson 32)

simplest form the form of a fraction whose numerator and denominator have only 1 as a common factor (Lesson 17)

square a rectangle in which four sides have the same length; it is also a rhombus with four right angles (Lessons 32, 34)

square unit the area of a square that has sides of 1 unit (Lesson 22)

term a number or figure in a pattern or expression (Lesson 4)

ton (T) a customary unit of weight; 1 ton = 2,000 pounds (Lesson 25)

trapezoid a quadrilateral with exactly one pair of parallel sides (Lesson 34)

triangle a polygon with three sides and three angles (Lesson 32)

two-dimensional figure a plane figure (Lesson 32)

unit fraction a fraction with a numerator of 1 (Lesson 24)

variable a letter or symbol used to represent a value that is unknown (Lesson 6)

vertex (plural: vertices) the point in which two line segments meet in a polygon (Lesson 32)

volume the number of cubic units needed to fill a three-dimensional figure (Lessons 27, 28)

weight a measure of how heavy something is (Lesson 25)

***x*-axis** the left-right or horizontal axis on a coordinate grid (Lesson 30)

***x*-coordinate** the first number in an ordered pair (Lessons 5, 30)

***y*-axis** the up-down or vertical axis on a coordinate grid (Lesson 30)

***y*-coordinate** the second number in an ordered pair (Lessons 5, 30)

yard (yd) a customary unit of length; 1 yard = 3 feet, or 36 inches (Lesson 25)

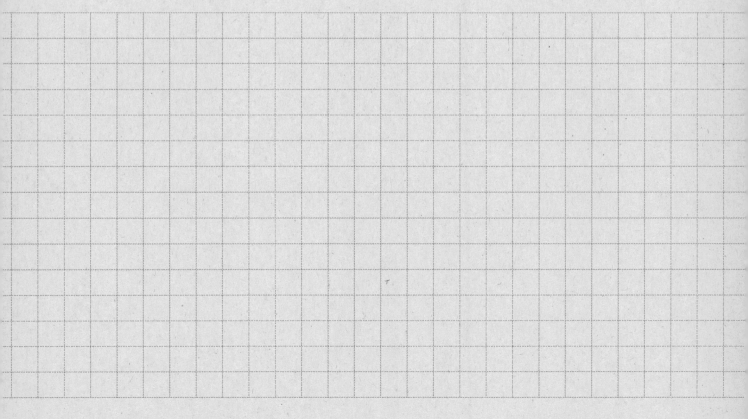

NOTES

NOTES

NOTES

NOTES

NOTES

NOTES

NOTES